God's Greatest Passion

H.L. Hussmann

Every Christian, Everywhere, Sharing Jesus

Requests for information should be addressed to:
PBL Productions, 302 South 5ᵗʰ Street, Suite 101, Murray, KY 42071
or see: http://www.godsgreatestpassion.com

Cover and Interior Design by: *PBL Productions*

Contents:

Acknowledgments

Without a certain three people, this book would not be a reality.

Becky Lile, who I am convinced will have a seat very close to the throne, should probably have her name on the cover alongside mine. Her editing skills (genius) have transformed this book from the ugly skeleton I presented to the glorious piece of grammatical artistry that you now hold in your hand. If there is anything wrong as far as grammar, form, or function, I am sure it is one of those times I foolishly chose to overrule her editing suggestions.

My wonderful mother, Susan Hussmann, deserves a huge thank you. As a single mom raising two unruly children, she did an amazing job. She was the one who taught me to place my concerns and dreams in God's hands and watch Him do His thing. Any credit I receive is surely a result of my upbringing.

Mark Randall, my good friend and campus pastor, has had an impact on my life that I am sure will not be understood until well into eternity. There is not a page in this book that does not bear the impression of his influence. He is, by far, the most consistent soulwinner I have ever met, and I am forever grateful to have observed him share the Gospel with literally thousands and thousands of people over the course of the last fifteen years.

Thank you to my wife for her faithful encouragement, support, and hard work during the writing of this book. I would be remiss if I didn't also thank her simply for being paradise in the form of a woman.

Thank you also to the following people who have played a part: Pastor Art and Kelli Heinz, Paul Lile, Justin Ferrell, Randy and Jennie Short, Scott and Amanda Pitt, Jerry and Rita Hendley, Brandon and Kimby Decker, Lee and Dottie Williams, Jim and Deborah Hereford, Eric and Treva Kelleher, Crystal Rieheman, Bill and Suzie Burnett, Darin and Janna Beth LeFever, Craig and Laura Prater, Steve and Deanne Turley, Bill and Lena Shrader, Dr. Steve and Margaret Bergquist, Greg Brotzge, Jonathan Watkins, Eric and Gloria Small, Rick and Jerri Mjos, Jenni Siler, Erin Powell, Leah Blackketter, Jeff and Candice Dowdy, Jason and Karla Tucker, Ned and Debbie Galloway, Mike and Bea Cornett, Bill Barger, Savannah Isaacs, the members of Hope Harbor Church and Murray State Christ Ambassadors, and Barry Morris for fixing my bike.

I would also like to thank my good friends Ryan and Kathleen Brooks for all of the incredible hard work they have done in my place at MSU. I am not ashamed to admit that you do a much better job than I ever did. Thank you for taking my load and running with it.

Thanks also to Dennis Gaylor, Bob Marks, and Scott Martin for reviewing the initial draft copy of this text and considering it for national distribution. You are making a difference worldwide, and I am thankful to play a small part.

Thank you to Dave Davidson, who unknowingly played a major role in inspiring me to write in general, and Marilyn Harris, who, on very short notice, did an amazing amount of proofreading for me in a very short time, and inspired me to take a second look at some of my discussion questions.

Finally, thank you to Paula Shelton, for patiently walking a first time author through the printing process. I can't possibly express how much I appreciate your contribution to this book.

If I forgot you, I beg you, please forgive me. Chalk it up as stress overload from nearly four hundred pages of writing, culminating in two pages of thanks. Call it brain fry and realize that I love you.

Prologue

I was absolutely terrified.

In fact, I was so scared that for about two and a half days I spent a great deal of the time in my hotel room either hugging the toilet and vomiting or lying in bed and moaning with a throbbing migraine headache. I was literally almost paralyzed with fear. I had no idea, however, that I was about to live out one of the most amazing and life-changing experiences I would ever know.

I was frightened, and I was clueless.

It had all begun about three days earlier. I was a college student at Murray State University in Kentucky and had flown out West to Phoenix, Arizona, for a conference with my campus pastor, Mark Randall. We arrived a few days early, rented a beautiful silver convertible, and headed off to Las Vegas for what I thought would be a few days of relaxing and sightseeing. I had no idea what I was getting myself into.

On the way up Highway 93 from Phoenix to Vegas, we stopped at Hoover Dam, and I can vividly remember standing against a guard rail looking at that amazing structure and feeling very small. It was about that time that Mark casually remarked, *"I can't wait to get out there in Vegas and start witnessing on the strip."* It may have been precisely that moment that my head began to hurt. Had I heard him correctly? Witnessing in Vegas? On the streets? What about seeing the sights, eating steak and lobster, watching shows? Surely I had misheard him. Either way, it did cross my mind that jumping the guard rail, falling from a great height, and having my frail body dashed on the concrete at the bottom of the dam seemed like a pretty reasonable and attractive alternative. The concept of any kind of public witnessing in such a wild place was just about too much for me. I am not sure how I managed to get back in the car with him. I thought to myself, *"Maybe I should start hitchhiking home."*

A few miles later we topped a hill and I saw, for the first time, Vegas in all of its glory. Even at night from miles away, the millions and millions of lights from the strip lit up the sky as though a section of Vegas had twenty-four hours of daylight. It was glorious, brilliant, mind-blowing, and just plain intimidating. In the back of my head was a voice, saying, *"Get out while you can; it's not too late."*

Cruising the strip only made things worse. What I had thought were millions of lights turned into what seemed like billions. There were marquees vying for the attention of anyone passing by, restaurants offering ridiculously low prices in the hope that once diners were inside they would gamble, and thousands of people everywhere, most of whom could accurately be described as "shady." There were men passing out literature that no Christian should want to view. There were women who were scantily clad and doing what they could to attract men's attention. There were security guards who looked like they would much rather beat people up than protect them. The place was flat-out wild, and I was flat-out petrified. Mark was excited. I was ready to cower in the hotel room.

The truth is, I really wanted to reach out to people. I loved Jesus, and I desperately wanted other people to love Him, too. I knew that part of being a Christian and wholeheartedly serving Jesus meant sharing His love with others. I also knew that His love was to be shared with all

> I had more questions than I had answers.

people, of all kinds, in all places, and that included the strip of Las Vegas. I just had no idea what to do. I had no idea what to expect, no idea how to reach those people effectively, and no idea how they would react. As much as I knew I wanted to reach out to them, and as much as I knew that God actually expected me to reach out to them, I was still terrified because of all of my questions: *How do I do it? Why should I do it? What will happen to me? Will my efforts really matter?* I had more questions than I had answers.

I believe most Christians feel the same way. They have an overwhelming number of questions and concerns about evangelism. They know they should reach out, and, deep down, they really want to, but they don't know how, and they don't know what to expect. They feel unequipped, unmotivated, unworthy, and incapable. The goal of this book is to change all of that. My prayer is that those who read it will be greatly motivated to reach our world, and specifically their personal sphere of influence, with the Gospel of our Lord Jesus. Whether you currently are confident about sharing your faith or are as terrified as I was, my desire is that this book will be a great resource for you and will assist you in reaching the world around you. I pray that it will motivate you, challenge you, stretch you, equip you, and ultimately send you out into the world with the unbelievable message that Jesus is alive and changing lives today.

So, how did my story end?

I have heard my friend Mark referred to as the "John Wayne" of evangelism, and from my experiences on that trip, I can see why. Both nights (while I stayed in the room throwing up and moaning) he would go out on the strip of Vegas and share Jesus with people. Eventually, after much deliberation, praying, worrying, and downright pleading with God, I decided that I would at least go down on the strip and watch him. I wasn't quite ready to be involved, but I eventually talked myself into standing at a distance and watching Mark do his thing.

There were dozens of men, as I mentioned earlier, standing on the street corners handing out literature about where to find a prostitute or a strip club. Mark would walk out on the streets, stand nearly shoulder to shoulder with a group of them, and begin handing out Gospel literature, all the while saying things to passersby such as, *"You don't need what they are handing out. This is what you need. It's about Jesus, the King of Kings, and the*

Lord of Lords." I'll admit, I thought he was a little bit crazy, and I wasn't the only one. The guys passing out literature must have thought he was a bit off his nut as well. They were mad. They cussed him, they made up lies about the legalities of handing out literature on the strip, they made fun of him, and they mocked him. It was ugly . . . at first.

> They were mad.
> They cussed,
> they mocked him.
> It was ugly . . .
> at first.

Mark stood his ground, and I was compelled. I kept moving closer and closer, mostly just trying to hear the conversations. Before I knew it, I was standing next to Mark, also handing out Gospel tracts, and also engaging these men in conversation. Once I overcame my initial fear, the whole experience became amazing. Over the three or four hours that we stood there, the atmosphere changed. The men eventually began asking us questions such as, *"Why are you doing this stuff, anyway?"* We would reply something along the lines of, *"To let you and all these people know that Jesus loves you and can change your lives."* We showed them a firm love that night, and it didn't take very long until they began to warm up to us. They began to "forget" to pass out their literature and instead engaged us in conversation. When we would challenge them that there was a better life than promoting prostitution, they would respond by saying, *"I know, but I gotta have a job. It pays the bills,"* to which we would respond, *"God could give you a better job."* We explained that if they would put their faith in Him and trust Him, He would meet their needs.

I couldn't believe the change in attitude that came over those men. Perhaps even more incredible was the fact that something was changing in me. I was excited. Actually, I was beyond excited – I was ecstatic. I was having an absolute blast. It was wonderful.

After several hours of passing out tracts and talking with these men, we decided it was time to go. When we announced we were leaving, one of the men actually began to get tears in his eyes and said gently, *"Will you be back tomorrow?"* Even more amazing than that was the fact that none of his friends ridiculed him for this but instead looked to us expectantly, hoping we had plans to return. Another of the men pulled us aside privately and asked if we could give him a ride home. We agreed. On the way, he pulled out a Gideon's New Testament from his coat. He said he always carried it with him. He confessed that he had been raised in church and knew a lot about the Bible, but had walked away from God and knew that he needed to recommit his life to Jesus. We were able to challenge him to live for Jesus, and, before we dropped him off, we were privileged to pray with him. He thanked us repeatedly.

> Perhaps even more incredible was the fact that something was changing in me.

I am convinced that at least some of those men were different after that night. For some of them, it may have been the first time that anyone ever loved them enough to challenge them and confront them. Some of them may have heard truth that really shook them up. At least one man was reminded of a time earlier in life when he was interested in following Jesus, and we challenged him to return to that mind frame. But, as much as it may have impacted those men, I am convinced that it impacted me more. I have never been the same. From that day forward, my life took on an entirely new purpose. There is no doubt whatsoever that it was one of the most pivotal moments of my entire life.

For thirteen years now I have dedicated my life to reaching out to people with the Gospel of Jesus. I have shared Jesus with my friends and family and with students at universities from Ohio State to Harvard. I have shared with people online, people on buses, people on planes, and people on trains. I have shared Jesus with Buddhists, Muslims, Taoists, atheists, and Bible-belters. I have shared Jesus from L.A. to Toronto, and from Trinidad to Thailand. It has been an absolutely amazing adventure. My goal is to challenge you to make sharing the Gospel of Jesus your lifelong adventure as well. I am convinced that sharing this message is man's highest destiny, and I will do my best to convince you of that. I am not necessarily going to challenge you to witness on the streets of Vegas, but I am going to challenge you, in the name of Jesus, to do something – anything – to reach this world with our perfect message of hope.

> ★ Courage is being scared to death but saddling up anyway. ★

John Wayne (the real John Wayne, not my friend) once said, *"Courage is being scared to death but saddling up anyway."* I relate my story to you to let you know that I was once scared terribly. I had no clue what to do, what to say, how to say it, or even why I should say it. Over the years, I have been changed, equipped, and motivated, and I believe that you can be too. Are you willing? You may not know what to do. You may not feel confident. You, too, may be completely terrified. Are you willing to "saddle up" anyway? I challenge you to take the content of this book, pull out your Bible, a pen, and a notebook, and begin to learn the answers to many of the questions you may have about sharing Jesus.

With that said, please do both of us a favor as you read and study: Don't skip the Bible verses. Many Christians today, especially those who are very familiar with the Bible, have a tendency to skim over, or skip entirely, passages of scripture when they read Christian books. Please don't do this. Instead, when you see passages of scripture, give special attention to them. Take the time to meditate on them and think them through. Be sure that the points I am making really do line up with the Word of God. Ultimately it will not be my words or ideas that will change you, but rather the *"living and enduring Word of God"* (1 Peter 1:23).

To reiterate this point: Don't skip the Bible verses, don't skip the Bible verses, and don't skip the Bible verses.

Ok. Are you ready? Go to the first chapter and let's *"saddle up."*

Note: If you are not currently a follower of Jesus, I strongly recommend first reading chapters 20 – 22 concerning the identity of Jesus, and chapters 12 & 13 concerning the message of Jesus before beginning Chapter 1.

Mission Statements

"Is it possible to get close to the Master's heart without getting close to the Master's mission?"
– Larry Moyer

What are the top three things you have prayed about over the last few months?

Take time to think about it. If possible, grab a pen and paper and write down your answer. (If you don't pray regularly, this exercise is going to be very difficult.) It is important that you complete this step before you read any further. Before you turn the page, please at least make a mental list. What are the top three things you have prayed about over the last two or three months? Make sure you list the things you have actually prayed about and not the things you think you should have prayed about.

Once you have your list, please turn the page and continue reading.

The reason I ask the question, *"What are the top three things you have been praying about?"* is that I believe people can make a clear connection between what they pray about and their highest priorities. It only makes sense that the things I consistently bring before God in prayer are things that are very important to me. I believe you can look at your list and tell very quickly what is most important to you.

If I had a meeting with the President of the United States (at the time of this writing, George W. Bush), and he gave me fifteen minutes of his time to tell him my wants and needs, you can be assured I wouldn't beat around the bush. (Forgive the pun.) He would know very quickly my highest priorities. If my highest priority was the environment, you can be sure I would not waste time talking about taxes or education. If my top priority was national security, I wouldn't spend my precious minutes chatting about gun control or social reform except where those topics related to national security. If nothing else, I certainly wouldn't spend time making small talk about fishing or baseball. Because I know he is a man with authority, I would make sure he understood clearly what was important to me. My priorities would be seen easily through my petitions.

It is also very easy to tell what is important to us based on what we bring before Jesus, the King of Kings and the Lord of Lords. I realize the analogy isn't perfect, as we can spend limitless time bringing our needs before God, but I also know that most people, if they will take an honest look at their list, will be able to see without difficulty what is really important to them. For many, it is family. For others, it is finances or a job situation of some sort. It also is not uncommon for many single people to include on their list a relationship with the opposite sex. Other common prayers include physical healing for ourselves or our loved ones, direction in life, peace for those who have experienced loss, peace in political situations, and God's grace in current events.

Based on your list, what is important to you? Take another second to think about it. Looking at the list you have made, what does your list say is really important to you?

Now, keeping your list in hand (or head, as the case may be), how do your priorities, as expressed through your prayer life, line up with the mission statement of Jesus?

> This one statement by Jesus sums up His entire reason for coming to Earth.

The mission statement of Jesus is found in Luke 19:10: *"For the Son of Man came to seek and to save what was lost."*

This one statement by Jesus sums up His entire reason for coming to Earth as a man, His entire mission while He was here, and His highest priority for those who follow Him today.

A mission statement can be called a *"statement of purpose."* When a company issues a mission statement, its intention is to lay out, in no uncertain terms, why it exists. The mission statement of Coca-Cola, for example, is to *"benefit and refresh everyone who is touched by our business."* A phone call to Wal-Mart shows that Wal-Mart's (unofficial) mission statement is *"to provide the best quality merchandise at the lowest possible price while providing exceptional customer service."* And when Walt Disney World opened in 1955, their mission statement was summed up in only three simple words: *"We create happiness."*

> Jesus has made it clear what our number one priority should be if we follow Him.

Each of these statements makes it very clear why the company is in existence; moreover, each paints an easily understandable picture of what is expected of the company's employees. In the case of Disney World, for example, the mission statement makes it obvious that the company exists to make people happy. This means that if the employees are not working toward the goal of making people happy, they are not actually working for Disney. Whether an employee works at ticket check-in, backstage at a show, or in a Goofy outfit parading around the grounds, the universal vision is clear: making people happy.

In the same way, Jesus has issued His mission statement, and in doing so, He has made it clear what our number one priority should be if we follow Him. The entire reason for His life and ministry on Earth was to bring people into fellowship with God. Our reason for living should be the same. This is expressed time and time again in the New Testament in many different ways:

Luke 4:18 - *"He has sent me to proclaim freedom for the prisoners and recovery of sight for the blind, to release the oppressed . . . ."*

1 Timothy 1:15 - *"Here is a trustworthy saying that deserves full acceptance: Christ Jesus came into the world to save sinners . . . ."*

John 3:17 - *"For God did not send his Son into the world to condemn the world, but to save the world through him."*

Matthew 20:28 - *"The Son of Man came . . . to give his life as a ransom for many."*

1 John 3:5 - *"He appeared so that he might take away our sins."*

Mark 2:17 - *"I have not come to call the righteous, but sinners."*

Read through this list of scriptures again carefully and you will see one common theme. Each of them describes *why* Jesus came to planet Earth. They describe why He came, why He was sent, and why He appeared, and in each case they are connected directly with the salvation of people.

A quick web search for the definition of the word "Christian" will produce results similar to the following:

-*"A follower of Jesus Christ"* (the most common definition)

-*"Following the teachings or manifesting the qualities or spirit of Jesus Christ"*

-*"The name given to the followers of Jesus Christ"*

-*"A disciple (follower) of Jesus Christ"*

> The Cross was entirely about saving people.

In other words, even by definition, to be a Christian means to follow Jesus Christ. It clearly follows that if we are to be a disciple of Christ, we must be on board with His mission statement, which is to *"seek and save that which was lost."* Just as the people who clock in for Disney World are expected to make people happy as their number one, absolute highest priority, we, as Christians, are expected to make seeking and saving people our highest priority in life.

The number one priority on God's list is to save people. This is clearly evidenced in the Cross. Ask yourself this question: Why did Jesus die on the Cross? Even a basic understanding of Christianity and a cursory study of the New Testament will tell you – the Cross was entirely about saving people. It was wholly about making a bridge between God and man so that people could be saved from their sin. The Cross was the place where God made a way for man to be saved. It was the culmination of the life and teachings of Jesus in the world. It was the most pivotal moment in human history. And it was all about lost people. The Cross was the *"It is finished"* of the mission of Jesus on Earth.

Is the mission of Jesus your highest priority? What if someone asked you, *"What is your mission statement? What is the focus of your life?"* Would your mission statement be the same as His?

Many people are looking for their purpose in life. What they really need is a mission statement. My hope and prayer is that after today you will say that your personal mission statement, the one chief principle that governs your life, will be the same as that of our Lord Jesus, *"to seek and save that which was lost."* I pray that from now on, reaching people with God's message will be your highest priority and will continue to be until the end of your days on Earth.

In Matthew 10:38 Jesus said, *"And anyone who does not take up his cross and follow me is not worthy of me."* The cross was a place where Jesus gave up *everything* for lost people. Are you willing to do the same? Are you willing to follow in the footsteps of Jesus; surrender your life to His cause; and dedicate your life, energies, and resources towards winning people to Him?

> Many people are looking for their purpose in life. What they really need is a mission statement.

Jesus had one central purpose for His ministry on Earth, and that was to reconcile men to God. Now, in His physical absence, He has left that task to us as expressed in 2 Corinthians 5:18-20, *"All this is from God, who reconciled us to himself through Christ and gave us the ministry of reconciliation: that God was reconciling the world to himself in Christ, not counting men's sins against them. And he has committed to us the message of reconciliation. We are therefore Christ's ambassadors, as though God were making his appeal through us. We implore you on Christ's behalf: Be reconciled to God."*

As a follower of Jesus, you have been given a position as an *"ambassador"* for Christ. It is your responsibility and amazing privilege to share His message of reconciliation with the world around you. It is the most remarkable lifestyle that a person can live, but it requires a change of focus that very few people ever experience. The life of the believer is intended to be a life that is focused outwardly on God and the people around them. It was never intended to be an inwardly focused lifestyle. In the coming pages we will explore what it means to take the focus off ourselves and place it on God and the people around us.

Discussion Questions:

-How does your prayer life reflect your priorities?

-Until now, what have been the highest priorities in your life?

-How does your lifestyle currently reflect the mission of Jesus on Earth?

-What does it mean to be an *"ambassador"* for Christ?

-What are some ways you can take up the mission of Jesus?

Big Fat Christians

"We have the means of evangelizing our country, but they are slumbering in the pews of our churches."
                                                                    - John Stott

Lambert's is a restaurant in Sikeston, Missouri, known as the *"Home of the throwed rolls."* During a meal, servers come around with huge, delicious, fresh-baked rolls and throw them to you from across the room (and occasionally they accidentally hit you with them). Afterwards, another server comes by with a bucket of molasses to dump on your roll. That server is followed by another with fried okra, followed by another with fried potatoes, then macaroni and tomatoes, then black-eyed peas, and much more. Usually, at this point you haven't even seen your entrée, which, when it arrives, could be bigger than your head. The soft drinks come in only one size: humongous. If you ask the server for *"just a little bit,"* you are still going to end up with a pile of food that no two people could ever hope to finish in one sitting. It is not a restaurant for the faint-hearted, and in the dozen or so times I have eaten there I can think of at least two occasions when one of my companions went to the bathroom and vomited before leaving. (One more did so on the drive home.) If you are looking for a place to totally gorge yourself on food, Lambert's is your restaurant.

Before I go any further, let me make one thing clear: I am not opposed to feasting. As a matter of fact, plugging the word "feast" into an online concordance (NIV) yields ninety-nine results, and a brief scan shows that God endorses nearly all of them. However, we all know that consistent and uncontrolled feasting without bounds is gluttony, and gluttony is a sin. Proverbs 23:2 says to *"put a knife to your throat if you are given to gluttony."* This is a grave warning indeed!

> Many Christians today are taking in as much spirituality as possible, but giving away very little.

Gluttony pertaining to food is sin because God recognizes that consistent overeating has deadly consequences. Perhaps this is why gluttony always makes it into the list of the seven deadly sins with which most of us are familiar. It is common knowledge that consistent overeating leads to obesity, and obesity is one of the leading health problems in the world. The World Health Organization website labels obesity an "epidemic." Essentially, eating too much will make you fat, and being fat can kill you.

At this point you might be thinking, *"That's great, but what does being fat have to do with winning people to Jesus?"*

It is my contention that many Christians today are becoming *spiritually gluttonous.* They are taking in as much spirituality as possible, but giving away very little or none at all.

Some Olympic athletes can consume 5,000 calories a day and remain very healthy; far healthier, in fact, than the average person because, although they may consume 5,000 calories a day, they burn those calories daily through a vigorous exercise and training regimen. They have a great deal of caloric intake, but they also have a great deal of caloric outflow. They take the calories in, and they burn the calories. If a person is obese it is because, without exception, that person is taking in more calories than he or she is burning.

Many Christians today have a great deal of spiritual intake. It would not be unheard of for a Christian to say something along these lines: *"I read my Bible all the time, I pray several times a day, and I am in church every time the doors are open. I am learning more about Jesus. I am growing in the fruits of the Spirit, and I am being used in the gifts of the Spirit. I am being discipled, I am being touched by God in worship regularly, and I am in a better place with Jesus than I have ever been before."* However, if you read this again, you will see one word repeated over and over: *"I."* Many Christians have a faith that is very much *"I"*-centered. *"I want God to touch me, I want to grow closer to Jesus, I need to be more righteous, I want to dance and raise my hands, I want to learn more about the Bible, I, I, I, me, me, me."* For many Christians the Christian faith has become a very "me"-centered faith rooted in spiritual selfishness. The

> A selfish faith is not the faith of Jesus Christ.

problem is this: A selfish faith is not the faith of Jesus Christ. The faith that Jesus established is one of living outside yourself and sacrificing your own needs, even your own life, for the lives of others. It always has been and always will be.

Please don't misunderstand. I believe in all of the Christian disciplines. Worship is amazing. Studying the Bible is essential. Knowing Jesus personally and intimately is the cornerstone of the Christian faith. Going to church is invaluable in reaching God's potential for our lives. I am not at all even remotely suggesting that we should lower our spiritual intake. What I am saying is that we should not only continue at a very high level of spiritual intake but also dramatically increase our level of spiritual outflow. The lessons we learn from God's Word, the times we spend in God's presence, and the joy we feel in worship should all be tools that we place in our belts to equip us for our primary mission: reaching the world with the Gospel of Jesus Christ. We should continue to take in massive amounts of spiritual calories daily, but we must be very, very careful that we are burning these calories through outreach, lest we blimp up and die spiritually.

Consider this very powerful and disturbing passage where God speaks through the prophet Amos:

Amos 5:21-24 & 6:1-8 - *"I hate, I despise your feast days, and I do not savor your sacred assemblies. Though you offer burnt offerings, I will not accept them, nor will I regard your fattened peace offerings. Take away from Me the noise of your songs, For I will not hear the melody of your stringed instruments. But let justice and righteousness* *run down like water . . . Woe to you who are at ease in Zion . . .* **Woe to you who put off the day of doom** *. . . who lie in beds of ivory, stretch out on your couches, eat lambs from the flock . . .* **who sing idly to the sound of stringed instruments** *. . . and anoint yourselves with the best ointments but are not grieved. . . .* **Those who recline at banquets shall be removed.** *"* (New King James Version)

Is it fair to say that this passage could very much apply to many Christians today? Are we as individuals unmoved by the lost state of the world? Are we *"putting off the day of doom"* as if God's day of judgment will never actually come? Are we living our lives as if lost people are not at risk? Are we spending a great deal of our time *"singing idly to the sound of stringed instruments"* but not letting justice and righteousness flow down like water into the lives of the people around us? Ecclesiastes 7:2 says, *"It is better to go to a house of mourning than to go to a house of feasting, for death is the destiny of every man; the living should take this to heart."*

In Matthew 22 a religious leader asked Jesus what the greatest commandment is. Jesus replied that the greatest commandment is to love God first with everything you are, and the second greatest is to love others as you would love yourself. He said that these two rules sum up everything it takes to obey God. You will notice that both of these greatest commandments are *outwardly* focused. Loving God is external. Loving others is external as well. The entire Christian faith is designed to be, from start to finish, an outwardly focused faith. As long as people are inwardly focused, even in their spiritual lives, they still will be missing the main point of the Gospel: escape from our own lives and investment in the lives of others.

Many Christians would never consider going a day without reading their Bible. Many Christians also would never consider going a full day, or even a few hours, without praying. Christians worship regularly, attend church regularly, and read Christian books regularly, but, sadly, most Christians today will go months and even years without sharing Jesus with the people around them. This is a travesty.

The question remains: What is a Christian to do?

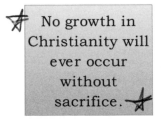

No growth in Christianity will ever occur without sacrifice.

Just as a person who has been eating too much and exercising too little, Christians must change their lifestyles. In this case, they should continue a great amount of spiritual intake through Bible reading, prayer, church attendance, and the like (taking in the right kinds of food). But they must change their exercise regimen to include working out spiritually, using those calories as energy for the real work of winning people to Jesus.

We are all familiar with the expression *"No pain, no gain."* This expression was never truer than in Christianity. No growth in Christianity will ever occur without sacrifice. As I mentioned in the last chapter, the cross of Jesus was the

It requires that we make choices that aren't always easy.

ultimate expression of sacrifice for the redemption of men. It is also intended as the ultimate example of the Christian lifestyle, laying down our lives for others. Living the Jesus-centered lifestyle requires that we become uncomfortable. It requires that we make choices that aren't always easy to make, and it requires that we give up the things we want in order that men might come to a saving knowledge of Jesus Christ.

Are you willing to give up comfortable, me-centered Christianity in exchange for the Christianity that God desires, which is centered on others? There is nothing in this world more important than the expansion of God's Gospel of Peace, and He is calling you, personally, to surrender your life to Him so completely that you will be a tool in His hands with only one purpose: reaching the world with His love. It is His plan for the world that the Gospel will go forth, and He wants to use you to do it. Will you play your part?

In Matthew 9:37 Jesus says, *"The harvest is plentiful, but the workers are few."* Continuing in Matthew 10 (a chapter almost entirely about the spreading of the Gospel), He says, *"Anyone who loves his father or mother more than me is not worthy of me; anyone who loves his son or daughter more than me is not worthy of me; and whoever does not take up his cross and follow me is not worthy of me. Whoever finds his life will lose it, and whoever loses his life for my sake will find it."*

> Make no mistake – the Gospel of Jesus requires your life.

Make no mistake – the Gospel of Jesus requires your life. It means moving past a religion that is all about your becoming more spiritual and into an abiding faith in Jesus that says to Him, *"My life is Yours; do with me what You will."* When He has you that completely, you can be assured He will use you to reach the nations with His message. It is His design for every believer.

This material is heavy. I understand that. I realize that it is a scary thing to give up your life to anyone for any reason. However, I also understand that God's ways are best, and living for His mission is the most fulfilling, amazing, and adventurous life a person can live. In the coming chapters I will begin a list of reasons that every Christian should be an active soulwinner (a person who brings people to Jesus). I pray you will be convinced not only that you *must* be a soulwinner but also that you *want* to be a soulwinner. Living the life of a soulwinner is the only way to go and the most excellent life a person can live. In the next few chapters you will begin to see why.

Discussion Questions:

-Is it possible to be spiritually selfish? Explain.

-What are some signs that a person is inwardly focused?

-What are some examples from the life of Jesus of living an outwardly focused life?

-What are some practical ways you could be more outwardly focused on a daily basis?

It Just Seems Good

"What is the greatest crime in the desert? Finding water and remaining silent."

-Arab Proverb

Did you know that your personal salvation hinges on your being a soulwinner?

Notice what I did not say. I did not say that your salvation *"depends"* on your being a soulwinner. I said that it *"hinges"* on it.

All your personal salvation depends on is the grace and mercy of Jesus Christ being active in your life through faith. That's it. However, scripture makes it perfectly clear that a genuine saving faith in the Lord Jesus Christ carries with it the earnest desire for others to come to faith as well. In other words, when you have a relationship with Jesus, it *"just seems good"* to share that relationship with others.

In Matthew 10:32-33 Jesus says, *"Whoever acknowledges me before men, I will also acknowledge him before my Father in Heaven. But whoever disowns me before men, I will disown him before my Father in Heaven."*

Jesus makes it very clear that the public proclamation of Himself as Lord is a salvation issue. Somehow a person's willingness to profess Jesus as Lord in front of people is directly tied to their salvation.

Jesus continues elsewhere to describe the expected lifestyle of those committed to Him:

Matthew 5:14-15 - *"You are the light of the world. A city on a hill cannot be hidden. Neither do people light a lamp and put it under a bowl. Instead they put it on its stand, and it gives light to everyone in the house."*

Matthew 10:27 - *"What I tell you in the dark, speak in the daylight; what is whispered in your ear, proclaim from the roofs."*

From these statements and many, many others it becomes blatantly obvious: Jesus desired that His followers would openly proclaim their faith and make it public. I have heard people say that their religion is *"a personal thing"* or that they like to keep it to themselves. If you are one who holds this belief, then I ask you this: What is your basis for that belief? It is certainly not a scriptural principle. In fact, the idea runs contrary to the teachings of Jesus.

In Ezekiel 33 the Lord speaks to the people and makes it clear that they are responsible for carrying His message to the people around them.

Ezekiel 33:8-9 - *"When I say to the wicked, 'O wicked man, you will surely die,'* **and you do not speak out** *to dissuade him from his ways, that wicked man will die for his sin, and* **I will hold you accountable** *for his blood. But if you do warn the wicked man to turn from his ways and he does not do so, he will die for his sin,* **but you will have saved yourself.**"

> *"I will hold you accountable for his blood."*

Once again, it is evident scripturally that the sharing of God's message with the people around us is a salvation issue and that those whom God calls His own are expected to speak out publicly on His behalf.

The first few verses of Luke are some of my favorites in the Bible:

Luke 1:1-4 - *"Many have undertaken to draw up an account of the things that have been fulfilled among us, just as they were handed down to us by those who from the first were eyewitnesses and servants of the word. Therefore, since I myself have carefully investigated everything from the beginning,* **it seemed good** *also to me to write an orderly account for you, most excellent Theophilus, so that you may know the certainty of the things you have been taught."*

I love it! Luke doesn't say something ultra-spiritual and sanctimonious here. He doesn't say, *"I, Luke, writing under the clear unction of the most Holy*

Spirit by divine revelation through the grace of the Lord Jesus Christ . . . ." Instead, he says, *"it seemed good"* to write. Can you believe it? *"It seemed good."* Every time I read it I get excited. One of the three synoptic Gospels, a book that has changed history for all time, that has changed my life personally, that rests between the covers of the Holy Bible, was written by a guy in the first century who thought *"it seemed good"* to write it. Yes!

Doesn't it *"seem good"* to share Jesus with others? When you consider all that God has done in the world, all that He has done and is doing in your own life, doesn't it just seem good to tell others about it? When you think about how amazing His principles are, how awesome His power is, how great His joy and peace are, and how beautiful it is to be with Him, how could you not tell others? In Jeremiah 20:9 the prophet of God describes what it would be like if he tried to keep from speaking about God and says, *"His word is in my heart like a fire, a fire shut up in my bones. I am weary of holding it in; indeed, I cannot."* And in 1 Corinthians 9:16 Paul says, *"I am compelled to preach. Woe to me if I do not preach the Gospel!"*

> The Gospel is not the Gospel until it is shared with others. Period.

Christians worldwide profess to a belief in the Gospel of Jesus. The word "gospel" literally means "good news," and the word "news" could easily be defined as "information that is shared." Information does not become "news" until it is communicated to others, so one way to define the word "gospel" would be "good information that is shared." The Gospel is not the Gospel until it is shared with others. Period.

34

Imagine a newspaper staff that goes to all of the trouble of going through a great deal of global information and news reports from around the country. Then they decide what items are newsworthy (i.e., worthy of being shared.) They compile the news in an attractive format, placing the most important items on the front page, secondary items on the second page, and so on. They sell advertising space and classifieds, accept letters to the editor, and do all of the other things that newspapers do regularly. They invest the time and resources every day to make the paper and to print massive quantities. However, this particular newspaper staff, when printing is completed, doesn't actually distribute the news. Instead, they keep a massive warehouse where there are stacks and stacks, row after row, of archived papers that have never seen the light of day and have never been read by a soul outside the newsroom. The people who work with the paper read it and know the information stored there, but it benefits only them, increasing their personal knowledge base. It never informs the public.

Does it make sense? Of course it doesn't. It defies logic. By definition, for a newspaper to be a newspaper, it must be distributed. In the same way, for Christianity to be Christianity, the message must be distributed.

Jesus came to Earth and lived a sinless, perfect life. He healed the sick, raised the dead, delivered oppressed people, walked on water, fed the hungry, and much more. He gave the world the greatest teachings on life and morality it has ever known. He suffered cruelly and died horribly on a cross. He rose from the dead and made His divinity known. His message is life transforming and good, offering peace, hope, love, and grace. It is the pinnacle of newsworthiness.

As Christians, we take the time to learn the message. We go to church. We listen to preachers. We read and study our Bibles diligently. And then, when the process of learning and compiling the Good News is done, we store it away and do nothing with it except edify ourselves. Just like the journalist who never distributes the news, we have a distribution problem that defies logic.

Just as the news isn't the news until someone else hears about it, the Gospel isn't the Gospel until others hear the message.

Jesus said in Mark 1:17, *"Come follow me . . . and I will make you fishers of men."*

By Jesus' own words we see that it is a defining characteristic of His followers. They are soulwinners. He doesn't say that if we will follow Him, He *might* make us fishers of men or that it is *possible* we will reach out to others. He says that if we follow Him, He *will* make us fishers of men. Those who follow Jesus become outreach oriented, without exception. If people are not outreach oriented, they are not following Jesus in the truest sense. Jesus' statement above could be rephrased, *"If you follow me it's inevitable, unavoidable even: Following me means a life centered on outreach."*

> By Jesus' own words we see that it is a defining characteristic of His followers. They are soulwinners.

Bringing judgment or condemnation is not my intent here. What I am attempting to do is challenge people to seriously examine their lives and lifestyles to see whether they are legitimately following Jesus. I am not trying to figure out who is saved and who isn't based on a set of rules – Romans 10 expressly forbids that. But I also know that the New Testament teaches that you can tell a lot about people based on the *"fruit"* you see in their lives.

Matthew 3:10 - *"Every tree that does not produce good fruit will be cut down and thrown into the fire."*

Luke 6:44 - *"Each tree is recognized by its own fruit."*

John 15:2 - *"He cuts off every branch in me that bears no fruit."*

Romans 7:4 - *"You also died . . . in order that we might bear fruit to God."*

Just as you can tell an orange tree by recognizing the oranges or an apple tree by the apples, one way to recognize a Christian – someone who is following Jesus – is by the fruit of a selfless, outreach-oriented lifestyle. It was the lifestyle of Jesus, and He intended for it to be the lifestyle of every person who bears His name. Just as oranges naturally grow out of orange trees, so outreach and evangelism are natural *"growths"* in the life of every Christian. Followers of Jesus become soulwinners, if for no other reason than that *"it just seems good."*

How about you? Is your lifestyle outreach oriented? If you examine yourself and find that you are not outreach oriented, it is easy to turn around. You can begin today. Repent. Confess to God that outreach has not been a priority in your life and that you need His grace to help you. Jesus told a parable in Luke 13:6-9 about a fig tree that was failing to produce figs. After three years of fruitlessness the man was ready to dig up the plant and destroy it. But the man who *"took care of the vineyard"* pleaded for one more year, and the owner consented. In the same way, I believe Jesus is pleading for you, even now, before God the Father. You can begin producing the fruit of outreach in your life today if you will allow God to shape you. Ask Him. He will help.

Discussion Questions:

-What does it mean to be a *"follower"* of Jesus Christ?

-What is so *"good"* about the *"Good News"*?

-What good things has God done in your life that are worth talking about?

-Who do you know that could use some *"Good News"*?

Personal Growth

"You have nothing to do but save souls. Therefore, spend and be spent in this work."

- John Wesley

Focusing on personal spiritual growth is not the key to personal spiritual growth. It is focusing on others that will help you grow in Jesus like nothing else. It is the fastest and surest way to grow in your walk with Jesus and become what He wants you to be. In fact, without a central focus on others, genuine Christian growth is impossible.

In Romans 13:10 we read, *"Love is the fulfillment of the law."* 1 Corinthians 13:5 tells us that *"love is not self-seeking."* In other words, everything it takes to please God is summed up in love, and love is not about you. It is focused on others.

Many Christians I know would love to hear God's voice more clearly. They would love to understand the Bible more, and they would love to see their prayer times become more productive. They would love to walk at a greater level of purity and righteousness. In essence, they want to grow. Because the Christian faith is designed to be outwardly oriented, however, it is impossible to grow genuinely as long as our focus is centered on ourselves. The key is to take our eyes off ourselves and focus on helping others reach their potential in Jesus. If Christians will do this, their personal spiritual lives will take off like a rocket. It is unavoidable. As we will discuss in the following pages, a focus on others will motivate you even more to be all that you can be in Jesus. It won't hinder your time in prayer, at church, or in the Bible. It actually will propel you further on in those pursuits. The actions will be the same; the motive – and the end result – will be different.

Growing in Christianity requires following Jesus intimately. Following Jesus intimately requires taking up His mission and goals. As we have discussed in previous chapters, taking up His mission and goals means laying down our lives – our time, resources, and efforts – so that others might come to a saving knowledge of Him.

Giving your life to the mission of Jesus and sharing His love and message with the world around you are not only the clearest marks of Christian maturity, they are also the only path that leads to real and lasting personal growth in Him.

I heard it said in a sales presentation once, *"The surest way to achieve your dreams and goals is to spend your life trying to make the dreams and goals of others become reality."* It is true. It's a spiritual law as sure as gravity. Time and effort invested in the lives of others is time and effort well spent. If I will plant spiritual seeds in the lives of others, I will reap spiritual results in my own life. If I will motivate and help people come to know Jesus, I will come to know Him more than I ever would have trying to reach Him through personal effort alone.

Let me say it one more time: The fastest and surest way to grow in Jesus is to spend your life helping others grow in Him.

The next few chapters will look at some ways that focusing on sharing Jesus with others will turbo-charge your own personal spiritual life.

Hearing God's Voice: John 10:4 says, *"His sheep follow him because they know his voice."*

It is necessary, as followers of Jesus, that we are able to hear from Him, and there are many ways that can happen: through His Word, through His quiet voice whispering in our heads, through people He has placed in authority over us, through our circumstances, through friends and family, and even through our emotions or conscience. The question is, how can we discern what is God and what isn't? There are so many voices and forces pulling us in so many directions at all times. How can we hear God's voice clearly? In order to do so, it is necessary to tune in to His frequency.

> How can we discern what is God and what isn't?

I heard a story about a military man who had gone in for an interview to be a telegraph operator. The job required extensive knowledge of Morse code.

When the man arrived at the site for the interview, he found a room filled with about a dozen other candidates who were applying for the same position. They were sitting at various locations in the room with their heads buried in books. They were all studying their codes, knowing they soon would be tested.

> It is necessary to tune in to His frequency.

For approximately an hour and a half they all sat there studying and occasionally looking around, wondering why no one had come to greet them. The time dragged on and on as no one appeared.

Suddenly, after a great deal of time had passed, one candidate stood up, cleared his throat, straightened his uniform, and walked through a door on the other side of the room. He had been gone for only a few minutes when the door reopened and an officer stepped through. The officer announced, *"I'm sorry, gentlemen, but the position has been filled, and we have no need for any further interviews. Thank you for your time."*

As it turned out, the entire time the candidates had been sitting in the room studying, Morse code was being faintly, but discernibly, tapped out over the P.A. system. The message had been repeated over and over until one of the candidates had finally tuned in and heard it. It said, *"The first person who hears this code and walks through the door in the back of the room will be given the job."* Finally, one of the candidates had tweaked his focus enough to get his head out of his book and hear the subtle message. As a result, he had heard what he needed to hear, and the job became his.

Hearing from God works very similarly. It takes being in tune with Him. It means focusing on the right thing. The problem most people have trying to hear from God is that they are not on His frequency. Mark these words: God never speaks anything unless it makes His Kingdom bigger. If you are trying to hear from God for personal reasons it is going to be very, very difficult, if not impossible. Clarity in hearing from God comes when you lay down your own motives and desires and begin saying to Him, *"I want what You want. Whatever You say goes, and whatever You want from my life is Yours."* At that point you can bet that you will begin hearing from Him more clearly. You can also bank on the fact that He will begin using your life for one purpose alone, reaching people with the Good News that He loves them and is available to them.

> God never speaks anything unless it makes His Kingdom bigger.

God wants to speak to you, but His communication with you will be, one hundred percent of the time, about reconciling man to God in one way or another. If you will give Him your ear with the attitude that you want to hear about His plan and want to be a part of reaching people for Him, you can rest assured that you will hear from Him like never before.

Cleaning Up Your Life: Nothing will clean you up like a focus on winning others to Jesus. When you come to the conclusion that your life is supposed to be spent sharing God with the people around you, it suddenly becomes more important than ever to make sure you live an upright and Godly life. When we focus on ourselves, the question always seems to be, *"How much can I get away with and still be right with God?"* When the question instead becomes, *"How can I effectively reach out to others?"* things begin to change. Instead of stretching the limits to get away with whatever we can, suddenly the standard becomes much higher. We realize that effectively reaching people for God requires a change in lifestyle that is apparent to others.

We all know that it is going to be difficult to convince a friend of the life-changing power of Jesus if that same friend knows that we are sleeping with someone who isn't our spouse, that we are viewing things online that we have no business viewing, that we talk about others behind their backs, or that we are out at the clubs getting drunk on the weekends.

People hate hypocrites. In talking with people about Jesus for the last decade I have heard it time and time again: *"I can't stand people who are out getting drunk every Saturday night and sitting in church on Sunday morning."* What this means, of course, is that if we become serious about reaching people for Jesus, it becomes necessary that we do our best to live as an example for Him. We realize that as His *"ambassadors"* (see 2 Corinthians 5:20) we should represent Him well.

> People hate hypocrites.

Please understand, I am not talking about a works-based faith here. I am talking about a life that has been transformed by Jesus (and there is a big difference). There can be no doubt scripturally that the lifestyle of a disciple of Christ is designed to be a lifestyle that emulates Him and His character. When Jesus enters a person's life, He changes them. Our lives should reflect this clearly.

1 Peter 1:15-17 - *"Just as he who called you is holy, so be holy in all you do; for it is written: 'Be holy, because I am holy.'"*

1 John 2:6 - *"Whoever claims to live in him must walk as Jesus did."*

1 Thessalonians 3:13 - *"May he strengthen your hearts so that you will be blameless and holy . . . ."*

The list of passages describing the lifestyle of a Christian as *"pure,"* *"holy,"* *"blameless,"* *"righteous,"* *"honorable,"* *"upright,"* or even *"perfect"* could go on and on.

The righteousness and perfection of a Christian come through Jesus Christ and Him alone. It is only through faith in Him that a person will ever be declared right in God's sight. The moment people begin to believe that their own personal holiness makes them something special is the moment they begin to abandon the teachings of God's Word. However, the same Word of God makes it very clear time and time again that a saving faith in Jesus changes people and puts them on a path that leads toward being like Him in thought, word, and deed.

If we are serious about reaching people for Jesus it is inevitable that we will become very committed to leading a Godly lifestyle because we realize that setting a Godly example for others is imperative if they are going to take us seriously when we share our faith. Matthew 5:16 tells us that seeing our *"good deeds"* should be at least one way by which people are propelled toward praising our Father in Heaven. Realizing this takes us a long way toward understanding what God really expects of us. Romans 12: 2 says that we are supposed to have our minds renewed in order that we may *"test and approve what God's will is – His good, pleasing and perfect will."* When our minds become renewed to think of loving others and sharing God's love with them as our life's goal, it naturally follows that we will come to understand what kind of lifestyle God expects of us. When our sincere desire becomes the salvation of others we will be more motivated than ever before to choose what is right.

Genuine love pushes us toward genuine goodness in every area.

Love is the highest ideal. It is the highest motive and the final authority on what is right and good. Real love will propel us to treat people with honor, respect, and compassion. It refuses self-destructive behavior, and it abhors behavior that hurts others. In other words, real love drives us toward Godly perfection. Genuine love pushes us toward genuine goodness in every area.

A lifestyle and mindset centered on loving God and others ahead of ourselves requires many changes in our behavior. An outward focus centered on sharing Jesus with others will always be the clearest path toward behaving in a way that pleases God. It is both the motive and the method toward living a Godly lifestyle as seen in Philippians 1:9-10, which says, *"This is my prayer: that your love may abound more and more in knowledge and depth of insight, so that you may be able to discern what is best and may be pure and blameless . . . ."*

When I was a sophomore in college I learned a valuable lesson about the correlation between living a Godly lifestyle and reaching out to others. At that point in my life, I was an active member of a Christian organization on campus. I was active in outreach, sharing my faith with people on a near-daily basis. People who knew me knew that I was serious about my faith and that I was serious about others coming to know Jesus. I was also living in compromise. I was spending the night regularly with the girl I was dating. At that time in our relationship, we were not physically "involved." In fact, we hadn't even kissed. We did, however, sometimes share a bed for the night and sleep together. I justified this by saying that our relationship wasn't sexual so it was *"no big deal."* That was before the night the fire alarm went off.

It was about 3 o'clock one morning, and she and I were staying together in her room in an all-girls dorm. (I had snuck in through a back stairwell.) When the fire alarm went off, everyone was required to leave the building and wait outside while the fire department came and made sure everything was okay. So, it was a couple hundred girls, a handful of other guys who had also snuck into the dorm, and me, standing in the cold and looking around at one another. I distinctly remember seeing the faces of those who knew me. The looks on their faces made it clear that they wondered what in the world I was doing there. That's when it hit me. The behavior was wrong! When people saw me coming out of her dorm room at 3 a.m., you can imagine the impression it left. I was compromising, and it was ruining my witness – potentially rendering me ineffective in sharing the Gospel. I was, at that point, betraying Jesus. The behavior had to change, and it did. When I realized that others were watching my behavior and that my actions made an impact on their lives, I began making better decisions. My life changed when I realized that God expected me to be an example for others, and I am so thankful that it did.

He expects right decisions from you, too. You are designed to be a shining example of God's light in a dark world that loves compromise. You are designed to be a witness of Jesus. Whether it is a matter of the way you talk, the things you look at, your attitude toward your boss, or the places you

> Let people see Jesus in you without compromise.

choose to visit, people need you to be an example for them. Let people see Jesus in you without compromise. Let them see that Jesus really can change a life and make people new. Be the person God has called you to be. Just as it would be difficult for me to convince others I have the cure for cancer if I have open sores and am doubled over in pain, so it also is nearly impossible to convince people that we have the cure for sin and selfishness if we are walking in compromise and rebellion. A focus on reaching others demands a lifestyle that glorifies God. If we are to reach others with the Gospel, we must clean up our lives.

Discussion Questions:

-What are some of the distractions that might keep us from hearing God more clearly?

-How would focusing on others help us hear God's voice more clearly?

-How would focusing on others propel us toward living a more Godly lifestyle?

-What behaviors would others view as "hypocritical" in our lives?

"The first time that Jesus came in the flesh, He died for the lost of the world, gladly laying down His precious life that others might have true life! Now that He is enfleshed in you, I wonder what He wants to do?"
                                                                    -John Willis Zumwalt

Personal Growth II

"If the church would only awaken to her responsibility of intercession, we could well evangelize the world in a short time."

— T.S. Hegre

Do you want to know the single most important key to unlocking everything that is available to us as followers of Jesus? The answer is found in Philemon 1:6, which says, *"I pray that you **may be active in sharing your faith, so that you will have a full understanding of every good thing we have in Christ.**"* Paul tells us here, very explicitly, that actively sharing our faith is the key to understanding everything that it means to be in Christ Jesus. One area that a lifestyle of outreach opens is prayer because prayer and evangelism go hand in hand.

There are many situations in nature in which two organisms exist in a mutualistic relationship – helping each other. One example of such a relationship is the interaction between certain species of ants and the tiny, pear-shaped insect known as an aphid (or plant louse). Aphids excrete a shiny, sticky substance known as honeydew, on which some ants feed. As such, it is not uncommon for ants to fight off the natural predators that threaten aphids. Their food supply depends on it. In turn, when the aphids are well protected, the ants have a limitless supply of food. It is a win-win situation for both organisms. If you want to get rid of the ants, get rid of the aphids. If you want to eliminate the aphids, a good beginning would be to get rid of the ants. The relationship between ants and aphids is circular. The ant helps the aphid, who then helps the ant, and the relationship continues. You can have one without the other, but neither will be as strong as it would be with the other. Prayer and evangelism have a similar relationship. They can exist separately, but, to maximize their potential, they are best together.

Prayer empowers evangelism. Nearly every time I go fishing, I find myself praying that I will catch fish. I talk to the water (*"here, fishy, fishy"*), but, almost without exception, I also find myself saying, *"Lord, please help me catch some fish today."* How much more should we be praying that the Lord will help us in our efforts to be fishers of men?

I have heard it said that trying to win people to Jesus without prayer is like trying to drive a car without gas. It simply doesn't work. While I don't think the illustration is perfect (God's Word is still God's Word, and it *will* bear fruit), there is no question that, if we want to be as effective as we possibly can be in reaching the world with the Gospel, we must pray. We must pray diligently and faithfully. E.M. Bounds said it like this: *"The keynote of apostolic success is this: Put the saints everywhere to the task of praying. The Gospel moves with slow and timid pace when the saints are not at their prayers early and late and long."* Elsewhere he said, *"No person is a soulwinner who is not an expert in the ministry of prayer."*

A lifestyle centered on outreach opens doors of prayer that will never be opened otherwise. A person with a sincere heart for the nations must learn to pray if he or she is to succeed. Evangelism is, and always will be, both a natural and a supernatural work. The conversion of a person from death to life and from darkness into light will always be a work of the Spirit of God on the spirit of a man. There is no effort on our part, no argument, no logic, and no understanding that can produce this spiritual change. It is only God's supernatural power working through our natural efforts that can do the job, and one way that God releases His power is in response to faith-filled prayer.

> A person with a sincere heart for the nations must learn to pray.

Ephesians 6:12 says, *"Our struggle is not against flesh and blood, but against the rulers, against the authorities, against the powers of this dark world and against the spiritual forces of evil in the heavenly realms."* The fight we are fighting is not a fight taking place in this world. It is other-worldly, and prayer is our chief means of doing battle.

Prayer does a few very significant things where outreach is concerned:

Prayer prepares us for the work of God's Kingdom: A life of prayer can mean the difference between walking in fear or walking in great courage.

It can mean the difference between having on-the-spot wisdom and having nothing profitable to say. It can fill us with a heart of compassion for people, and that compassion will be noticed. It can motivate us when desire is lacking. It is the difference between an effective and inspiring Christian and one who is feeble and uninteresting.

Prayer prepares those who will hear our message: Prayer can soften the hardest heart. It can cause someone to listen to us intently who normally would never even consider our message. It can put us in the right place at the right time. It can shape circumstances in the lives of unbelievers

> Prayer is the difference between an effective and inspiring Christian and one who is feeble and uninteresting.

and remove confusion, doubt, and turmoil. It can be the difference between a person who is receptive and one who isn't.

Prayer opens up channels of communication: Anyone who studies communication will tell you that there are several important factors. A message is passed from an information source through a transmitter to a destination through a receiver. In most cases of human interaction, this means one person speaks and another person hears. In between the transmission and reception, however, the signal can be distorted through noise or interference. Prayer can be a huge step toward eliminating interference – in making sure the message gets from point A to point B without becoming distorted in between. It can cause the message to bypass walls and barriers that have been erected because of past pain and can clarify signals normally distorted by bias, pride, hatred, or countless other hindrances. Prayer is even powerful enough to help people hear what God needs them to hear, even when the message sender may not be the most educated or articulate. Prayer can make the message effective, regardless of the source or situation.

As *"fishers of men,"* because prayer does all these things, we need to stay prayed up. Great opportunities to share Jesus can arrive without notice (and, coincidentally, the more a Christian prays, the more these spur-of-the-moment witnessing opportunities seem to happen). Usually we will not have time to withdraw and pray. It is very important that we pray continually. We need to ask God to touch the people around us, soften their hearts, and change their ways of thinking. We need to pray for boldness, wisdom, and supernatural insight into the lives of those with whom we come in contact. We need to pray that God will fill us with His love for the people of the world.

It is important that we learn how to pray for the lost if we are to be successful in our efforts. Prayer should be a lifetime pursuit for all believers, and it is some of the most demanding work in which a believer can engage. While there are thousands of lessons that one could learn about prayer, it must have two main attributes if it is to be effective. One is that prayer must be faith filled. The other is that it must be persistent.

There is one kind of prayer I am confident displeases God, and it goes like this: *"Dear Lord, I need (insert need here) from You. Please do it for me."* A short time passes – a few days, a few hours, or even a few minutes. And then, *"Lord, I prayed for something, and it didn't come yet. Why don't You ever answer my prayers?"*

Prayers like this are not prayers of faith, but rather prayers based on doubt. The Word of God tells us in James 1:6, *"But **when he asks, he must believe and not doubt**, because he who doubts is like a wave of the sea, blown and tossed by the wind."* Unfortunately, it is all too common for us to pray once, or even a few times, and then give up when we don't see the results we desire as quickly as we would like to see them.

Jesus taught us exactly how He would like us to pray:

Luke 11:5-9 - *"Suppose one of you has a friend, and he goes to him at midnight and says, 'Friend, lend me three loaves of bread, because a friend of mine on a journey has come to me, and I have nothing to set before him.' Then the one inside answers, 'Don't bother me. The door is already locked, and my children are with me in bed. I can't get up and give you anything.' I tell you, though he will not get up and give him the bread because he is his friend, yet **because of the man's boldness he will get up and give him as much as he needs.** So I say to you: Ask and it will be given to you; seek and you will find; knock and the door will be opened to you. For everyone who asks receives; he who seeks finds; and to him who knocks, the door will be opened."*

Luke 18:1-8 - *"Then Jesus told his disciples a parable to show them that they should **always pray and not give up.** He said: "In a certain town there was a judge who neither feared God nor cared about men. And there was a widow in that town who kept coming to him with the plea, 'Grant me justice against my adversary.' For some time he refused.*

But finally he said to himself, 'Even though I don't fear God or care about men, yet **because this widow keeps bothering me, I will see that she gets justice,** *so that she won't eventually wear me out with her coming!'" And the Lord said, "Listen to what the unjust judge says. And will not God bring about justice for his chosen ones, who cry out to him day and night? Will he keep putting them off? I tell you, he will see that they get justice, and quickly. However, when the Son of Man comes, will he find faith on the earth?"*

Prayer that works is prayer that absolutely refuses to give up, no matter what. Prayer that pleases God is tenacious, persistent, and even a little bit impudent. It is like Jacob, who wrestled with God and refused to let go until the blessing came. Faith-filled prayer never surrenders.

> Prayer that pleases God is tenacious, persistent, and even a little bit impudent.

Prayer that reaches Heaven and accomplishes results is comparable to a tiny person trying to ring a very heavy church bell. It just isn't possible with a simple tug here and there. You can't pull on the rope once, or even a few times, and expect the bell to ring. Pulling, walking away, walking back, and pulling some more doesn't get the job done. It is only through persistence and consistency that the bell will ring loud and clear. It takes grabbing the rope, pulling it, riding it to the top and back down, pulling it again, and pulling it again. It takes putting your entire weight into the work. It takes diligence and hard work. If we would never give up on prayer we would see results. We must continue to pray for unbelievers, even when hope seems bleak.

In Daniel 10, an angel appears to Daniel and explains to him that, although he has been praying for quite a while with no results, God heard his prayer as soon as it was uttered. However, from the time of his prayer until the time the angel appeared, 21 days later, a battle had been taking place in the spiritual realm and was continuing even at that moment. The results had not been seen yet, but the battle was raging. Help was on the way. It just hadn't arrived yet.

It is the same way when we pray for others. Sometimes we will not see immediately the results we want to see. But, if we will continue to believe God, trusting Him to fulfill His promises, we will see results in due time. Remember this when praying for your family, friends, and other loved ones: the battle is going on now. Prayer is one force capable of turning the tide in the war that is raging on planet Earth for the souls of men. As long as Christians place the salvation of men as their highest priority, they will learn to pray.

> If we will continue to believe God, trusting Him, we will see results in due time.

Prayer is such a powerful force in the battle for the lives of people that one might even consider it a method of evangelism. When all else fails, when a person refuses to listen to the Gospel message, prayer can result in the breakthrough needed. When a person has heard and yet failed to respond to the Gospel many times, prayer may be the only hope. Prayer can accomplish things that nothing else can. Christians want to know how to pray. They want their prayers to become more effective and want to see God answering when they call. Outreach is the key to all of this.

When a person's life is centered on loving God and loving others, many walls that once hindered prayer come crashing down. A life of outreach is a huge key toward a life of prayer, and a life of prayer is a huge key toward a life of outreach. The two cannot be separated.

Discussion Questions:

-How do prayer and outreach go hand in hand?

-Why must prayer be both faith-filled and persistent?

-What are some ways we can pray for those who are not following Jesus?

-What are some times in your life when God answered prayer?

"Let us not glide through this world and then slip quietly into heaven, without having blown the trumpet loud and long for our Redeemer, Jesus Christ. Let us see to it that the devil will hold a thanksgiving service in hell when he gets the news of our departure from the field of battle."
                                                                                    - C.T. Studd

Personal Growth III

"Worship and evangelism are inextricably intertwined, but the first is the goal and the second is the means."
                                                                      - Marva Dawn

I am not a big fan of chocolate.

I know most people can't relate to that, but it's true. In fact, many times, chocolate gives me a headache. When a person gives me a gift, pretty much the last gift I would want to receive would be chocolate. In fact, if a person knew me well and gave me a gift of chocolate, I might consider the person somewhat thoughtless. I would wonder why the person didn't at least go through the effort to find out what I like and what I don't like.

Part of blessing someone is making the effort to find out what is important to them – finding out what they like – and then giving it to them. We don't (at least, we shouldn't) give gifts based on what we would want or based on what we consider convenient or comfortable to give. To be a good gift giver, we must consider what is desired by the person who will receive the gift.

If a person we are shopping for has one overwhelming passion in life, gift giving can become very simple. We look for a gift that is related to that passion. For example, my mother-in-law loves photography. She loves taking pictures; she does research on the latest photographic technology; and she has even set up a makeshift photography studio in her basement, complete with the appropriate lighting, backdrops, and even a few props. When I am buying a gift for her, I always consider buying something related to photography. I know she loves photography, and so, when I want to bless her, gifts related to photography are almost always on target. She has several other hobbies, including gardening, bike riding, and quilting. She may like those things, but she *loves* photography. I can never go wrong if I go that route.

> Worshiping God is a process of finding out what is most important to God and then giving Him what He desires.

Worshiping God can be very similar. It is a process of finding out what is most important to God and then giving Him what He desires.

If you ask the average churchgoer today, *"What is worship?"* the first images many will think of are keyboards and guitars, drums and singers. We imagine people lifting their voices and hands to God in song and prayer. We might imagine people bowing, crying, or dancing. These are, of course, all manners in which we may worship, but these actions are not worship in and of themselves. True worship goes beyond action and takes place deep within a person's heart. It is more an attitude or a motive than it is an action. True worship is placing oneself in a posture of humility and submission before God that says, *"Do with me whatever You want. I am Yours."* Romans 12:1 illustrates this clearly when it says, *"Therefore, I urge you, brothers, in view of God's mercy, to offer your bodies as living sacrifices, holy and pleasing to God – this is your spiritual act of worship."*

This condition of complete surrender to God will often result in the actions described above. People surrendered to God may do all of these things and more. They will sing, they may clap, they might dance, and they will pray. However, worship that stops there falls tremendously short of the worship that God desires. God desires that we find out what is most important to Him and then give Him what He wants. As we have already established, people are His greatest passion. He wants us to reach them. It is the greatest gift we can give Him and the act of worship He appreciates most.

There are many acts of worship that God appreciates in addition to the actions of singing, clapping, and praising described above. Financial giving can be an act of worship. Showing kindness or charity can be an act of worship. Fasting and praying also can be acts of worship. But the greatest act of worship, the gift we can give God that means the most to Him, is a gift of our lives in service to His Kingdom. It is a gift that says, *"God, I recognize that You have a passion that all men everywhere would come to know You. I see there is nothing more important to You. As such, I want to do all I can to make sure that happens. Here I am. Send me."*

Just like my buying photography equipment for my mother-in-law, God will always be excited when you give Him a gift related to His greatest passion. The sacrifice of a life dedicated to evangelism will always be pleasing in God's eyes. It is His favorite act of worship, superseding every other gift we could present. Let us never claim to be true worshipers of God as long as we ignore His greatest passion. It is impossible to be identified as a "worshiper" of God as long as we ignore the masses of people who don't know Him. He loves them passionately and desires them with a fervor we cannot possibly understand. To knit our hearts to Him in worship requires that we take up His passion and pursue people with our heart, soul, mind, and strength. Most Christians desire to grow in their experience of God in worship. A life centered on others is the key. As Dick Eastman, author of *The Hour That Changes the World* said, *"To evangelize the lost glorifies God on the highest level."*

In the end of the ninth chapter of the book of Luke, we find what I believe are some of the hardest statements Jesus made to anyone. He was calling people to follow Him, and the people wanted to comply – they just had a couple of items they wanted to take care of first. One man's father had just died, and he wanted to attend the funeral. The other man simply wanted to return home and say goodbye to his family. Both of these reasons seem completely valid. In fact, most people I know would not fault these people for their desires. Jesus, however, was not "most people."

To the man who wanted to attend to his dead father, Jesus said, *"Let the dead bury their own dead, but you go and proclaim the kingdom of God."* To the one who wanted to say goodbye to his family, Jesus exclaimed, *"No one who puts his hand to the plow and looks back is fit for service in the kingdom of God."*

Even now as I read this, I am struck with the thought, *"Wow, Jesus was harsh."* To us, this kind of all-encompassing demand seems nearly over the line, if not totally over the line. But this is the kind of sacrifice Jesus requires. The worship He desires from us is that we would lay down our lives to follow Him and serve His Kingdom and mission. The sacrifice of worship that we offer Him is our entire lives. When a person grows in the area of evangelism, growth in worship is a natural result. Where outreach is lacking, worship is lacking as well.

> Where outreach is lacking, worship is lacking as well.

Another area that goes hand in hand with evangelism is growth in the Word of God. To illustrate this point imagine a car mechanic who has learned his trade from reading books. This particular mechanic has studied the ins and outs of car design and repair very thoroughly and knows his stuff. You need your brakes fixed? He can do it in a flash. Want your radiator flushed? He's your man. But wait. He does have one minor problem. In all of his reading, he has never grasped the fact that cars were meant to go somewhere. As far as he is concerned, cars are beautiful pieces of modern ingenuity. He sees them as amazing tributes to the car maker. He doesn't understand, however, that they are not only beautiful but also functional. This mechanic has built cars from the ground up, but the cars he has repaired have never gone anywhere. He has never seen the need for them to travel.

As such, portions of his car manuals just don't make sense to him. He can understand why it's important to change the Freon in the air conditioning unit because it keeps people cool when they sit inside. He knows why it's good to have a functional windshield wiper motor – it allows people to see through the windshield, even on a rainy day. But the need for the car engine just baffles him. Sure, it fires up, and it makes noise; sure, he has learned how to build one; but, because he doesn't understand the basic purpose of a car, the roar of the engine ultimately confounds him. He just doesn't get it. So, remaining perplexed about the purpose of the car, he fails to understand completely the manuals about car repair. And, failing to understand the manuals, his eyes are never opened to the practical nature of the automobile, traveling from point A to point B.

Many people today are in a similar boat as that of this mechanic. They have never come to understand the underlying principles of Christianity. As such, the service manual – the Bible – just doesn't do for them all that it could. To them it is a great book. It helps them keep their lives in some semblance of beauty and order. But, because they fail to understand the basic purpose of their lives – loving God and loving others – much of what is contained in the Bible misses them completely. It is just as ridiculous for a mechanic to misunderstand that cars were meant for driving as it is for a Christian who studies the Bible to miss the point that Christians were meant for outreach.

Just as we studied concerning prayer, a life of outreach and a life consumed with God's Word go hand in hand. They are in a symbiotic relationship. A life in God's Word points people toward their purpose: reaching other people. Conversely, a life consumed with reaching others must always be a life consumed with the study of God's Word. God's Word is inspiration for those whose will is lacking, strength for those who feel incapable or afraid, instruction for those who feel ill-equipped, and a recharging station for those who feel drained. A true soulwinner will be a true student of the Word every time. In the same way, a true student of the Word should become a soulwinner without exception.

There are several ways in which the Word of God and evangelism are connected:

The Word of God only makes sense in light of God's greatest passion: The Bible is God's story of the redemption of mankind. From the fall of Genesis to the life, death, and resurrection of Jesus, all the way through to His second coming and the establishment of the Kingdom of Heaven, the Bible is about man's relationship with God. Understanding this goes a long way toward understanding the Bible as a whole. It is, for all intents and purposes, the Bible "code." Just like trying to read a car manual without understanding the basic functionality of a car, trying to understand the Bible without a basic understanding of God's passion for people is destined to end in perplexity.

The Word of God provides the commission and inspiration for reaching people: In many ways, the Bible reads like a letter from a *Mission Impossible* episode. It essentially says, *"Your mission, should you choose to accept it"* is to reach the world for Jesus. The Bible lays it out for us in no uncertain terms: We are God's agents in the world. He has a job for us to do.

The Word of God is the means of fulfilling His mission: As we will explore in a later chapter, sharing the Word of God with people is the method that God has chosen for reaching the world. It is the Word of God, received and planted in the life of a person, that promotes change. Our mission is to share the Gospel around the world. The Gospel is the Good News of God's Word. Where the Word of God is absent, evangelism is impossible. For people to be born into the Kingdom of God, they *must* receive His Word into their lives. In order for that to happen, we must share it with them. Having a life centered on others will, by default, drive Christians toward the Word of God. When a person desires to share a message with others, he or she must become familiar with that message. When a person we are sharing with asks questions we don't know how to answer, it should most definitely drive us toward the Word to seek answers. In that way, we will become more and more capable as we go. The next time we are confronted with the same questions, we will know how to respond.

> We are God's agents in the world. He has a job for us to do.

The desire to share with others will also go a tremendous way toward prompting us to memorize scripture. When sharing the Gospel with others, we will not always have the time or ability to look up passages of scripture. The more we can memorize, the better equipped we will be to minister to people in every situation. Scripture memorization seems to be a lost art in Christian circles today. Those who are serious about sharing their faith should become serious also about familiarizing themselves with the Bible to a point where they are prepared *"in season and out of season"* (2 Timothy 4:2) to share the Gospel with others.

Deuteronomy 6:6-9 - *"These commandments that I give you today are to be upon your hearts. Impress them on your children. Talk about them when you sit at home and when you walk along the road, when you lie down and when you get up. Tie them as symbols on your hands and bind them on your foreheads. Write them on the doorframes of your houses and on your gates."*

Joshua 1:8 - *"Do not let this Book of the Law depart from your mouth; meditate on it day and night, so that you may be careful to do everything written in it. Then you will be prosperous and successful."*

Psalm 37:31 - *"The law of his God is in his heart; his feet do not slip."*

Psalm 119:11 - *"I have hidden your word in my heart that I might not sin against you."*

If we desire to be as effective as we can be in reaching others, we must be people who passionately consume God's Word. As we grow in intimacy with the Word of God, we will grow in confidence, in love of others, in faith, and in authority. The love of the Word of God is absolutely necessary for us to complete our mission. A Christian going into the mission field needs the Word of God as much as a soldier going into battle needs food and water. It is our sustenance, the source of our energy, and, unlike food and water, it is the very weapon by which we do battle.

Hebrews 4:12 - *"For the word of God is living and active. Sharper than any double-edged sword, it penetrates even to dividing soul and spirit, joints and marrow; it judges the thoughts and attitudes of the heart."*

Ephesians 6:17 - *"Take . . . the sword of the Spirit, which is the word of God."*

The Word of God and a life of outreach are completely inseparable. As people who love God and desire to serve Him, we must be people who love His Word and incorporate it into our daily lives. We must read it, listen to it, proclaim it, memorize it, repeat it, and share it with any who will listen. We must consider it our lifeblood and treat it accordingly. Without it, we have no message to share and no reason for sharing.

Discussion Questions:

-How do you answer the question: *"What is worship?"*

-How can evangelism be considered an act of worship?

-In what ways are studying the Bible and outreach connected?

-How can regular memorization of scripture help us reach out to others?

Famous Last Words

"The Bible in its totality ascribes only one intention to God: to save mankind. Every task of the church makes sense and has a purpose only as it leads to the mission."

- George F. Vicedom

In the 2002 movie *John Q*, Denzel Washington plays a man whose son has become fatally ill because of a heart problem. Because his insurance will not cover the expense of a heart transplant, Washington's character takes matters into his own hands, enters the hospital with a gun, and takes several hostages, demanding that his son be put on the list for a transplant.

At one point in the movie, Washington's character realizes that his son is not going to receive the heart that he so desperately needs, and he makes a very difficult decision: He decides to take his own life. He commits himself to donating his own heart so his son can survive.

In a touching scene, before John Q attempts to take his life, he sits down with his son to share his last words. With tears in his eyes he begins:

"I want you always to listen to your mother . . . .

Girls? You're too young for them now, but when the time comes, treat them like princesses because that's what they are . . . .

If you say you'll do something, do it. . . . your word should be your bond . . . .

Don't be a knucklehead like your father . . . .

Don't smoke . . . .

Try to be kind, but . . . be a man and stand up for yourself . . . .

Don't get caught up in the bad things; there's too many great things out there."

Essentially, in his last words to his son, this man tried to cram a lifetime's worth of teaching into only a few brief words. He knew he needed to stress his priorities.

In 1814 Napoleon Bonaparte stood before his remaining loyal Old Guard and issued his final farewell before going into exile. He proclaimed: *"I have sacrificed all of my interests to those of the country. I go, but you, my friends, will continue to serve France. Her happiness was my only thought. It will still be the object of my wishes."*

In 1796 the Father of our country, George Washington, issued his farewell address to the nation, in which he declared, *"Observe good faith and justice toward all nations. Cultivate peace and harmony with all . . . ."*

In each of these examples and in countless others, it becomes clear that, when given time to prepare, a man's last words usually reflect his passions and priorities. Jesus was no different.

Matthew 28:18-20 contains the farewell speech of Jesus to His followers.

"Then Jesus came to them and said, 'All authority in heaven and on earth has been given to me. Therefore go and make disciples of all nations, baptizing them in the name of the Father and of the Son and of the Holy Spirit, and teaching them to obey everything I have commanded you. And surely I am with you always, to the very end of the age.'"

> A man's last words usually reflect his passions and priorities.

You can be certain that Jesus had carefully determined His last statement. It was this: *"Go!"*

I have heard it said that meticulous studies have been conducted to determine the precise meaning of the word *"go"* in this passage - with shocking results. In the original Greek manuscripts, the word *"go"* actually means, *"go."* Can you believe it?

Jesus doesn't say here, *"When you get the chance, try and do something for My Kingdom, you know, when it is convenient and you sense that it is a really good time for witnessing, and it fits nicely into your schedule and lifestyle, then maybe, sometime, kind of, you could maybe possibly do some work toward spreading My Word."* No, instead He says, *"I am redefining your life right now. Whatever else you think is important, lay it down. I am giving you a new mission. Go win the world for Me."*

We have been issued a direct order from our Commander in Chief to go into the world with His Gospel. Failure to do so is insubordination.

Paul, too, just before his death, in his last words to Timothy, said the following in 2 Timothy 4:

"In the presence of God and of Christ Jesus, who will judge the living and the dead, and in view of his appearing and his kingdom, I give you this charge: Preach the Word; be prepared in season and out of season; correct, rebuke and encourage—with great patience and careful instruction . . . . Do the work of an evangelist . . . . For I am already being poured out like a drink offering, and the time has come for my departure."

> We have been issued a direct order from our Commander in Chief.

So, Jesus, the Son of God, was not the only one who considered the great commission of reaching the world as worthy of His last words. Paul the apostle did as well.

In Mark 1:17, when Jesus calls His first disciples, He makes this statement: *"Come, follow me, . . . and I will make you fishers of men."* In other words, He tells them from the very beginning, before they ever sign on to be His disciples, what the results will be if they choose to follow Him. He says to them, *"If you follow Me, I am going to change what you do for a living. I'm going to change your very identity to the point where your entire life is centered on My mission, and that is to bring men into a relationship with the Father."*

Jesus continues to say the same thing to us today. If you follow Him – really follow Him – it's going to happen. You are going to become a fisher of men. You inevitably will be a soulwinner.

> If you follow Him, it's going to happen. You are going to become a fisher of men.

In John 20:21, when Jesus first appears to His disciples following His resurrection, He greets them with these words: *"Peace be with you! As the Father has sent me, I am sending you."*

Not only are Jesus' last words to His disciples about His mission for the world, but His first words after His resurrection are also about the same topic. When He says, *"As the Father has sent me, I am sending you,"* what He means is, *"Now it is your turn. You can take over from here. My mission of reaching the world is now in your hands. You're hired."*

> This desire to *"feel led"* has resulted in multitudes of Christians who are doing virtually nothing.

Many people want to *"feel led"* in matters concerning evangelism. Because they rightly believe that we should be led by the Spirit, they sometimes think that every outreach experience should be a mystical occurrence of some sort during which God speaks and makes Himself very clear that a particular person is to be ministered to in a particular way at a particular time with specific and expected results. This desire to *"feel led"* has resulted in multitudes of Christians who are doing virtually nothing to advance God's Kingdom. God's desire is that Christians will be not only sensitive to His voice, but also proactive.

Several years ago the pastor at my local church preached a sermon that I considered brilliant. In this sermon he passed out fishing sinkers to every member of the congregation. Once every member had a sinker he instructed them to roll them between their fingers and then between their palms. He then explained that the sinkers were made of lead and proceeded with his sermon, exclaiming, *"Now that you have all 'felt lead,' get out there and do something!"*

The truth is, we have been commanded to go and do something. We have our orders in writing, and action requires no particular unction from the Holy Spirit. To be led by the Spirit is to be obedient to God, and to be obedient to God is to follow His Word. The Word of God has already established that we are to go and do something. We either obey or disobey. As Christians, some things are very clearly Biblical mandates. Showing kindness, helping those in need, forgiving others, and telling the truth are all qualities that are expected of Christians without any particular *"leading"* to do so. Sharing the Gospel is no different.

The Holy Spirit does lead and direct. He will prompt people into particular circumstances, ministries, and conversations. The problem is that many Christians use a lack of specific direction as an excuse for no action at all. If they don't *"feel led,"* they do nothing. A better policy is this: Do something, and if God directs, do something different. Only do nothing when God specifically and directly leads you to do nothing. One example of this is found in Acts 16:6-7, which says, *"Paul and his companions traveled throughout the region of Phrygia and Galatia, having been kept by the Holy Spirit from preaching the word in the province of Asia. When they came to the border of Mysia, they tried to enter Bithynia, but the Spirit of Jesus would not allow them to."* It becomes obvious in this passage that the disciples assumed the responsibility to go out and preach the Gospel was theirs unless specifically *"led"* otherwise.

Many Christians today (both consciously and subconsciously) follow this rule: *"If I don't sense God leading me to witness, I am not going to do so."* A better rule would be this: *"Unless I sense the Lord leading me not to witness, I am going to do so."* There are a few good reasons that this is a better policy. The first is, of course, as we have

> Do something, and if God directs, do something different.

discussed: God's Word instructs us to do so directly. Second, that seems to be the policy the apostles followed. Third, most of us are not as good at hearing God as we think we are.

From God's perspective, knowing how people are wired, which policy do you think He would choose in the area of evangelism? The sad truth is, most Christians are looking for every excuse *not to* share their faith. If they must be depended on to hear from God in every circumstance and react accordingly, there would be very little outreach going on at all. As we discussed in Chapter 4, people simply are not tuned in to God in this area. As such, God, instead of expecting us to hear from Him about all of the particulars, has issued broad and sweeping statements about outreach and expected us to respond to His commands. It can be a form of arrogance to think that we are going to get it right every time if we depend on *"being led."* In effect, when we say that we will witness when we *"feel led"* to witness, we are also saying that we are fully capable of *"feeling led"* every time God wants to lead us. It is an attitude that says, *"I never miss His voice, and I am always perfectly obedient when I hear Him."* I would say that is unlikely, even in situations when we *want* to hear from God every time. It is even less of a reality in areas of evangelism, where the average Christian isn't exactly excited about what God might say. I am confident that God is aware of all of these dynamics. As such, His policy is as it is: *"Go do something for my Kingdom. If I want you to stop, I will make it clear."* The souls of men hang in the balance. To leave evangelism as a matter of discernment in the hands of men is a risk God is unwilling to take. Instead, He simply says, *"Go."*

So, if for no other reason, we should be soulwinners because Christ commands us to be soulwinners. To be otherwise is to exist in rebellion and disobedience.

When we consider the last words of Jesus (and the last words of the apostle Paul) we see quite clearly not only that obedience in this area is expected, but that it tops off the list of

> **Christ commands us to be soulwinners**

commandments that are considered most important. The Great Commission to go and reach the world with the Gospel is not merely an option to be considered, and it is not a directive that governs just a portion of our lives as believers. The last words of Jesus were His way of summarizing the entirety of what it means to be a Christian. In essence He was saying, *"Everything I have taught you up until now concludes in this thought: I am calling you to reach the world. Now, go do it. I am leaving it in your hands."*

Discussion Questions:

-If you knew you were dying today, what would be your last words?

-What do you think Jesus meant when He said, *"As the Father has sent me, I am sending you?"*

-What are some ways that God leads people in the particulars of sharing the Gospel?

-Do you always hear from God perfectly?

"Most Christian ministries would like to send their recruits to Bible college for five years. I would like to send our recruits to hell for five minutes. That would do more than anything else to prepare them for a lifetime of compassionate ministry."

-William Booth

The Reality of Hell

"Would that God would make hell so real to us that we cannot rest."

– James Hudson Taylor

Hell is real. I've seen it.

Before you immediately dismiss me as crazy, let me explain. In the fall of 1992 I had a dream about Hell that I believe was from God. The dream I am about to describe is, in my opinion, a good description of what Hell is *like*. Notice, I did not say that it is an accurate description of the specifics of Hell. I only present it as an easily explainable example of the horrible *nature* of Hell. If you are a bit squeamish, be prepared. This may be difficult to read.

In this dream I was falling. The hole I was falling into was perfectly round with silver metallic walls. If I had to guess, the diameter of the circular wall was about a hundred or a hundred and fifty feet. I was falling into what I perceived as pitch-blackness, but as is often the case in dreams, I was able to see the events around me despite the absolute darkness. The terror of this hole was what waited for me on the floor below. The best way I know to describe the floor was as a machine. It may be difficult to imagine accurately. A huge flat machine made up of interlocking gears covered the entire floor. The gears were perfect globes that interlocked together to cover the entire expanse. Each gear was covered with inch-long razor-sharp needles, and each little globe was spinning and whirring in all directions at thousands of rotations per second. Tens of thousands of these little globes were spinning and humming together, creating what might be best described as a "chainsaw floor." I knew that when I landed, this horrible floor was going to shred me alive. I was naked as I fell, and there was nothing to protect me from the torture waiting below.

When I landed I screamed in agony as the terrible machine bit into my shoulder and my hip. It literally and instantly shredded all of the flesh from those parts of my body, and it ground all the way into my bones. The pain was beyond explanation, and, despite the total destruction of all of my nerves, there was no diminishing the torture.

My first instinct was to place my hands and feet on the surface and try to pull away from the pain. As soon as I did this, the torture machine ripped the flesh from my hands and the pads of my feet. I specifically remember the piercing agony as the webs between my fingers were pulled into the floor and severed. Again, after the nearly instant destruction of my flesh, the barbs continued to tear into my bones, which felt the agony yet seemed only superficially damaged. The lightning bolts of pain shooting through my hands and feet and up my arms and legs were overwhelming, and I collapsed forward with the same horrendous results to my chest, pelvis, and stomach.

> I knew I would always be there, alone and in torment forever.

At this point in my dream I somehow skipped forward what seemed like several months and found that my situation had not changed. I rolled around helplessly on the floor in constant agony. First my shoulder, then my upper and lower back, my hands, my face. The torture never lessened. I would have given anything if I could just die. I would purposefully press my face against the chainsaw floor; desperately hoping the barbs would penetrate my skull into my brain and finally kill me. The needles would instantly shred my eyes and tear into the bones and flesh around my face and forehead, but they were always just a little too short to kill me. I would press my face as hard as I could against the whirring needles, and as my lips where pulled down and destroyed I would cry out to die, but death would not come. Somehow in the back of my mind I knew that death would never come and that my situation was hopeless. I knew I would always be there, alone and in torment forever.

Reading this makes me uncomfortable. I'll admit that I don't like talking about it. and, if I am completely transparent, at times I have been a little bit embarrassed or apologetic about the fact that my religion believes in such a terrible place. As far as I am concerned, the doctrine of Hell is probably the most difficult teaching of the Bible to come to grips with. The concept of Hell brings up so many difficult questions: Why is Hell necessary? How could a good and loving God create such a place? Isn't an eternity of torment a bit much? The questions could go on and on. My hope and prayer for this chapter is that as we come to understand the realities of Hell more completely we will be motivated to share the love of Jesus with greater passion and immediacy. Make no mistake: Hell is real, it is a terrible place, and real people are going there.

God gives you what you live for: On the final day there will be two kinds of people: 1) Those who have received God's free salvation and surrendered their lives to Him. 2) Those who never received God's free gift and lived their lives committed only to themselves.

Essentially, every person's life is finally dedicated either to God or to self. On the day when men stand before God He will give them exactly what they lived for. To those who surrendered to God and lived their lives in service to Him, He will give a *"crown of life"* (Revelation 2:11) and invite them to *"share [their] Master's happiness."* (Matthew 25:23) However, for those who choose to reject God's gift of salvation through Jesus and choose to live for themselves, God turns them over to what they have lived for: an eternity of self without God. If people live their lives purposefully separated from the life and plan of God, in eternity they will forever remain so – separated from Him.

2 Thessalonians 1:8-9 - *"He will punish those who do not know God and do not obey the gospel of our Lord Jesus. They will be . . . **shut out** from the presence of the Lord and from the majesty of his power."*

Matthew 7:23 - *"I will tell them plainly, 'I never knew you. **Away from me,** you evildoers.'"*

Matthew 25:41,46 - *"Then [the King] will say to those on his left, '**Depart from me,** you who are cursed, into the eternal fire prepared for the devil and his angels.' . . . Then they will go away to eternal punishment . . . ."*

The meaning of these verses is clear. Separation from God is the punishment that awaits those who reject His plan of salvation. But I can hear it now. Many will say, *"Separation from God? That doesn't sound too bad."* What these people don't understand is that separation from God means separation from all that is good.

> Separation from God means separation from all that is good.

Light comes from God.

Genesis 1:3 - *"And **God said, 'Let there be light,'** and there was light."*

John 8:12 - *"When Jesus spoke again to the people, he said, '**I am the light of the world.** Whoever follows me will never walk in darkness . . . .'"*

If God is light, and Hell is separation from Him, then all that remains is absolute, impenetrable darkness.

Matthew 22:13 - *"Then the king told the attendants, 'Tie him hand and foot, and throw him outside, into the **darkness**, where there will be weeping and gnashing of teeth.'"*

2 Peter 2:17 - *"These men are springs without water and mists driven by a storm. **Blackest darkness** is reserved for them."*

All pleasure comes from God.

1 Timothy 6:17 - *"Command those . . . to put their hope in God, who richly provides us with everything for our **enjoyment**."*

Everything enjoyable, all pleasure, comes from God. When we are separated from God, nothing is left but pain and torment. This pain that remains when God is gone is often described in scripture as related to fire, the only thing humanly imaginable that could adequately compare.

Luke 16:23 - *"In hell where he was in **torment** . . . ."*

Jude 1:7 - *"They [are] an example of those who **suffer the punishment of eternal fire**."*

Revelation 14:10 - *"He will be **tormented with burning sulfur** in the presence of the holy angels and of the Lamb."*

All hope and rest come from God.

Psalm 62:5 - *"Find rest, O my soul, in God alone; **my hope comes from him**."*

Romans 15:13 - *"May the **God of hope** fill you with all joy and peace."*

Matthew 11:28 - *"Come to me, all you who are weary and burdened, and **I will give you rest**."*

If all hope and all rest come from God, but God is eternally absent, all that remains is an eternity of unrelenting despair. The terrors of Hell are eternal and without pause. Hell has no escape and no interruption.

> The terrors of Hell are eternal and without pause. Hell has no escape and no interruption.

Revelation 14:11 - *"And the smoke of their torment rises **for ever and ever**. **There is no rest** day or night . . . ."*

Psalm 95:10-11 - *"They are a people whose hearts go astray, and they have not known my ways.' So I declared on oath in my anger, '**they shall never enter my rest**.'"*

One of the most difficult things for people to grasp concerning Hell is that it is, quite literally, forever and ever. Many would like to believe that it is temporary. It is difficult to grasp how any sin here on Earth could merit such a seemingly out-of-balance punishment. It simply does not seem fair that a short lifetime of sin here on Earth could merit torment of such magnitude with no end. We find ourselves asking the question, *"Why would God torture someone forever without hope, no matter how bad they were?"* Forever seems unjust. We could cope with the thought of a thousand years, even a million years. Perhaps a billion years or more might seem just for people like Adolph Hitler, Pol Pot, Charles Manson, child molesters, and rapists. But forever? Forever seems too long.

> **When people are completely consumed with self, they would never, ever choose God or His Kingdom.**

The answer lies in the fact that when people are completely consumed with self, they would never, ever choose God or His Kingdom. Once God withdraws His hand of grace from their lives they are completely without hope. The only way a man can be saved is to respond to the grace of God while it is available. Man can never reach God until he gives up his own selfishness and accepts the hand that God has extended through His Son Jesus. Once that hand is unavailable, salvation becomes unavailable as well. C.S. Lewis sums this up best in his book *The Problem of Pain* when he writes, *"The doors of Hell are locked on the inside."* Once people are separated from God they experience total and complete self-implosion. They retreat completely and irrevocably behind a wall of self that they would never allow to be breached. Given the chance, no residents of Hell would ever accept an extended hand of God's grace to save them. As unthinkable as it seems to be, the bitter reality of Hell is that once people are condemned to be there, they will be there for all eternity.

Jesus satisfies.

John 4:14 - *"Whoever drinks the water I give him will never thirst. Indeed, the water I give him will become in him a spring of water welling up to eternal life."*

John 6:35 - *"Then Jesus declared, 'I am the bread of life. **He who comes to me will never go hungry**, and **he who believes in me will never be thirsty.'"***

Revelation 7:16-17 - *"**Never again will they hunger; never again will they thirst.** The sun will not beat upon them, nor any scorching heat. For the Lamb at the center of the throne will be their shepherd; he will lead them to springs of living water. And God will wipe away every tear from their eyes."*

Jesus is the thirst quencher. He satisfies every deep desire of men, and outside of Him there is no satisfaction. Those who walk with Jesus will find an eternity filled with amazing contentment, fulfillment, and satisfaction. Those who do not will spend eternity cut off from the possibility of ever having their "thirsts" quenched.

> They will exist perpetually in a state of wanting and craving with no respite available.

They will exist perpetually in a state of wanting and craving with no respite available. Scripture seems to indicate this thirst will be literal as well as figurative.

Luke 16:23-24 - *"In hell, where he was in torment, he looked up and saw Abraham far away, with Lazarus by his side. So he called to him, 'Father Abraham, have pity on me* *and send Lazarus to dip the tip of his finger in water and **cool my tongue, because I am in agony in this fire.**'"*

Isaiah 5:13-14 - *"Their masses will be **parched with thirst** . . . . The grave enlarges its appetite and opens its mouth without limit; into it will descend their nobles and masses with all their brawlers and revelers."*

Hell is terrible. I am not trying to imply that I know what Hell will be like specifically. In researching this topic I find that debates rage on and on endlessly as to whether the flames of Hell, the lake of fire, the utter darkness, and so on are meant to be taken literally or if they are all meant to be analogies describing what Hell is like. One thing is certain, though: Hell is the absence of God, and the absence of God is as bad as it gets.

> Hell is a place of inescapable fear and mind-wracking chaos.

This list of what God is, and what Hell is not, could go on for page after page. God is love. Hell is a place filled with hate. God is peace. Hell is a place of inescapable fear and mind-wracking chaos. God is righteousness. Hell is inconceivably wicked. God is tender. Hell is harsh. God is compassionate. Hell is a place without mercy. God is joy. Hell is a place of total despair. God is eternally living, and Hell is eternally dying. Jonathan Edwards was correct in his sermon "Charity and Its Fruit" when he said, *"Everything in Hell is hateful. There is not one solitary object there that is not odious and detestable, horrid and hateful."*

Hell is loneliness. Perhaps worst of all, God is the God of fellowship and community. When God is absent there is nothing left but loneliness and abandonment. God is the designer of all things relational: friendship, romance, community, and family. Where God is, people connect in amazing and meaningful ways. Where He is not, there is no alternative except complete and unending loneliness.

Sometimes I imagine what the world would be like if, suddenly, I was the only human alive and all others had vanished. Take a moment to think what living would be like with no families, no children laughing, no coins jingling in others' pockets, no crowded lines of unfamiliar faces in which to stand, no people answering the phones, no one to celebrate holidays with, no one to eat meals with, and no one to laugh at your jokes. Imagine no contact with any other human being, ever. Vast museums would stand empty, abandoned cars would be hauntingly scattered across the globe, and somehow nights would always seem horrifying. There would be no one, anywhere, to offer security or help in a time of need. Empty buildings, empty streets, and empty living would seem the worst fate imaginable. To me, the concept of absolute loneliness is paralyzingly frightening. It is also the reality of Hell. Where God is absent, connection with others is absent as well.

Christians must intervene: I have heard it said that *if Christians really believed in Hell they would crawl on their hands and knees over thousands of miles of broken glass to share the Gospel of Jesus with just one person who might be going there.* The sad truth is, most Christians today will not even cross the street to share Jesus with another person. Most Christians will not give up time in front of the television to minister to the people in their community, and many Christians spend more money on material things, such as golf clubs, fishing boats, and jewelry than they do on global missions. This is because Hell is not a reality in our minds and our hearts. We need to pray that God opens our eyes.

The existence of Hell should be one of the highest motivating factors in our lives. Do you believe in Hell? Do you *really* believe that people can go there? If so, what could matter more? If our aunts and uncles, our children, our friends, waitresses, bank tellers, and teachers have even the slightest chance of spending eternity separated from God, how can we remain quiet? How can we remain inactive? I challenge you to let the reality of Hell sink in. Allow it to motivate you into action in your circle of influence, in your community, and in missions around the world. You can help change a person's eternal destiny. Are you willing?

Discussion Questions:

-How do you imagine Hell?

-Of all the conditions of Hell described in this chapter, which seems the worst to you?

-What are you willing to sacrifice in order to help others avoid Hell?

Great Rewards

"Here I am, Lord, send me; send me to the ends of the earth . . . send me from all that is called earthly comfort; send me even to death itself if it be but in Thy service and to promote Thy Kingdom."
                                                -David Brainerd

Imagine two kinds of soldiers.

Soldier number one is highly trained. He knows military strategy. He is equipped with every piece of modern warfare equipment that a soldier could possibly want. He is big, strong, tough, and fast. He is a world-class marksman capable of bringing down a target nearly a mile away. He looks like G.I. Joe with his crew cut, square jaw, and biceps that nearly burst his sleeves. He talks like a grunt, walks like a grunt, and eats like a grunt. To the casual observer, he is the epitome of what it means to be a man of war.

He does have one major problem, though. He refuses to fight. In fact, he never strays very far from the command post.

His theory is, the closer he can stay to the general, the better off he is going to be. As long as he can remain in the presence of the general, he is going to learn more about warfare techniques. He is going to hear about any new equipment that might come down the line. As far as he is concerned, the best way to "be all that he can be" is to spend all of his time learning how to be a better soldier.

If he had his way, he would stay in basic or advanced training his entire life. Somehow, even though the general has made his orders very clear, soldier number one thinks that he knows best how to spend his time in the military,

> Surely the general wouldn't subject him to such potential pain, violence, and danger, would he?

and he has chosen to ignore his orders. He is sure the general will appreciate his efforts to learn all that he can. After all, the old saying is that "war is hell." Surely the general wouldn't subject him to such potential pain, violence, and danger, would he?

Soldier number two is a different soldier entirely.

Soldier number two is only about 5'7". He weighs about a hundred and thirty-five pounds. He doesn't look the part of a "killing machine." He, too, went through basic training and, although he didn't receive any special honors, he managed to make it through. He isn't the greatest marksman in the world, but he can manage to hit his target after a few shots. He works with whatever equipment he is given. He continues to learn warfare techniques, but most of his training comes hands-on through combat experience. He has been involved in several gun battles and has actually been shot twice. After his second injury he was offered a simple job pushing pencils near the command center, but he refused. As far as he is concerned, time between battles is used for recouping and refocusing before entering the battle again. As soon as he is able, his desire is to go out and play his part in winning the war. He sees that every mission in which he participates is important to the overall victory. He is committed to the cause. When the general speaks, he listens and obeys. He isn't overly concerned with the pain and the suffering that he might experience on the front line. He has spent cold, sleepless nights in trenches. He has sheltered behind trees, avoiding enemy fire. He has watched his friends die. Regardless, he remains a faithful soldier.

> He has been in several gun battles and has actually been shot twice.

Now ask yourself this question: Which of these soldiers will be rewarded when the war is over? The answer is obvious. It is also obvious that none of us wants to be soldier number one. He is not only on track to receive no reward, he is on track to be court-martialed and sent to jail.

Soldier number two is a different story. He is due a great reward and will more than likely receive great accolades and honor. He is the kind of soldier who would do his duty regardless of the reward, but chances are, his efforts will be recognized and he will receive the honor that is due him. He doesn't look as good, and he is a little rough around the edges, but he is faithful and obedient, and when the medals are handed out, that will be what matters. God's Kingdom is no different. For the faithful, the rewards are sure. There will come a time when God will reward generously those who served Him and His Kingdom and punish those who did not.

Consider the following list of passages concerning this topic:

Matthew 16:27 - *"For the Son of Man is going to come in his Father's glory with his angels, and then **he will reward each person according to what he has done.**"*

Daniel 12:3 - *"Those who lead many to righteousness [will shine] like the stars for ever and ever."*

1 Corinthians 3:12-15 - *"If any man builds on this foundation . . . his work will be shown for what it is, because the Day will bring it to light. It will be revealed with fire, and the fire will test the quality of each man's work. **If what he has built survives, he will receive his reward.** If it is burned up, he will suffer loss; he himself will be saved, but only as one escaping through the flames."*

Colossians 3:23-24 - *"Whatever you do, work at it with all your heart, as working for the Lord, not for men, since you know that **you will receive an inheritance from the Lord as a reward.** It is the Lord Christ you are serving."*

Revelation 22:12 - *"Behold, I am coming soon! **My reward is with me**, and I will give to everyone according to what he has done."*

These, of course, only touch the tip of the iceberg where this topic is concerned. The parable of the talents in Matthew 25 emphasizes this concept clearly. In this parable, Jesus describes three servants who were each given a certain amount of resources to manage. One was given five talents, one was given two talents, and another was given one talent. The first two servants put their talents to good use, doubled their resources, and presented their earnings to their master, who was pleased with them. The third servant was a different story. This servant did nothing but hide his talent away, losing nothing but also gaining nothing. The master was not pleased.

> Our reward is sure.

In the end, the servants who utilized their resources to expand the master's kingdom were greatly rewarded. The servant who did nothing was thrown into darkness and abandoned.

In Mark 10:29-30 Jesus says, *"I tell you the truth . . . no one who has left home or brothers or sisters or mother or father or children or fields for me and the gospel will fail to receive a hundred times as much in this present age (homes, brothers, sisters, mothers, children and fields—and with them, persecutions) and in the age to come, eternal life."*

It is clear in Scripture. Those who work for God's Kingdom and the expansion of His Kingdom will be rewarded both in this life and in the life to come. While our motive is devotion to Christ and a desire to do what pleases Him, His promises are still true. Our reward is sure.

John 14:1-4 - *"Do not let your hearts be troubled. Trust in God; trust also in me. In my Father's house are many rooms; if it were not so, I would have told you.* **I am going there to prepare a place for you.** *And if I go and prepare a place for you, I will come back and take you to be with me that you also may be where I am. You know the way to the place where I am going."*

Revelation 21:3-4 - *"And I heard a loud voice from the throne saying, "Now the dwelling of God is with men, and he will live with them. They will be his people, and God himself will be with them and be their God. He will wipe every tear from their eyes. There will be no more death or mourning or crying or pain, for the old order of things has passed away."*

> Heaven is being eternally consumed with God.

Heaven is a very real place. In the last chapter we talked about how Hell is eternal separation from God. Heaven, on the other hand, is just the opposite. Heaven is being eternally consumed with God. Everything good comes from God. Everything about God is amazing, pleasurable, wonderful, and awe-inspiring. As such, we can expect that Heaven will be amazing, pleasurable, wonderful, and awe-inspiring as well. In an age where the word *"awesome"* is used to describe everything from soft drinks to skateboards, it seems a shame to use it here, but because the word literally means "inspiring awe," it is appropriate. Heaven is going to be awesome. It will inspire awe. Heaven will be awesome because God is awesome. The depth of God's goodness is beyond measure. No one can know the extent of His joy or His pleasure. No human could ever imagine the vastness of His love. It is the same way trying to imagine

Heaven. Because, essentially, God is Heaven, it would be impossible for me or any other human being to describe what Heaven will be like specifically. The apostle Paul, in 2 Corinthians 12, talks about being *"caught up to paradise"* and how things seen there were *"inexpressible things, things that man is not permitted to tell."* There is no question that the specifics of Heaven are indescribable and unimaginable, but Heaven will be even better for some than it is for others.

> In Heaven, some will be rewarded more than others.

Many Christians may not realize this, but there will be varying degrees of reward in Heaven. It is not perfectly clear what this will entail, but from some of the passages mentioned above and many more, it becomes clear that in Heaven, some will be rewarded more than others. The passage from 1 Corinthians 3, which was quoted earlier, shows unambiguously that some people will receive great rewards based on the work they did for Jesus during their lives, while others will barely make it into Heaven at all and will *"suffer loss."*

In the parable of the talents, we find that those who put their resources to good work will be given even more resources to work with upon entering the Kingdom of God.

Jesus says several times that in Heaven the last will be first and the first will be last. In Matthew 18 the disciples ask Jesus who will be the greatest in the Kingdom of Heaven. He doesn't rebuke them (which He was apt to do when their theology seemed wrong or their question seemed foolish). Instead, He instructs them, saying that those who humble themselves like a little child will be the greatest in the Kingdom of Heaven. In Matthew 5 Jesus described some people as *"great"* in the Kingdom of Heaven and others as the *"least"* in the Kingdom. In Matthew 15 Jesus said that, although John the Baptist was the greatest person to have ever been born, even the *"least"* in the Kingdom of Heaven was greater than he.

Jesus taught that in Heaven some will be greater than others. He taught that there will be varying rewards in Heaven based on what Christians do with the time, talents, and resources they are given.

In Luke 17 the disciples approach Jesus, asking Him to increase their faith. Jesus replies to them by saying, *"If you have faith as small as a mustard seed, you can say to this mulberry tree, 'Be uprooted and planted in the sea,' and it will obey you."* He goes on to say, *"Suppose one of you had a servant plowing or looking after the sheep. Would he say to the servant when he comes in from the field, 'Come along now and sit down to eat'? Would he not rather say, 'Prepare my supper, get yourself ready and wait on me while I eat and drink; after that you may eat and drink'? Would he thank the servant because he did what he was told to do? So you also, when you have done everything you were told to do, should say, 'We are unworthy servants; we have only done our duty.'"*

In other words, Jesus affirms their request for more faith by telling them how good it is. He then follows this up by telling, in a short parable, how to receive more faith. He basically says, *"It is good that you ask for more faith because with faith you can accomplish anything. But here is how you get more faith: Do what you are supposed to do. Do what the Master requires of you. Consider it your duty, expecting nothing in return."* Obedience is the key to faith.

It is when we realize that we are soldiers in a battle, serving our Commander in Chief and obeying His commands regardless of the consequences, that we earn the favor of God. Like so many subjects in the Word of God, it appears somewhat paradoxical. When we serve and expect no reward is when we are rewarded. If we want to save our lives we must lose our lives. If we want to be considered great we must humble ourselves and become the *"least"* of people. It is through giving our lives to a cause outside of ourselves that we receive the greatest personal blessing and reward, both in this life, and in the life to come.

> When we serve and expect no reward is when we are rewarded.

In Heaven you will be able to worship God constantly in ways you have never dreamed of . . . forever. You will be able to read and study His Word in ways that will blow your mind . . . forever. You will be able to pray to Him, learning how to touch His heart and receive His favors . . . forever. You will fellowship with others and experience relationships filled with more love than you can now comprehend . . . forever. You will *not*, however, be able to help people come to Him any longer. It is one thing you cannot do in Heaven.

You have been given one life on Earth with the express purpose of introducing others to Jesus so that they, too, can enter into God's Kingdom and live with Him for all eternity. It is the reason you have breath in your lungs at this moment. God desires to use you, for a little while longer, to spread His message of love to others. He has placed you in a unique place that no other person, ever, will occupy. He has surrounded you with people whom He desires to influence through your life.

Are you willing to make Heaven your ambition, not only for your own life, but also for the lives of others around you? I am convinced one of the greatest joys of Heaven will be the people there whom you influenced for God's Kingdom. I can imagine knowing no greater joy than having a friend with me in Heaven who is there as a direct result of God's Word working through me to touch and change his

> Are you willing to make Heaven your ambition?

or her life. God will receive all of the glory because it is His Word that does the work, but if nothing else, I will enjoy the reward of having a best friend for all time.

There is no doubt that in Heaven we will be eternally thankful for every moment that we spent sharing God's Word with others. We will never think, *"If only I had wasted more time."* Instead, we will praise God with everything that we are because of the amazing things that He accomplished through our small efforts at reaching people.

God wants to fill Heaven with people and has set it up where you, as an individual, are His tool to do so. Will you, as expressed in Luke 14:23, *"Go out to the roads and country lanes and make them come in, so that my house will be full"*?

Discussion Questions:

-What are your thoughts concerning soldiers number one and number two from the beginning of this chapter?

-How do you think God rewards those who serve Him?

-What might it mean that there will be *"greatest"* and *"least"* in the Kingdom of Heaven?

-What are you doing to make Heaven full?

"Brother, sister, I want to tell you calmly and quietly, I am resolved, God helping me, to stretch this poor body of mine across their pathway to a burning Hell, if perchance some may stumble over it and land in a happy Heaven. I am resolved, God helping me, my time, my talents, my money, my strength, my all, shall be thrown between them and their hopelessness and helplessness here and hereafter if perchance some may hear the gracious invitation, accept and be saved. Beloved, what will you say? What will you do?"

– William Hesslop

Adrenaline Junkies

"From subtle love of softening things, from easy choices, weakenings . . . from all that dims Thy Calvary, O Lamb of God, deliver me."
-Amy Carmichael

Imagine it: You are about to jump.

You are standing up in the back of a pickup truck as it rolls across a huge bridge. At just the right moment, you intend to take the plunge. You know that over the guardrail awaits a several thousand foot drop to the river, rocks, and trees below.

You know that if things don't go exactly as planned – if your chute doesn't open properly, if you catch the guard rail with your foot, if you don't time everything perfectly – you may free fall to the ground below with nothing to stop you or slow you down. You know that you won't have much time to open your chute before you hit the ground.

> You may free fall to the ground below.

Your pulse is racing, your face is flushed, and you are breathing much, much faster than normal. You are BASE jumping. At just the perfect time you place your foot on the outside rim of the truck's bed and push off as hard as you can into the open air. Gravity takes over.

> Your pulse is racing, your face is flushed, and you are breathing much, much faster.

To some people, it's insanity. To others, it is as exciting as life gets, a thrill worth risking their lives over.

Jimmy Tyler (BASE 13) is known as the first person ever to BASE jump from a moving vehicle when he launched from a pickup truck crossing the Pine Valley Bridge in San Diego, California. He was also the first jumper to die jumping from Half Dome in Yosemite National Park when, in 1982, he slammed into the cliff wall and fell to the earth below.

In the Frequently Asked Questions section of www.bridgeday.info – a website committed to BASE jumping, the question is asked, *"Is BASE jumping dangerous?"* The answer: *"Even if you've had extensive training, the best gear, perfect weather conditions, and you're smarter than the rest of the jumpers in your group, you can be injured or killed. Canopy openings are not always predictable and can open facing a cliff wall or towards an antenna. Some of the smartest BASE jumpers in the world have recently been injured or killed BASE jumping. It's not "if" but "when" you get busted up in this sport, so be prepared and get good medical insurance."*

In other words, *"Yes! It is dangerous."* However, the danger is what makes it so exciting to so many people. If there were no risk, there would be no

thrill. It is just like countless other activities that are sometimes described as "extreme." People throughout history have done what it takes to introduce a thrill in their lives. They climb Mount Everest. They explore deep underwater caves. They race cars at speeds over 200 mph. They parasail, hang glide, skydive, and surf. They snowboard, mountain bike, bungee jump, and cliff dive. I have even heard of a sport called "noodling," in which people catch catfish with their bare hands. Basically, they reach into muddy catfish holes with their bare hands and try to pull out whatever they

> If there was no risk, there would be no thrill.

find. The problem is that sometimes it isn't a catfish they encounter but instead turns out to be a snapping turtle or an angry beaver. The sport is called "stumping" by some because of the number of noodlers who are missing fingers. Yes, people really do this stuff!

I have personal knowledge of a man who would hunt alligators in the bayous of Louisiana using what could only be described as "unconventional" methods. He would float along in his boat, silently searching for gators. When he found one, he would attempt to float up close enough, pull out his pistol, and shoot it in the head. The crazy part was what he would do next. After he shot the gator in the head, he would throw his gun into the boat and immediately jump in the water so he could wrestle with the creature while it thrashed about and died. Like I said . . . crazy.

The point is this: People worldwide are looking for adventure, excitement, and an adrenaline rush, and some of them will do anything to find it. Many of them become adrenaline junkies, always looking for the next high.

> When the rush comes, they turn tail and run.

Compare this to the average Christian today. Most Christians I know of do whatever they can to produce just the opposite effect. They consider a rush of adrenaline to be a sign that something is very much wrong. When that rush comes, they turn tail and run. I don't believe that is how it is supposed to be.

In my opinion, the life of a Christian should be a life full of excitement, daring, and adventure. It should be a life filled, at least sometimes, with a whole lot of adrenaline. With the proper mindset, living an outreach-centered life can easily go from being a burden and a horror to being an adventure and a thrill. It simply requires saying *"Yes!"* to the rush instead of quenching it.

Living the life of a soulwinner is the single most exciting life that a person can possibly live on earth, hands down. When you are an active soulwinner, even the most mundane tasks can turn into thrills that parallel bungee jumping. Whether you are at the Laundromat,

> The life of a soulwinner is the most exciting life a person can live.

sitting in a classroom, or shopping at Wal-Mart, if you are constantly looking for the next opportunity to share Jesus with someone, life becomes exciting and challenging to a level that it never could be otherwise.

In the summer of 2004 I took an amazing vacation. I had saved money for more than a year and marked off an entire month in my calendar so I could go backpacking in Thailand. It was just me and a backpack for an entire month. I was thousands of miles from home and totally without an agenda. It was amazing.

While I was there, I spent about a week on a small island called Koh Tao. It is one of the most inexpensive places in the world to become certified to scuba dive, and I wasn't going to pass up the opportunity.

One thing about scuba certification, at least in the PADI (Professional Association of Diving Instructors) system, is that you are trained to use the "buddy system." The buddy system hooks you up with another diver for the course of your training in order to help each other in case of an underwater emergency. Essentially, if something goes wrong, you are always supposed to be within a few feet of your buddy so you can reach his alternate air or seek other assistance. My buddy's name was Nathan. (OK, I confess, I changed the name to protect his identity.)

> That was my chance, and I took it. I wish you could have seen his reaction.

I remember sitting with Nathan between dives on the second day of our training. We were on top of the sundeck eating fresh pineapple and watching the coastline go by. After he talked a little while about drinking alcohol and smoking marijuana, he began asking me about my interests and asked me about what kind of music I liked. That was my chance, and I took it.

I told Nathan at that point that I mostly listened to Christian music. I explained to him that a few years ago I had given my life to Jesus and that He had changed everything about me, including the kind of music that I listen to. I then asked him something along the lines of, *"What do you think about Jesus?"*

I wish you could have seen his reaction.

Nathan came across as a wealthy European who had it all together. He was good looking, well traveled, charming, and healthy. He seemed to have a live-it-up attitude about life, and it seemed like girls and the next party were probably the only things on his mind. That is why it surprised me when he stood up and began pacing back and forth on the sundeck. With tears in his eyes he put his hands over his chest and began to exclaim, *"Man, this is too weird . . . I, uhm . . . man, this is weird . . . I . . . whoa . . . God works in mysterious ways . . . I uhm . . . oh man . . . this is weird."*

When I finally got him to calm down a little and sit back down, he tearfully explained to me the truth about what was going on in his life. He was so shaken up that he was breathing fairly heavily the whole time he talked. He explained to me that he had actually just gotten out of jail a very short time before his trip to Thailand. He said that he had gone on the trip to try and *"get his life back together."* He confessed that he had lied to me about his job and life back home. He even confessed that his Rolex watch was a fake that he wore to convince people that his story about working at a prestigious car dealership was true. He said that while he had been in jail he had read the New Testament through four times and that he desperately wanted to live for Jesus, but he didn't know how and didn't think that he could really pull it off.

Over the course of the next four or five days, Nathan and I spent quite a bit of time together talking about the Lord and the things of God. The day before he left, on a gorgeous white-sand beach, thousands of miles from home, I had the privilege of praying with him that the Lord would reveal Himself to him and help him live his life for Jesus. We have stayed in touch somewhat since then, and even though he cannot visit me in the States (he is not allowed in the U.S. because his crimes involved firearms), I am sure that he will be a lifelong friend.

> . . . the exact right place, at the exact right time.

I can tell you for certain that there is nothing more exciting in the world than knowing you are in the exact right place, at the exact right time, doing and saying exactly what you are supposed to be doing and saying. There is nothing better than feeling God smile on you as you carry out His mission, even when you are thousands and thousands of miles away from familiar territory.

I could tell story after story of similar circumstances that have happened either in my own life or in the lives of friends I know who are active soulwinners. Sometimes it blows my mind when I consider all of the amazing things I have experienced and the relationships that have been established as I have been willing to step out and share Jesus with the people around me.

Contrary to the rush of BASE jumping, snowboarding, or parasailing, the excitement generated from even one divine encounter through soulwinning has a lasting effect that creates excitement and joy for the rest of a person's life. With the world's form of excitement there may be a rush, there may be a few fleeting moments of pure adrenaline and fun, but when the activity is over the rush is gone, the fun has stopped, and normal ho-hum living sets back in. Soulwinning is different because the effects are lasting, both in the soulwinner's personal life and in the lives of the people ministered to. In other words, conquering the fear of soulwinning and embracing the rush produces results that have eternal consequences for all involved. The results of soulwinning are lasting and important. The results of other ways of excitement are typically short-lived and somewhat trivial.

> Embracing the rush produces results that have eternal consequences.

Reaching other people with the Gospel and the hope of Jesus is an exciting life because it is a life (and really the only life) that lends itself to real and eternally lasting purpose.

Probably every person on the planet would like his or her life to mean something important. Most people, upon thinking of their own funerals, would never want it said of them that they lived for nothing other than their own pleasures and desires. If people have any kind of morality or decency whatsoever, they would want it said of them that their lives made a positive difference in the lives of others. I believe that deep down every person on the planet knows that it is right to use their energy and resources for the betterment of others.

There is no greater way to make a positive difference in the lives of people, and even in the world in general, than to help other people come to embrace Jesus Christ.

Think about it. If a doctor helps prolong comfortable life for people, but then those same people die without Jesus, has that doctor, from an eternal perspective, actually helped anyone? If an environmentalist spends years trying to save trees or endangered species but does nothing to draw people into a relationship with the One who created those trees and animals, has that person done anyone any favors? If someone were to feed and shelter the homeless, end world poverty, stop war as we know it, and do all manner of amazing things which comforted people physically, and yet those same people passed into eternity without God, what good has the comfort done them? To an honest Christian thinker there can be no doubt. If the end result of a lifetime of work does not involve anyone's entering God's Kingdom, that life was ill spent. If, however, a lifetime is spent bringing people into an eternal relationship with God, that lifetime has been well spent. In the end, it will be seen as the only lifestyle that was worth pursuing. This is not to minimize the importance of meeting people's temporal needs, but rather to emphasize the great importance of meeting people's eternal needs.

So, what is a Christian to do? Perhaps you are like I was and the idea of sharing Jesus with someone is terrifying to you. Don't worry; you're in good company. I have heard of pastors conferences where, when the time came to hit the streets and share Jesus, pastors were seen actually climbing out of their hotel windows, trying to avoid being seen, as they clambered to their cars and left the conference before they were forced to witness for Jesus. And, like I said in the prologue, I know what it is like to be afraid. I also know that fear can be overcome. In the next chapter we will discuss several tips to overcoming the fear of soulwinning.

> They clambered into their cars and left before they were forced to witness for Jesus.

Discussion Questions:

-What's the most fun you've ever had being scared?

-What does it mean to live a life of adventure?

-How could a daily focus on others be an exciting life?

-What fears do you have about sharing your faith with others? How could you overcome those fears?

Adrenaline Junkies II

"Make it an object of constant study, and of daily reflection and prayer, to learn how to deal with sinners so as to promote their conversion."
- Charles Finney

John Wesley once said, *"Give me one hundred preachers who **fear nothing but sin and desire nothing but God**, and I care not a straw whether they be clergymen or laymen; **such alone will shake the gates of hell and set up the kingdom of heaven on Earth.**"*

If we are to become everything that God wants us to be, it is imperative that we learn to deal with fear. The difference between living free from fear and living bound by fear is the difference between victory and defeat, especially in the area of soulwinning. As Christians we *must* learn to overcome our fears. In this chapter we will explore different ways to receive God's freedom from fear in soulwinning.

> The difference between living free from fear and living bound by fear is the difference between victory and defeat.

Think about the worst that could happen: In all of my years of active soulwinning I cannot think of a time when I really thought I was in physical danger. I have had a few people mad at me. I have seen a very few who have cussed and screamed and stomped their feet. I have had maybe a handful walk away. But, all in all, the number of people who have responded positively have outweighed the number of people who have responded negatively by at least a hundred to one, literally. Remember, Jesus said it Himself in Luke 10:2, *"The harvest is plentiful, but the workers are few."* People are ready to hear the Gospel. There is no lack of receptive people out there if we are willing to look. What we are missing is enough people who are willing to go out and share the Gospel with others.

Realize this: In Jesus, there is quite literally nothing to be afraid of. First, chances are good, at least in America today, that very little suffering is likely to arise as a result of your efforts. Probably the worst that is going to happen is that you will be verbally mocked or made fun of. Second, this life is simply a passing breath in light of eternity. Heaven is the eternal destination of the followers of Christ. So, no matter what happens, it all ends well. Christians should have no worries. According to God's Word, even if we are persecuted, it is to our benefit. (We will discuss this concept more in a later chapter.)

Also, consider those who have gone before you in the Christian faith. Be encouraged by their willingness to proclaim Jesus despite intense persecution. Compare the level of suffering they faced to the level that you might face if you are bold enough to speak out for Jesus.

For centuries Christians have been persecuted worldwide. They have been beaten to death. They have watched as their children were mutilated before their eyes. They have been burned alive, been held under water with spears until they drowned, had their tongues cut out to shut them up, had their homes destroyed, and had their eyes plucked out. They have endured sleepless nights of not knowing whether they would ever see their spouse again, spent years in cold, damp prisons, and been subjected to public humiliation. The list of atrocities that Christians have endured is inexhaustible. I suggest reading *Jesus Freaks* by DC Talk and The Voice of the Martyrs, along with *Foxe's Book of Martyrs* by John Foxe for very enlightening and challenging material about the strength of Christians in the face of great persecution. It is unbelievable what people have gone through in the name of Jesus. It is also amazing to reflect on the incredible courage of Christians throughout the centuries who have been unwilling to bow down in fear.

> The list of atrocities that Christians have endured is inexhaustible.

Jesus Freaks includes the story of a congregation of believers in North Korea during the 1950's who were captured by Communist leaders. They were brought before a crowd of 30,000 people and told, *"Deny Christ or you will die."*

> *"Deny Christ or you will die."*

After watching four of their children hanged to death, not one of the twenty-four other believers was willing to renounce the faith, and a steamroller was called in. The believers were forced to lie in its path and were given another chance to renounce Christ. Not a single one of them did so, and they were all crushed together as they sang in unison: *"More love to Thee, O Christ, more love to Thee. Thee alone I seek, more love to Thee."* The execution was reported in the North Korean press as an act of suppressing superstition.

Can you imagine what they must have been feeling as they lay on the ground, hearing the roar of the steamroller's engine as it approached, listening to the voices of their closest friends and family being cut off as they were crushed and their bones shattered? Can you imagine anything more horrible or more fearful? And yet, they stood their ground.

What a shame it is that in today's world Christians can be silenced by something as simple as public ridicule or a reputation of being "one of those." We love our lives too much and the message of the Gospel too little.

> We love our lives too much and the message of the Gospel too little.

People throughout history have given up their families, their homes, and even their lives in order that the Gospel might go forth. The Gospel of Jesus requires that we be willing to give up our lives for the message of salvation, but many Christians today are not even willing to give up their public image. God forgive us!

Pray: The battle we are fighting is a supernatural battle. One of the greatest keys to walking in freedom from fear is to realize that in the world there are very real and very powerful supernatural beings that absolutely hate your guts and will do anything to destroy you or keep you from reaching your potential. They are a huge source of fear, but the good news is that they are also defeated through Jesus.

I understand that I am going to lose some people here. I know that to some people, talk of demons and devils seems just a bit too much "out there" for their tastes. However, the Bible has a tremendous amount to say on the topic. In fact, in the NIV the words "the devil" are mentioned, describing a real and personal evil entity, thirty-four times. Demons are mentioned thirty-two times. Satan is referred to forty-seven times. These numbers fail to account for the other names by which Satan is described: Lucifer, Mammon, the enemy, the adversary, prince of the power of the air, the ruler of this age, and more. Notice that he is called *"the"* devil and *"the"* enemy. Make no mistake: Despite the world's and the media's attempts to make a mockery of those who believe in a real and personal devil, the devil is truly alive and well on planet Earth. In fact, the existence and activities of the devil should be considered one of the central themes of the Bible.

1 Peter 5:8 - *"Be self-controlled and alert. **Your enemy the devil** prowls around like a roaring lion looking for someone to devour."*

Luke 8:12 - *"**The devil** comes and takes away the word from their hearts. "*

1 John 3:8 - *"**The devil** has been sinning from the beginning. The reason the Son of God appeared was to destroy the devil's work."*

Hebrews 2:14 - *"So that by [Jesus'] death he might destroy him who has the power of death – that is, **the devil**."*

> The scariest thing on the devil's horizon is Christians who are not afraid to open their mouths.

This same devil that Jesus Himself describes as our enemy is out to get you. He wants to shut you down from winning souls. The truth is, he hates soulwinners and will go way out of his way to keep Christians from sharing their faith. The scariest thing on the devil's horizon is Christians who are not afraid to open their mouths and let God's Word come out. He despises soulwinners.

One of the devil's chief weapons against soulwinning is fear, and our chief weapon against fear is prayer. Understanding where fear comes from is a central key to understanding how to defeat it. Because worldly fear has a supernatural origin, it must be battled in a supernatural way. It must be battled with prayer.

Pray that the Lord will allay your fears. Pray that He will be a wall between you and the devil and his plans. Pray like David in Psalm 18, *"The Lord is my rock, my fortress and my deliverer; my God is my rock, in whom I take refuge. He is my shield and the horn of my salvation, my stronghold."* Pray also that the Lord will replace your fears with boldness as Paul prayed in Ephesians 6:19-20, *"Pray also for me, that whenever I open my mouth, words may be given me so that I **will fearlessly make known the mystery of the gospel**, for which I am an ambassador in chains. **Pray that I may declare it fearlessly**, as I should."* If the apostle Paul felt it necessary to pray for boldness, how much more should we?

Allow the Lord to replace your fears with boldness and strength. Call out to Him and let something rise up in you that says through Jesus you are stronger than your fears. In the name of Jesus, you are not a coward or a wimp. You are intended to make the devil tremble and not the other way around.

A few years ago my brother Andy attempted to quit smoking and was successful. I later found out his secret. He said that every time he was tempted to pick up a cigarette he would say the following words to himself: *"Smokers are weak, and I am not weak!"*

You are not weak. You can learn to share your faith with others, and the power of the Lord Jesus is available to you. When an adrenaline rush comes to you and threatens to shut you down, learn to embrace it instead. Call on Jesus

> Call on Jesus and jump in headfirst.

and jump in headfirst, all the while saying, *"I am not a coward; I am not weak."* The Lord will honor your courage in the face of fear. He will be there with you.

God answers prayer. If you ask Him to diminish your fears and you believe Him, He will do it. Being with Him and knowing Him is the easiest way to overcome fear.

1 John 4:18 - *"There is no fear in love. But **perfect love drives out fear**, because fear has to do with punishment. The one who fears is not made perfect in love."*

2 Timothy 1:7 - *"For **God did not give us a spirit of timidity**, but a spirit of power, of love and of self-discipline."*

The first step to overcoming fear is to ask God for help and walk with Him. He will help, as we see in Isaiah 41:10: *"So do not fear, for I am with you; do not be dismayed, for I am your God. I will strengthen you and help you; I will uphold you with my righteous right hand."*

Start small and then work toward more: I remember one of my first experiences in public speaking. I was a second-semester freshman at Murray State University, and I was teaching a Physics lab.

> I was so nervous that my hands were visibly shaking.

To say I was tremendously nervous would be an understatement. As I stood in front of my class of about twenty people for the first time, I was so nervous that my hands were visibly shaking. The chalk was audibly clacking against the chalkboard as I attempted to write because I couldn't control the tremors. I was breathing heavily, and sweat was literally pouring off my forehead and drenching my clothes. I was an absolute wreck, and the students could tell. Eventually, one of the students in the front row had to try to calm me down by saying, *"Hey man, calm down; everything is going to be okay."*

Familiarity conquers fear, and practice breeds familiarity.

Can you imagine how humiliating that was, to have a student try to calm the teacher down in front of the entire class? However, fourteen years and hundreds of public speaking opportunities later, I am a changed man. Public speaking now holds very little, if any, anxiety for me whatsoever. The truth is, it is now my passion, and I can think of very little that I would rather spend my time doing than preaching God's Word to people. And the way I see it, the larger the crowd the better because the larger the crowd, the more people who hear the message.

My point is this: Familiarity conquers fear, and practice breeds familiarity. In other words, if you are afraid, keep pressing on. Eventually, the fear will subside to a great extent. The first time a pilot lands a plane is probably an adrenaline rush like very few others. But, I am sure, after a pilot has landed a plane a thousand times, things are different. It might even become quite routine. I can assure you, at least to a great extent, that soulwinning can be quite similar. The longer you do it, the more actively you practice, the easier it will become. I promise.

If you are afraid, I suggest you start small. For some, that may mean sharing the Gospel with yourself in a mirror, finding a trusted Christian friend who will role play with you, or even talking to your dog, cat, or goldfish first. It may seem silly to some, but I am convinced that as the Word of God comes out of your mouth at home it will become easier for you to share with others outside your home.

In later chapters we will discuss many different ways that Christians can practically share Jesus with others. Some of them should present very little or no fear at all, even for the most timid among us. Literally anyone can leave a Gospel tract where it can be found, and most anyone can casually invite someone to go to church with them. So I challenge you to start somewhere. Hand someone a tract, ask people if you can pray for them, invite your neighbors to go to a Bible study with you. As you do this you will find more and more that you are able to overcome your fear. But don't stop there. Continue to stretch yourself on a daily basis. Ultimately, the goal is that you will be a vessel in the hands of God that is willing to go anywhere, anytime, and do whatever He asks, no matter what. A huge key to arriving at that place is being willing to consistently step out and do something that may make you uncomfortable. The minute your Christianity becomes really comfortable is the minute it becomes less than the Christianity God desires for you.

Educate yourself: I have asked many people throughout the years: *"What fears keep you from sharing your faith with others more often than you do?"* Without exception, the most common answer I get is that people don't want to come across as stupid. When I ask them to elaborate I tend to hear, *"I am afraid that people are going to ask me questions, and I am not going to know how to answer."*

It is understandable. If we feel like we don't know enough about our topic to share it intelligently, it makes sense that we would have anxiety about sharing at all. It is for that reason that I believe all Christians should do their best to become thoroughly acquainted with what we believe and why we believe it.

1 Peter 3:15 tells us, *"Always **be prepared to give an answer to everyone who asks you** to give the reason for the hope that you have. But do this with gentleness and respect."*

Upcoming chapters will be dedicated to equipping you to share the Gospel with others effectively. We will talk about how to answer difficult questions, what to do if you don't know how to respond, and, basically, what the message is that we are really trying to share in the first place.

Discussion Questions:

-What is the worst thing that could happen if you share your faith?

-What should you be willing to give up for the Gospel?

-How could prayer help you overcome fear?

-What are some ways you can start small and work upward?

"I am driven to keep going for Christ by the filling of the Holy Spirit and the knowledge that the harvest is not forever. It will soon be past."   -Bill Bright

What is the Gospel

"Nothing makes one so vain as being told that one is a sinner."

-Oscar Wilde

The Good News about Jesus begins with some pretty bad news.

> The Good News about Jesus begins with some pretty bad news.

Every person, everywhere, throughout human history has been a dirty, rotten sinner consumed with selfishness. They were born that way, and, unless something miraculous happened, they lived that way and died that way. Besides Jesus Christ, there have been absolutely no exceptions in the human race. Every person you have ever met or ever will meet was born selfish to the core and incapable of even the most elementary act of true goodness or righteousness.

The truth is, people are bad . . . really bad . . . and there are no exceptions.

I realize that this could be one of the most unpopular chapters in this book. I also believe it is one of the most necessary. Until we realize the true state of lost people (which includes our own state outside of the grace of God), it will be very difficult for us to stay motivated to reach out to them. And, as long as we see people as basically good, it is going to be next to impossible to convince them that they have a desperate need for a savior. We need to realize this truth and effectively convey it to others. As long as I see myself as a good person, I will never see a real need to call out to Jesus. When I finally

> For many, the self-righteousness of denying sin is actually the pinnacle of their own sin.

see my selfishness and sin for what it is, I am taking a huge step toward calling out to Him for help. The first step toward fixing a problem is admitting that we have one. For many, the self-righteousness of denying sin is actually the pinnacle of their own sin.

> In order to escape their situation, they must humble themselves before God.

The bottom line is this: Every single person, because of his or her own unrighteousness, deserves eternal punishment and separation from God. All people are on a one-way street toward eternal damnation, which they justly deserve. In order to escape their situation, they must humble themselves before God and receive His free salvation. In order to do that, they have to be awakened to the reality of their situation and their own guilt before God.

It can be phrased in dozens of ways, including *"Every person is selfish,"* *"No one is good enough for Heaven,"* *"Every person has broken God's law,"* *"All are sinners,"* and *"No one is right before God."*

No matter how you phrase it, the truth is that we have all fallen short of God's desire for our lives. We are imperfect. As such, we have no place in God's perfect Kingdom on our own.

> No matter how you phrase it, we are imperfect.

The first few chapters of the book of Romans are essential to understanding this topic. The first chapter explains that Gentiles (non-Jews) are sinners in their lifestyles of greed, sexual immorality, idolatry, gossip, and slander. The second chapter covers Jewish people and declares that they are sinners because of their hypocrisy, pride, and judgmental nature. Then, in chapter three, the author sums it up saying that *all* are sinners.

Romans 3:9-18 - *"What shall we conclude then? Are we any better? Not at all! We have already made the charge that Jews and Gentiles alike are all under sin. As it is written:* **'There is no one righteous, not even one; there is no one who understands, no one who seeks God. All have turned away,** *they have together become worthless;* **there is no one who does good, not even one.** *Their throats are open graves; their tongues practice deceit. The poison of vipers is on their lips. Their mouths are full of cursing and bitterness. Their feet are swift to shed blood; ruin and misery mark their ways, and the way of peace they do not know. There is no fear of God before their eyes.'"*

Romans 7:18 says, *"I know that **nothing good lives in me,** that is, in my sinful nature. For I have the desire to do what is good, but I cannot carry it out."* And Galatians 3:22 says, *"But the Scripture declares that the whole world is a prisoner of sin . . . ."*

To many, the idea that all people are inherently sinful is enormously repugnant. I have heard it said many times, *"I just don't believe that. I think people are, in general, pretty good."*

It is definitely true that there are a lot of *"good"* people out there, but only when compared to other people. 2 Corinthians 10:12 says, *"When they measure themselves by themselves and compare themselves with themselves, they are not wise."* The problem is that the standard of what is good is not the standard set by other people. The standard for what is good is the standard that God has set, and it is a standard of absolute moral perfection. A flock of sheep looks brilliantly white against a backdrop of green grass but appears absolutely filthy when standing in freshly fallen snow. It is the same with our sin. James 2:10 says, *"For **whoever keeps the whole law and yet stumbles at just one point is guilty of breaking all of it.**"* And Matthew 5:48 adjures us to *"be perfect, therefore, as your heavenly Father is perfect."*

> There are a lot of *"good"* people out there, but only when compared to other people.

To this, many would reply, *"That's impossible; nobody's perfect."* And that is the point. No one *is* perfect. We are all sinners.

130

Consider this. When a child is born and raised, do you have to teach that child to hit his brother, to kick and scream when she doesn't get what she wants, to write on the walls with crayon, or to have a *"mine, mine, mine"* mentality? Of course you don't. Everyone knows that you have to teach a child to be nice. You have to teach him to share with his friends. You have to teach her not to take things that don't belong to her. Basically, you have to teach children to be good. Why? It is in their nature to be bad. It is their nature to be selfish. (*side note available at chapter's end)

The Bible teaches that selfishness leads to every kind of sin. James 3:16 says, *"For where you have envy and **selfish ambition**, there you find disorder and **every evil practice**."* Think about it. People steal because they selfishly want what others have. They are sexually immoral because they have selfish sexual desires that they refuse to submit to God's boundaries. They lie because they have a selfish need to hide something. No matter what the sin, whether it is discord, hatred, jealousy, envy, drug abuse, or witchcraft, somewhere at its root is the basic, fundamental truth that every human being, without exception, is inherently selfish.

Many times I will hear people say something along the lines of, *"There are some really good people out there."* When we consider some of the good things people do, it is understandable to think so. However, let us not be guilty of mistaking people who do good things for good people. There is a difference. If, at some point in his life, Adolph Hitler walked an old lady across the street and gave money to charity, even a very large sum, we still would not mistake him for a good person. We would recognize him for what he was, an evil person who sometimes did good things. (In fact, believe it or not, Hitler was *Time Magazine's* "Man of the Year" in 1938 – years before the world saw his real character.)

We are all in a similar boat. Unless God touches us with His grace, we are simply evil people who sometimes do good things. Some do more good things than others. Some look better on the outside. It doesn't change the reality that all of us are sinners.

Imagine two trashcans. One trashcan has been beaten up. It has dents and scratches, the paint has chipped off, and the lid doesn't quite fit.

> Hitler was *Time Magazine's* "Man of the Year" in 1938.

Trash seeps out the top and runs down the side. Bugs and worms abound, and the stench nearby is horrible. It is a trashcan that no one would want on their back porch, much less inside their home.

The other trashcan, however, looks good. It is practically brand new. The outside doesn't have a scratch on it. It has no dents, and the lid fits nice and tight. It even seems like someone has sprayed it down with perfume because the surrounding air smells quite nice. It has been jazzed up with some art-deco painting, and the pull handle is hand carved. This is one nice trashcan. Many people would have no problem keeping it on display in their home. This trashcan looks sharp. Do you see where I am going with this? They are both still trashcans. They are receptacles for dumping waste, and even if the outside of one trashcan looks really nice, if you take off the lid and look inside you are still going to find nothing but garbage: stinky, funky, rotten garbage that belongs nowhere near anything but the local landfill.

When I consider this analogy, something rises up in me that says, *"Wait a second! People are not trashcans! People are worth infinitely more than that."*

Yes, it is true. People are not designed to be vessels filled with the trash of selfishness. They are designed to be vessels filled with God's Spirit. This is God's desire for each and every person. The problem is, God's Spirit and a spirit of selfishness cannot both exist in the same vessel. In order for God to fill the vessel, He must first clean it out. In order for Him to do this, we must realize the garbage that is actually contained within us, "open the lid" so to speak, and allow Him to clean us up.

> People who proclaim their own goodness show their own sinfulness.

Jesus alluded to this concept in Matthew 23:25-26 when He said, *"Woe to you, teachers of the law and Pharisees, you hypocrites!* **You clean the outside of the cup and dish, but inside they are full of greed and self-indulgence.** *Blind Pharisee!* **First clean the inside of the cup and dish, and then the outside also will be clean."**

For some, the sin that makes them most filthy is the sin of denying their own filthiness. It is spiritual pride – the sin Jesus spoke against most often. People who proclaim their own goodness show their own sinfulness by their claim. They have proven themselves to be prideful and liars.

Still not convinced? One of the fastest and most obvious ways to see the truth about mankind's sinful and selfish nature is to look at the Ten Commandments and compare their requirements to the life and lifestyles of human beings. Romans 7:7 says, *"**I would not have known what sin was except through the law.** For I would not have known what coveting really was if the law had not said, 'Do not covet.'"* This essentially means, *"The easiest way to see that you are a sinner is to look at what God demands of you. If you will compare His rules with your behavior, you will see really quickly that they don't match up."*

Consider just a few of the Ten Commandments. The first commandment, found in Exodus Chapter 20, is *"You shall have no other gods before me."* Do you know anyone who has consistently, throughout his or her entire life, followed this commandment? Have any of us without exception put God first at all times? Only a liar or a fool would claim to have done so.

The sixth commandment tells us, *"You shall not murder,"* which, for most people, is not an overly difficult commandment to keep. However, Jesus expands on this commandment in Matthew 5:21-22, saying, *"You have heard that it was said to the people long ago, 'Do not murder, and anyone who murders will be subject to judgment.' But **I tell you that anyone who is angry with his brother will be subject to judgment** . . . ."*

The seventh commandment tells us, *"You shall not commit adultery,"* of which Jesus says in Matthew 5:27-28, *"You have heard that it was said, 'Do not commit adultery.' But I tell you that **anyone who looks at a woman lustfully has already committed adultery with her in his heart.**"*

The other commandments tell us not to lie, not to steal, to honor our parents, and more. We are even commanded not to covet what other people have. Do you know anyone who has never wanted what someone else had?

When we compare humans to other humans, we inevitably will come to the conclusion that some people are "good." We will see that some people come across as kind, loving, generous, and helpful. This is a very important point. As long as our standard of what is good is a standard of our own choosing, a standard whereby the goodness of people is determined by comparing them to other people, we will most definitely come to the conclusion that some people are inherently good. We will also most definitely be completely wrong in our conclusion. The standard for judging the goodness of people is, and always has been, God's law. What God says is good is good and what God says is bad is bad. His rules determine guilt or innocence, and based upon the rules He has given us in the Ten Commandments (and many other places) we are all guilty. We deserve to be punished.

> What God says is good is good and what God says is bad is bad.

This is where the Gospel begins. It begins with the truth that we are all, by nature, sinners. No matter who you are, no matter how relatively good you have been, unless God has done a supernatural act of grace in your life, you are rotten to the core. It may not be popular. It may not be fun to think about. You might even be so deceived that you are, even now as you read this, justifying your behavior and lifestyle or the behavior and lifestyle of others. But it is the truth. The question is, once people realize their own sinful condition, once they realize that their eternal separation from God is not only well deserved but also imminent, what can they do about it?

We are all going to stand before God and be judged someday. Matthew 12:36 says, *"But I tell you that **men will have to give account on the day of judgment** for every careless word they have spoken."*

> We are all going to stand before God and be judged.

Romans 2:5 - *"But because of your stubbornness and your unrepentant heart, you are storing up wrath against yourself for **the day of God's wrath, when his righteous judgment will be revealed.**"*

2 Corinthians 5:10 - *"**For we must all appear before the judgment seat of Christ**, that each one may receive what is due him for the things done while in the body, whether good or bad."*

Based on our own merits or favor, we will all be declared guilty. We have all broken God's law and have no place in Heaven, a place governed by that very law. So the question is: What can we do to be saved? That will be the topic of our next chapter.

Discussion Questions:

-Besides the Ten Commandments, what are some of God's other rules that people commonly break?

-Have you personally kept all of God's commandments and lived unselfishly for Him? Explain.

-What are some ways to convey to others that they have sinned against God?

-Do you believe all people are sinners? Are you?

*A side note – Do young children go to Hell?

Whenever the inherent selfishness and sinfulness of children is discussed, it inevitably leads to the question, *"Do children go to Hell when they die?"* While the scope of a question like this is too broad for this book, a general answer can be given. The short answer is, no, they don't.

In 2 Samuel 12, King David's newborn baby became very sick. After seven days, the child died. In verses 22 and 23, David says, *"While the child was still alive, I fasted and wept. . . . But now that he is dead, why should I fast? Can I bring him back again? **I will go to him**, but he will not return to me."*

We also know from Psalm 23:6 that King David fully expected to spend eternity *"dwell[ing] in the house of the Lord forever."*

When we consider both of these verses together, the answer is clear: David expected his dead newborn to meet him in Heaven. When combined with other passages from the New Testament such as Matthew 18:3-5, Luke 18:16-17, Mark 10:13-16, and many more, it can be said categorically that God takes children to Heaven. As far as at what age children become accountable for their sins and their decisions, we will not discuss that topic here, but we can rest assured that God is just and merciful. Let us do our best to introduce young people to Jesus as soon as possible to avoid even dealing with these issues.

What is the Gospel II

"Evangelism is just one beggar telling another beggar where to find bread."

-D.T. Niles

We have already established that we are all sinners. The question is: What can we do about it? The real truth of the matter is this: We can't do a thing! In our own power and effort there is absolutely nothing we can do to be free from our sin and our sinful nature.

As we read in the last chapter, Galatians 3:22 says, *"But the Scripture declares that the whole world is a prisoner of sin."* As prisoners of sin, we are trapped.

Just like a person who has been taken into a deep dungeon, chained hand and foot to a wall, locked behind another wall of iron bars, and left without any means of escape, there is no way that we can possibly escape our *"prison"* of sin. That is, unless someone *outside* the prison comes to our rescue.

139

Our sinful nature runs so deep through our minds, our bodies, and our souls that even our attempts at righteousness and goodness are tainted with sinfulness and selfishness. Even our best acts are stained with the idea of serving ourselves. Our attempts to escape the prison of sin are tainted with an attitude that says, *"I must escape sin for my own benefit."* Therein lies the problem: Even our attempts to escape sin are entrenched in selfishness. It is a never-ending paradox. We give to charity, partially out of a desire to help, but partially because it just makes us feel good. We don't steal, partially because we recognize that stealing is wrong, but partially because we think not stealing makes us good somehow. We say kind things to people, partially out of a desire to make them feel good and encourage them, and partially because we want them to like us. The list could easily continue for page after page.

> Even our attempts to escape sin are entrenched in selfishness.

While some of our motives might be true and upright, we also constantly have to deal with our selfish nature, which makes even our attempts at goodness come up short. Isaiah 64:6 says, *"All of us have become like one who is unclean, and **all our righteous acts are like filthy rags**; we all shrivel up like a leaf, and like the wind our sins sweep us away."* We cannot even cry out to God for help in a righteous manner. The truth is, I need God's mercy for *my* sake. I need to be saved. *I* do. Even in my efforts to reach God, I am still looking out for number one. When I say, *"God, have mercy on me, a sinner,"* I am still doing so out of a selfish motive. I am still self-seeking.

> We cannot even cry out to God for help in a righteous manner.

Paul describes our situation best in Romans 7: *"I am unspiritual, sold as a slave to sin. I do not understand what I do. For what I want to do I do not do, but what I hate I do . . . .* **I know that nothing good lives in me, that is, in my sinful nature. For I have the desire to do what is good, but I cannot carry it out. For what I do is not the good I want to do; no, the evil I do not want to do – this I keep on doing** *. . . . So I find this law at work:* **When I want to do good, evil is right there with me.***"* So, not only are we all sinners, but there is absolutely nothing we can do on our own to be saved. Left to our own devices, we are doomed.

> Left to our own devices, we are doomed.

But here is the Good News: God has declared a way for us to be saved, and His Word is true! If there is any part of this book that I believe is important and must be absorbed for the message to get across, it is this: God's Word is true. It works. Just as when God said, *"Let there be light"* and there was, when God says it, it happens, no matter what. When God declares in His Word that we can be saved, it becomes a fact. Hearing and applying God's Word to our lives is the single key to the Gospel. It is the way to salvation. If we want to be effective evangelists, we must become effective at sharing God's Word with others. Sharing God's Word with people is the most important aspect of evangelism.

When God says, as in Romans 10:13, that *"Everyone who calls on the name of the Lord will be saved,"* it is true. Regardless of who the person is, regardless of the person's motives, regardless of even the selfishness and unrighteousness of the person's calling out, when God says it, it becomes reality. God said everyone who calls on Him will be saved. That settles it. When a person hears that message and responds, regardless of the person's motive or condition, that person *"will be saved."* Period. In order for the person to respond, however, he or she must hear the message.

> When a person hears, receives, and clings to God's Word, God does what He said He would do.

When the Word of God says, *"Here I am! I stand at the door and knock. If anyone hears my voice and opens the door, I will come in and eat with him, and he with me (Revelation 3:20),"* it means it. If a person will open the door of his or her heart to Jesus, He will come in. It doesn't matter why the person opens up to Him. Whether it is to escape Hell (a selfish motive), to experience His peace (a selfish motive), or to become a "good person" (also a selfish motive), God still does the work. When a person hears, receives, and clings to God's Word, God does what He said He would do. He realizes that none of us can even respond to him righteously, but He loves us anyway and has demonstrated his love for us by sending His Son Jesus to pay the price for our sins and to destroy our sinful, selfish nature, replacing it with His perfect and holy nature, His Spirit.

Earlier we mentioned that we are all prisoners of sin and that we can do nothing to save ourselves. We must have an outside influence to redeem us from our corruption. Jesus is that influence, as we see in Romans 7:24-25: *"Who will rescue me from this body of death? Thanks be to God – through Jesus Christ our Lord!"* Psalm 103:12 says, *"As far as the east is from the west, so far has he removed our transgressions from us."* And Hebrews 10:17 says, *"Their sins and lawless acts I will remember no more."*

When a person calls out to Jesus and receives His Spirit into his or her life, He forgives that person completely. God can do this and remain a God of justice because the penalty for our sin has already been paid. Even though we are all deserving of eternal punishment, Jesus took our punishment upon Himself. The price has already been paid.

Galatians 3:13 - *"**Christ redeemed us from the curse of the law** by becoming a curse for us, for it is written: 'Cursed is everyone who is hung on a tree.'"*

1 Timothy 2:5-6 - *"For there is one God and one mediator between God and men, the man **Christ Jesus**, who **gave himself as a ransom for all men** . . . ."*

1 Peter 2:24 - *"**He himself bore our sins in his body** on the tree, so that we might die to sins and live for righteousness; by his wounds you have been healed."*

One of the most awesome and unique aspects of the Christian faith is that of the Atonement. There are many religions and philosophies in the world today that can help people become "better." There is no religion, philosophy, or method in the world that changes what someone has already been and eradicates their sinful past life – except Christianity.

Imagine a man who at the age of twenty-five committed premeditated and violent murder. If that same man is captured twenty years later, it will not matter how much he has changed. Even if he has become an upright citizen, a family man, and a community volunteer at several charities, it does not change the fact that he is a murderer. There is no statute of limitations on murder. Regardless of how much of a better person he may have become, he is still guilty. The price for his sins must be paid.

That is exactly what Jesus did. He paid the price! In modern day terms, He paid our speeding ticket. He served time in our place. He went to the chair for us. When we stand before God the Judge, if we have accepted Jesus' Atonement and received Him, He will declare us innocent. Even though before we had been murderers, thieves, adulterers, and liars, because His Son Jesus has paid the penalty for our sins, we are declared innocent. We are criminals against God and man no longer. We are free!

> We are criminals against God and man no longer. We are free!

It gets better. In John 3:3, Jesus says, *"I tell you the truth, no one can see the kingdom of God unless he is born again."* 2 Corinthians 5:17 explains what this means. *"If anyone is in Christ, he is a new creation; **the old has gone, the new has come**!"* Galatians 6:15 tells us that *"What counts is a new creation."*

When we call out to Jesus and receive Him, He gives us a new nature. Just like a tenant who moves into a filthy apartment, He cleans house. He utterly destroys the old, sinful nature and replaces it with a perfect nature. The spirit of a person who receives Jesus is utterly changed in its very nature. He gives people power (grace) to live for God. Where before it was impossible to do good, suddenly the potential for good exists. Because our nature is changed, goodness and righteousness become conceivable realities where before they were impossibilities. We quite literally get to start over as we see in Ezekiel 36:26, which says, *"I will give you a new heart and put a new spirit in you; I will remove from you your heart of stone and give you a heart of flesh."*

> Here is where things get interesting.

Here is where things get interesting. Once God has given us a new spirit, it is time for that spirit to begin controlling our lives. Instead of continuing in sin and ungodly behavior, the Spirit of God desires that we live our lives in reverence for God, allowing Him to live through us.

Galatians 2:20 - *"I have been crucified with Christ and **I no longer live, but Christ lives in me.** The life I live in the body, I live by faith in the Son of God, who loved me and gave himself for me."*

Romans 6:6, 11-12 - *"For we know that our old self was crucified with him so that the body of sin might be done away with, that **we should no longer be slaves to sin . . . . Count yourselves dead to sin** but alive to God in Christ Jesus. Therefore **do not let sin reign in your mortal body** so that you obey its evil desires."*

When we receive Jesus, our spirit has been changed, but our mind has not, and this is where many people become confused. Romans 12:2 tells us to be *"transformed"* by the renewing of our minds. Over the years that we have lived for ourselves, our mind has been conformed to the *"pattern of this world."* While we lived in selfishness, our minds were focused on self-centered thinking. Receiving Jesus is the starting point to a lifetime of transformation. In that way, salvation is not only an experience, it is also a process. It is a process in which Jesus not only forgives our sins, He not only changes our spirit, but He also comes alongside us to help us live our lives for Him. He removes our dead, selfish spirit, replaces it with His own Holy Spirit, and then overcomes our carnal mind and selfish thinking by that same Spirit that now lives in us. He then takes our lives and maximizes our potential by using us to deliver His message to others.

> Receiving Jesus is the starting point of a lifetime of transformation.

To sum up, the Gospel of Jesus is this: We are all sinners with a nature incapable of true righteousness. There is nothing we can do on our own to be saved because our very nature binds us to a lifestyle of sin. If no one intervenes, we will be separated from God for all time in Hell. But God, in His mercy and love, made a way for us. His Son Jesus paid the price for our sin, and through receiving Him we can be made right with God. He will come into our lives, destroy our sinful selfish nature, and remove from us the penalty and weight of our past sins. He will then take our lives and use them to further His Kingdom and His message, introducing to others the concept that saved us in the first place. He pours His love, mercy, and grace into our lives and expects that not only will we be made full but that we will overflow into the lives of those around us. It is good news indeed. It is the news that must be shared with others. In the next chapter we will begin diving into the practical aspects of sharing His message with others. How do we do it? What is the best way? What exactly can I do to reach people for Jesus?

Discussion Questions:

-How are we "prisoners to sin"?

-Can you relate to the idea that even our best attempts at goodness are tainted with selfishness? How? Can you give some other examples?

-How can we have our minds "renewed" after receiving Jesus?

"To me, it has always been difficult to understand those evangelical Christians who insist upon living in the crisis as if no crisis existed. They say they serve the Lord, but they divide their days so as to leave plenty of time to play and loaf and enjoy the pleasures of this world as well. They are at ease while the world burns; and they can furnish many convincing reasons for their conduct, even quoting Scripture if you press them a bit. I wonder whether such Christians actually believe in the Fall of Man."

-A.W. Tozer

Eating the Elephant:

"No one can do everything, but everyone can do something; and together, we can change the world."
-Ron Sider

Most people have heard the question: How do you eat an elephant? The answer is, of course: One bite at a time.

The question we as Christians must ask ourselves is this: "How do we reach the world for Jesus?" The answer: one person at a time, one event at a time, and one opportunity at a time. We would never try to eat an elephant in one sitting. Instead, we would break the elephant down into manageable chunks and try devouring it one meal at a time, one bite at a time. At first, the task of eating an elephant would seem nearly insurmountable, but, as days go by, eating one bite at a time, it *would* be possible, especially if there were a large group of people working together, bite after bite, meal after meal. It would be the small but consistent efforts of individual people over a long period of time that would make the task a possibility. It *is* possible to eat an elephant. In the same way, it *is* possible to reach people all over the world for Jesus, but it must be handled in the same way: people, working together, one person at a time, one conversation at a time, one event at a time, and one opportunity at a time. In order to reach the world with the Gospel we must each do our part. Each person's part may seem small in the grand scheme of things, but it doesn't change the fact that each person's part is very, very important.

What is the best way to reach people with the Gospel?

In Christian circles, there seems to be a great deal of debate concerning the best method. Some think public preaching, cold-turkey conversations with strangers, passing out tracts, and carrying signs are the most effective methods. Others think relational evangelism – making friends, allowing them to see your lifestyle and beliefs, and introducing them to a relationship with God – is the way to go. Still others consider acts of service – feeding the hungry, sheltering the poor, and providing help to the community as the best way to share the Christian faith.

The truth is this: All of these methods work because all of these methods can be used to introduce people to God's Word and it is God's Word that changes a life.

James 1:21 tells us to *"get rid of all moral filth and the evil that is so prevalent and humbly **accept the word planted in you, which can save you**."* 1 Peter 1:26 says, *"For **you have been born again**, not of perishable seed, but of imperishable, **through the living and enduring word of God**."*

Both of these passages state clearly that it is the Word of God somehow being planted in our life that saves us. It says it directly. The seed of the Word of God planted in people's lives can save them. What that means for us is this: If we want to live out the mission statement of Jesus – *"to seek and save that which was lost"* – we need to make it our life purpose to get the Word of God into the eyes and ears of lost people however we can. If it is the Word of God planted in a person

> It is the Word of God somehow planted in our life that saves us.

that saves them, it logically follows that if we want to see people saved, we must do what we can to introduce them to God's Word and the truths contained therein, regardless of the method.

Consider the Parable of the Sower (Contained in Mark 4), which comes from Jesus Himself. He teaches the disciples (v. 13) that this parable contains truths that are so basic to Christianity that if they do not understand this parable, it is going to be difficult for them to understand most any of His teachings. This parable is important. Depending on which version of the Bible you are reading, Jesus begins with the words *"Hearken! (KJV),"* *"Listen! (NIV, NLT, others),"* or *"Give attention to this! (Amplified)."* All of these are the equivalent of saying, *"This next part is really important. Make sure you are paying attention."*

Mark 4:3-8 - *"Listen! A farmer went out to sow his seed. As he was **scattering** the seed, some fell along the path, and the birds came and ate it up. Some fell on rocky places, where it did not have much soil. It sprang up quickly, because the soil was shallow. But when the sun came up, the plants were scorched, and they withered* *because they had no root. Other seed fell among thorns, which grew up and choked the plants, so that they did not bear grain. Still other seed fell on good soil. It came up, grew and produced a crop, multiplying thirty, sixty, or even a hundred times."*

He later explains that the seed that is sown is the Word of God. It is scattered in various places, and in different places it has different effects. In some places it takes root, and in others it doesn't. But notice that, regardless

> The behavior of the farmer remains the same. He scatters seed.

of the eventual outcome, the behavior of the farmer remains the same. He scatters seed. He throws it down in places that look inviting and in places that don't. He throws it on the road, on shallow soil, in with weeds, and on soil that looks good. His scattering appears almost arbitrary. Regardless of whether his scattering is completely random or not, there is no doubt that any other farmer who saw him would probably consider him a fool and tell him that he was doing it wrong. They would tell him to use wisdom in planting his seed and would instruct him to choose his targets more carefully. They would probably also instruct him to examine the area carefully and plow it up thoroughly before he even begins his work.

As ambassadors for Christ, we are expected to scatter seed. We are not expected to figure out what soil looks good and what soil doesn't. We are not expected to prepare the soil before we begin our farming. We are simply expected to scatter seed and see what happens. It is then and only then that the rest of the farming process (bringing people to a decision and discipling them) begins. Once a seed takes root and begins to grow, the process of nurturing (discipleship) begins. The ironic thing is, however, that nurturing and watering are done the same way, by sowing the seed of God's Word into the lives of those who are being nurtured (see John 8:31).

1 Corinthians 3:6-9 says, *"**I planted the seed, Apollos watered it, but God made it grow.** So neither he who plants nor he who waters is anything, but only God, who makes things grow. **The man who plants and the man who waters have one purpose,** and each will be rewarded according to his own labor. For we are God's fellow workers; you are God's field, God's building."*

Evangelism can be easily equated to farming. In essence, the ambassador for Christ scatters the seed of God randomly through many different methods, whether it is public preaching, holding a Christian event, or visiting people in nursing homes and reading the Bible to them. It means putting the Word of God and its principles out before people and giving them an opportunity to respond. And notice that the Christian worker is awarded according to the *"labor"* and not the *results* of the labor (vs. 8). It is we who do the work of spreading the Gospel, scattering it wherever we can by whatever means are at our disposal. The end result of that work is left in the hands of God. It is also true, however, that the more generously the seed is spread the larger the harvest will be. The more often we faithfully share the Gospel with others the more often we are going to see results.

Many Christians want to change the world for Jesus. We want to see "revival," where many people turn toward God and serve Him. We want to see God transform not only our family and friends, but our communities, our country, and the nations. What we don't realize, however, is that this is a process that begins with us, right here and right now through doing what we can, when we can, to share the Gospel with others.

> This is a process that begins with us, right here and right now.

Consider the following chain of events: A person most people have never heard of, Edward Kimball, was once a Sunday school teacher. One of his students was a young man who worked at a shoe store and one day Edward went to visit him while he worked. The young man was led to Jesus while he stocked shoes in the back room of that little store. His name was Dwight L. Moody, and he became one of the greatest preachers and evangelists of all time.

The story doesn't end there. While Moody was visiting the British Isles he preached in a small church where his stories made a tremendous impact, especially with their pastor, Fredric Brotherton Meyer, who later testified that his ministry was changed entirely as a result and that he owed everything to that moment when he knew what it meant to be brokenhearted about sin. It inspired him to reach others for Jesus.

Later in life, that preacher, Meyer, ended up preaching in Moody's school and said, *"If you are not willing to give up everything for Christ, are you willing to be made willing?"* The question changed the entire ministry of a young preacher named J. Wilber Chapman who also turned out to be one of the most effective evangelists of his time.

154

Chapman eventually turned his ministry over to a young man whom he had been training to preach the Gospel. This young man, named Billy Sunday, preached the Gospel to hundreds of thousands of people at a time when there was no TV, no radio, and no Internet. In 1924 he conducted a revival meeting in North Carolina. Out of those meetings a group of laymen determined to form a permanent organization to continue sharing Jesus in their community. In 1932 they arranged for a crusade in Charlotte and brought in an evangelist named Mordacai Ham.

At that same time, a man by the name of Albert McMakin was gathering together some of his friends to attend the Mordecai Ham services. There was a particular young man who, though he didn't really want to go, was persuaded when Mr. McMakin offered him the opportunity to drive his vegetable truck if he would attend. Wanting to drive the truck, the young man agreed and went with McMakin. During the service he dedicated his life to Jesus Christ. The young man's name was Billy Graham. Billy Graham, of course, has preached the Gospel to literally millions of people throughout the world from Moscow to Maine and from Germany to Georgia.

Can you imagine how much of an impact there has been from the millions of people who have heard the Gospel through the preaching of Billy Graham, D.L. Moody, and Billy Sunday? Chances are, if you think about it, you know someone personally who is living for Jesus today and would give Billy Graham credit for introducing him or her to the Gospel. The point is this: All of this began with one unknown man teaching a Sunday school class and sharing his faith in the back of a shoe store.

Another man, gathering a group of young people and taking them to a church service, made the story complete. There is no way we can possibly know how much even our smallest efforts to share the Gospel can impact the entire world.

There are more than two billion people in the world who claim Christianity as their religion. All of this began with a small group of people who were willing to actively share their faith regularly as we see in Acts 5:42,

> Even our smallest efforts to share the Gospel can impact the entire world.

which says, *"Day after day, in the temple courts and from house to house, **they never stopped teaching and proclaiming the good news** that Jesus is the Christ."* The question is, what are *you* doing? I implore you in the name of Jesus, begin doing something, anything, to reach the world with the Gospel. Your efforts will not be in vain. 1 Corinthians 15:58 says, *"Therefore, my dear brothers, stand firm. Let nothing move you. Always **give yourselves fully to the work of the Lord, because you know that your labor in the Lord is not in vain**."*

The vast majority of hospitals and institutions of higher learning worldwide were founded by Christians who wanted to expand God's Kingdom. Cannibalism has been virtually wiped from the globe as the result of Christian missionaries. People throughout the world have established countless homeless shelters, orphanages, and food dispensaries as a direct result of the Gospel of Jesus Christ and its reception. Most of the languages that have been codified have been done so by Christians seeking to bring the Word of God to illiterate tribes. There can be no doubt whatsoever that the spread of the Gospel from person to person has absolutely revolutionized the world, and it has been the efforts of individuals and collections of individuals working together that have made the difference. It is each person doing what that person needs to be doing, consistently over time, that has produced monumental change worldwide.

> Every day that goes by is a day that could make the difference for thousands, even millions of people.

You can change the world. Through personal effort on a consistent basis you can make the difference in the lives of countless people. My challenge to you is to begin today. Do something. Every day that goes by is a day that could make the difference for thousands, even millions of people. Please read the following passage of scripture very carefully and meditate on what it says.

Romans 10:13-14 - *"'Everyone who calls on the name of the Lord will be saved.' How, then, can they call on the one they have not believed in? And how can they believe in the one of whom they have not heard? And how can they hear without someone preaching to them?"*

This passage indicates that people cannot be saved unless someone preaches the Word to them. If we really think about it, it is a relatively obvious truth. Do you know anyone who is living for Jesus today who didn't somehow hear the Word of God? Whether it was through a Gospel tract, a sermon heard on the radio, a TV evangelist, or a conversation with a friend over coffee, somehow, some way, the Word of God was planted in them, they received it, and it grew up into salvation. Salvation always begins with the seed of the Word of God. The method to get it there is often as varied as the many personalities and ideas in the body of Christ.

In future chapters we will discuss several ideas for sharing the Word of God. We will talk about everything from open air preaching to distributing literature and from church invitations to giving surveys. They will all be methods that you can begin to apply and impact the world with the Gospel. First, however, we must confront some of the lies that people believe that keep them from sharing their faith.

Discussion Questions:

-What are some reasons that reaching the world with the Gospel seems like such a difficult task?

-What events led up to your testimony? How big are these events in the grand scheme of things?

-How could one opportunity to share the Gospel make a difference in millions of lives?

Thinking Clearly

"It is not our business to make the message acceptable, but to make it available. We are not to see that they like it, but that they get it."   -Dr. Vance Havner

It is very, very difficult for most Christians to think clearly when it comes to soulwinning. It can be hard enough to reach out to others when we have to deal with things like our own fears, laziness, or apathy. The battle becomes even harder if we believe ideas about evangelism that are incorrect. Some of the ideas we tend to hold are minor obstacles to overcome. Others are downright diabolical in nature and seriously undermine the spread of the Gospel. In the next few chapters we will examine the problems with several such ideas.

In Romans 1:25 we find a group of people who have *"exchanged the truth of God for a lie."* While this passage is talking specifically about sexual immorality, the point is made that it is possible for people to walk around believing something that is not true. It is possible that we could make decisions throughout our entire lives based on a false premise. As such, it is important that Christians examine themselves, their ideas, their doctrines, and the opinions that they hold dear.

Remember that lies can be extremely powerful and, when believed, have the ability to shape our lives for the worst. Consider a young girl who at the age of nine is told that she is stupid. She might be very bright, have a higher I.Q. than the rest of her classmates, and learn quickly, but if she ends up believing that she is stupid, it will affect her entire life. She might not try to accomplish things she normally would attempt to accomplish. She might not enroll in classes that she considers above her intellectual level. She might not go to college. In other words, believing the lie that she is stupid might affect many, many other areas of her life. She might have the intelligence of Einstein, but if she believes the lie that she is stupid, she will act accordingly.

> Remember that lies can be extremely powerful and, when believed, have the ability to shape our lives for the worst.

Lies have tremendous power to shape and change behavior. For that reason it is very important that we examine ourselves and humbly submit to God in a willingness that says to God, *"Tell me the truth. If I believe things that are false, reveal the truth to me, and help me accept what is right."*

2 Corinthians 13:5 says, *"**Examine yourselves** to see whether you are in the faith; **test yourselves**."* Psalm 139:23 says, *"**Search me, O God**, and know my heart; **test me** and know my anxious thoughts."*

As followers of Christ, it is imperative that we allow God to have His way with our minds. If we are in error, it is very important that we humble ourselves enough to seek God and allow Him to reveal the error to us.

Psalm 25:9 says, *"He **guides the humble** in what is right and teaches them his way."* My prayer is that you will take time to humbly ask God to reveal if there is any error in your thinking concerning evangelism. If nothing else, please take time to think through these phrases. See if they have somehow been used to keep you from being as effective as you could be in sharing the Gospel. The items listed in this and the next two chapters are some of the chief weapons that the enemy uses against the people of God to limit severely the expansion of God's Kingdom. They are lies that he propagates as extensively as any in his arsenal. He has established them firmly in the minds of countless believers and, as a result, has caused people who would normally be powerful soldiers for the Kingdom of God to lay down their arms and refuse to take any ground. These lies have, at best, limited severely the effectiveness of Christians around the world. At worst, they have made many Christians entirely ineffectual in spreading the Gospel of Jesus. Let's examine the first lie:

1. If you make people mad, you have done something wrong. There seems to be an unspoken rule in Christian evangelism today that says, *"If you make someone mad, you are doing it wrong."*

It is simply untrue. Not only is it untrue, it is the exact opposite of what Jesus and the Bible declare over and over. What the Bible teaches is that if you are doing it right, sometimes (not always, but sometimes) people are going to be mad. Get used to it. It may be difficult, but it is reality. Consider the following:

Matthew 5:11-12 - *"**Blessed are you when people insult you, persecute you and falsely say all kinds of evil against you because of me**. Rejoice and be glad, because great is your reward in heaven, **for in the same way they persecuted the prophets who were before you**."*

> Sometimes (not always, but sometimes) people are going to be mad.

John 15:20-21 - *"Remember the words I spoke to you: 'No servant is greater than his master.' **If they persecuted me, they will persecute you also**. If they obeyed my teaching, they will obey yours also. They will treat you this way because of my name, for they do not know the One who sent me."*

2 Timothy 3:12-13 - *"In fact, **everyone who wants to live a godly life in Christ Jesus will be persecuted**, while evil men and impostors will go from bad to worse, deceiving and being deceived."*

The truth is, for those who live the Christian lifestyle as it is designed to be lived, it is inevitable and absolutely unavoidable that people are going to be mad at you sometimes. It is part of the package. Jesus said in Mark 10:29-30, *"I tell you the truth . . . .. No one who has left home or brothers or sisters or mother or father or children or fields for me and the gospel will fail to receive a hundred times as much in this present age (homes, brothers, sisters, mothers, children and fields — **and with them, persecutions**) and in the age to come, eternal life."*

While the Christian faith offers many promises such as joy, peace, eternal life, and forgiveness of sin, one of the promises that we tend to try not to think about is the promise of persecution. In the above passage it is clear: Persecution is a promise as sure as salvation for those who live for Jesus.

> Persecution is a promise as sure as salvation for those who live for Jesus.

I can imagine what it would have been like in the early church if some of today's Christians had been around. In Acts 7 we read about the response of the crowds when Stephen preached to them.

Acts 7:54-58 - *"When they heard this, **they were furious and gnashed their teeth at him**. But Stephen, full of the Holy Spirit, looked up to heaven and saw the glory of God, and Jesus standing at the right hand of God. 'Look,' he said, 'I see heaven open and the Son of Man standing at the right hand of God.' **At this they covered their ears and, yelling at the top of their voices, they all rushed at him, dragged him out of the city and began to stone him.**"*

If today's church had been around at that time, you can bet they would have wanted to pull Stephen aside and correct him on his methods. I imagine it would go something like this:

"Look, Steve, I really appreciate your passion, your boldness, and your zeal. The Lord knows we need more people with that kind of courage, but, man, you're doing it all wrong. I mean, look at those people. They're gnashing their teeth at you, man; they are

really ticked off. You're turning people off, and you're making it harder for the rest of us to share Jesus in a way that's more effective. Let's try to use some wisdom here, okay, pal?"

Am I way off base here, or is this a realistic scenario?

I am not saying we should seek to make people mad. I am not at all suggesting that we should be rude, callous, or insensitive when we witness to others. Sharing the Gospel with others and even shouting it from the rooftops is a command of God, but so is treating people with love and dignity.

> Shouting it from the rooftops is a command of God, but so is treating people with love and dignity.

Romans 12:18 - *"If it is possible, as far as it depends on you, **live at peace with everyone**."*

Matthew 10:16 - *"Be as **shrewd as snakes** and **as innocent as doves**."*

Philippians 4:5 - *"Let **your gentleness be evident to all**."*

1 Peter 3:15-17 - *"Always be prepared to give an answer to everyone who asks you to give the reason for the hope that you have. **But do this with gentleness and respect**, keeping a clear conscience, so that those who speak maliciously against your good* *behavior in Christ may be ashamed of their slander. It is better, if it is God's will, to suffer for doing good than for doing evil."*

In Jesus we need to go out into the world around us with the message that Jesus is Lord and that He is transforming lives today. We need to do so in the fruit of the Spirit (see Galatians 5:22-26) with love, kindness, respect, and gentleness. However, even when we approach people in God's kind spirit, some of them may become angry. I don't want to lie to you, but rather I want you to be prepared, knowing that you have no reason to be afraid. Jesus said it best in Luke 12:4-5: *"I tell you, my friends, **do not be afraid of those who kill the body and after that can do no more**. But I will show you whom you should fear: Fear him who, after the killing of the body, has power to throw you into hell. Yes, I tell you, fear him."*

If you are faithful to share the Gospel, sometimes people are going to get mad. This doesn't mean that you did it wrong. If the truth be known, sometimes people need to get mad. Otherwise, how do you explain some of the harsher words of Jesus (see Matthew 23), John the Baptist (Matthew 3), and the apostle Paul (Galatians 5:12)?

How many of us at one time or another have become downright furious with someone only to later rethink our position and our response and realize that we were in the wrong? How many of us have ever apologized to someone and admitted that person was right after we took some time to think things over? Sometimes getting mad is the best thing for us because it reveals our real heart. Sometimes being kind means warning people of danger – emphatically if necessary.

The Gospel demands change from people. It says, *"You are wrong."* And people never like to hear that they are wrong. The Gospel is, understandably, offensive to people. That doesn't make it wrong. In fact, it is the Gospel's claim that it is the right way (and the only way) that makes it so offensive. It is impossible to think that we are able to adequately convey the message that all people are sinners, that going your own way is a sure route toward destruction, and that there is only one way to be saved, and expect people not to become angry with us sometimes. That doesn't mean that we shouldn't do it. Attempts to convey this message without the risk of making someone mad will always be doomed to failure.

> The Gospel is, understandably, offensive to people.

I admit, I wish it were different. I wish that I could be a friend with every person I come across and that everyone would see the truth of the Gospel instantly without anger. At the least, I wish people would always see that my motive is one of love and appreciate my efforts. Unfortunately, that is just not the case. If you do it right, sometimes people are going to become angry. In my experience, it is uncommon, but it does happen.

Now, let's examine the second lie:

2. **My efforts are going to turn people off.** This is a big one. Over the past thirteen years of sharing Jesus with people and doing my best to

encourage others to do the same, this is probably the concern most often expressed by Christians when it comes to sharing their faith: They are afraid of doing more harm than good. In some ways, it is understandable to think this way. We all realize our own shortcomings. We have all met people who say that they have been "turned off" by churches, preachers, and even friends whom they considered overbearing. Even humility requires that we don't view ourselves as having all of the answers for everyone and that we view ourselves as capable of doing things wrong and really messing things up. But that is why we must, without question, trust the methods that God has laid down in His Word as the "right way" to do things.

> We must, without question, trust the methods that God has laid down in His Word.

Ask yourself this: Which of the following sounds more like what the Bible teaches?

A: *"Be careful how you do things out there. If you don't handle things just right, people are likely to get the wrong idea and actually go the opposite way than they should as a result of your efforts. This Gospel has to be handled delicately. We don't want to ruin the world with it. Basically, if you are not sure that the time is right and the person is ripe and ready, don't do anything. If you aren't sure, do nothing. It is better to be quiet and do nothing instead of risking the damage you might do to a person's eternal soul by declaring the Gospel to them. Just think, if you say the wrong thing or act the wrong way at the wrong time, they might go to Hell forever."*

Or does the following sound more like the teachings of Jesus?

B: *"Go out and do something! Share My message with everybody you can and do your best to persuade them to come into My Kingdom. It is the only solution for mankind, and it has to be shouted from the housetops and declared, full-steam ahead, from coast to coast and continent to continent. There isn't enough time to worry about all of the particulars. Just trust Me! Get out there and spread this message to every single person who breathes. Let Me deal with the rest. If they won't listen to you, leave them behind and go find somebody who will. My message is truth. If they reject it, don't get too freaked out – it's bound to happen. Instead, you be concerned about who you are going to share with next."*

Anyone who honestly examines the New Testament must come to the conclusion that the latter sounds more like the teachings of Jesus. Consider the following passages and decide for yourself – which does the Bible teach?

Matthew 10:14-16 - *"**If anyone will not welcome you or listen to your words, shake the dust off your feet when you leave that home or town**. I tell you the truth, it will be more bearable for Sodom and Gomorrah on the day of judgment than for that town. I am sending you out like sheep among wolves. Therefore be as shrewd as snakes and as innocent as doves."*

Matthew 10:27 - *"What I tell you in the dark, speak in the daylight; what is whispered in your ear, **proclaim from the roofs**."*

Mark 6:12 - *"They went out and preached that people should repent."*

Isaiah 58:1 - *"Shout it aloud, do not hold back. Raise your voice like a trumpet. Declare to my people their rebellion and to the house of Jacob their sins."*

Acts 17:17 - *"So he [Paul] reasoned in the synagogue with the Jews and the God-fearing Greeks, as well as in the marketplace day by day with those who happened to be there."*

Acts 19:8 - *"Paul entered the synagogue and spoke boldly there for three months, arguing persuasively about the kingdom of God."*

Psalm 40:9-10 - *"I proclaim righteousness in the great assembly; I do not seal my lips, as you know, O LORD. I do not hide your righteousness in my heart; I speak of your faithfulness and salvation. I do not conceal your love and your truth from the great assembly."*

I could continue to list scripture after scripture to establish this point, but these should suffice. The Bible teaches proclamation, boldness, preaching, arguing, compelling, consistent outreach, reasoning with people, speaking out, declaring, sharing, testifying, and even shouting as the methods that God has chosen for His Good News to go out among people. The problem lies in the fact that we, in our pride, think that we can determine better than God which methods work and which methods don't. We are just arrogant enough to think that we can determine the best way and the right time to evangelize. We think that we can determine when a person is ready and when a person will be "turned off" by our methods or our message and that we have the wisdom always to know the difference. The truth, however, is that we don't know these things.

Remember these two equations:

1. The Seed of God's Word + Good Soil = Great Harvest

2. The Seed of God's Word + Bad Soil   = Bad Soil

> The Gospel cannot damage people, although it most definitely divides people.

Notice that for bad soil, the Word of God makes no change whatsoever. The truth of the matter is this: If people become offended, angry, or bitter as a result of the Word of God being presented to them, it is because of their condition. It is because they are already people with a propensity toward anger, bitterness, and offense. The Gospel has not damaged them. The Gospel cannot damage people, although it most definitely divides people. The presentation of the Word of God brings out the best and the worst in people.

Is it possible to turn off the lights in a dark room? Of course you can't. You can't turn off what is already off. Unless you bring light into the room, it is going to remain in darkness. The problem is, if you bring light into a dark room, some people are going to be angry and tell you to turn it off. We all know that once you have become adjusted to darkness, light burns the eyes and is unpleasant for a while. It is the same with people who are walking in darkness. When the light of the Word of God shines into their lives, many will react in a negative way. For some, it would not even matter at what rate you increased the brightness. They simply love life in the dark.

John 3: 19-20 says it like this: *"This is the verdict:* **Light has come into the world, but men loved darkness instead of light** *because their deeds were evil.* **Everyone who does evil hates the light***, and will not come into the light for fear that his deeds will be exposed."*

As mentioned above, when we present the Gospel, it is unavoidable that some people are going to become angry. Some will walk away bitter and blaming us for their bitterness. The truth, however, is that those people would be bitter with or without our message. They don't like the message. They don't like the concept that anyone (God or otherwise) would challenge their lifestyle. They don't want to be told what to do.

The Bible makes a very clear distinction between two kinds of people. Those who are chosen by God are those who are humble and teachable. Those who are rejected by God are proud people who refuse to submit to, or often even listen to, His teachings.

All people are sinners, but there is a difference between a humble sinner (one who admits his or her sin) and a proud sinner (one who refuses to believe or admit he or she is guilty). There are teachable sinners who will listen and consider the Gospel and unteachable sinners who refuse even to listen to God's method of redemption. The important thing to remember where this topic is concerned is that we, as soulwinners, cannot shape, determine, or even guess who is who. That is why we must present the Gospel to *"all creatures,"* regardless of who we think will or will not listen.

In the next chapter we will examine two more statements that Christians often make that seriously undermine the spread of the Gospel worldwide: *"I don't have the gift of evangelism"* and *"I just want to let my light shine."*

Discussion Questions:

-Have you ever been furious and later realized you were wrong? When?

-What are some examples of loving someone enough to tell them something that might anger them?

-What is a *"teachable sinner"*?

Thinking Clearly II

"Missions are the chief end of the Church . . . the chief end of the ministry ought to be to equip the Church for this. Each congregation is meant to be a training class."

– Andrew Murray

3. I don't have the gift of evangelism.

One time a group and I were ministering at a church, and after our team spent a considerable amount of time encouraging the congregation to be active in reaching out to the world and challenging them to consistently share their faith, the pastor of the church took over and prayed for the congregation. During his prayer, he mentioned probably three times that many people in the congregation didn't have the *"gift of evangelism"* and essentially said to them, *"If you don't have the gift of evangelism, don't worry about the sermon you just heard; it doesn't apply to you."* I was stunned! It was a pastor whom I respect greatly,

> I was stunned!

and I understand his motive and his heart to shelter his congregation, but the damage that he did in that short prayer was, in my opinion, beyond description. You can bet that several people in his congregation who had been challenged and convicted suddenly felt relieved of their obligation to share the Gospel. You could almost hear a sigh of relief as people went from challenged to complacent in only a few simple words. According to their pastor, it seemed, if you don't have the *"gift,"* you have no responsibility for the spread of the Gospel.

This thinking comes from a misguided view of Ephesians 4:7-13.

Ephesians 4:7-13 - *"But to each one of us grace has been given as Christ apportioned it . . . . 'He led captives in his train and gave gifts to men.'   . . . It was he who gave some to be apostles, some to be prophets, **some to be evangelists**, and some to be pastors and teachers, to prepare God's people for works of service, so that the body of Christ may be built up until we all reach unity in the faith and in the knowledge of the Son of God and become mature, attaining to the whole measure of the fullness of Christ."*

If you will read this passage carefully, you will see that it says something completely different than many people would have you believe. This particular passage is describing positions in the church. Some people are called to be apostles (a position in the church). Some are called to be pastors (a position in the church). Some are called to be teachers (a position in the church). And some are called to be evangelists. Are we to assume, because it is popularly taught this way, that *"evangelist"* is the only item on this list that means something different than the others? Of course not. The evangelist, like all of the others, is a position in the church. What does the evangelist do? The same thing as all of the other positions on this list: *"prepare God's people for works of service."* The position of the evangelist is twofold: to preach in public forums so that lost people will be won over to Jesus (see 1 Timothy 4:2-5) and also to train Christians in effectively sharing the Gospel with others, thus fulfilling their mandate to *"prepare God's people for works of service, so that the body of Christ may be built up."*

Not all people are called to be evangelists (holding a position in the body of Christ centered on evangelism), but all Christians, everywhere, are called to do the work of evangelism (reaching people with the Gospel of Jesus). In fact, the Bible nowhere mentions the *"gift of evangelism."* It simply says that some are called specifically to a life as an evangelist.

Romans 12:3-8 tells us, *"Do not think of yourself more highly than you ought, but rather think of yourself with sober judgment . . . Just as each of us has one body with many members, and these members do not all have the same function, so in Christ we who are many form one body, and each member belongs to all the others. **We have different gifts**, according to the grace given us. If a man's gift is prophesying, let him use it in proportion to his faith. If it is serving, let him serve; if it is teaching, let him teach; if it is encouraging, let him encourage; if it is contributing to the needs of others, let him give generously; if it is leadership, let him govern diligently; if it is showing mercy, let him do it cheerfully."*

Read this passage again from the perspective we are talking about. Some use a form of logic that says, *"I don't have the gift of evangelism, so I am, to an extent, released from the responsibility to evangelize."* Following the same logic, however, we can examine the passage above and come to the conclusion that, because we don't have a special *"gift of mercy"*, we are free from our obligation to show mercy to others, or, if we don't have a special *"gift of encouragement,"* that we are free from the need to encourage others. This is, of course, ridiculous. It would be like saying, *"I am not good with my money, so I am free from the need to give to the poor."*

Evangelism isn't even mentioned in this passage because all of these gifts are tools in God's belt that are to be used for the evangelism of the world. Spreading His mercy, encouraging others, teaching, and giving to the poor

> It would be like saying, *"I am not good with money, so I am free from the need to give to the poor."*

are all methods God uses to expand His Kingdom. The gifts that God gives each person are to be used for that great purpose. The question is never *"should I reach out to the world around me?"* but instead, the gifts God gives people determine *how* to reach out to the world around them. Make no mistake: You are absolutely required and expected to spread the Gospel. It is your giftings that, to an extent, determine how you will do that. Your giftings will determine what methods you will use.

I read recently on a website the following list of questions to ask yourself to find out if you have the *"gift of evangelism"*:

1. Do you like to talk about Jesus to those who do not know Him?

2. Are you able to share the Gospel in a way that makes it clear and meaningful?

3. Do you wish to relate to non-Christians so you can share your faith?

4. Are you are at ease in sharing how Christ has changed your life?

5. Do you get frustrated when others do not seem to share their faith with unbelievers as much as you do?

6. Have you been instrumental in leading others to believe in Christ as their Savior or in helping believers find their ministry?

I'll be honest with you – this list made me angry. If we were to believe that this list determined our giftedness or lack thereof in terms of evangelism, how many of us would ever share Jesus with anyone? I won't dwell on this point for long, but I will cover a couple of the points.

First, this list mistakenly assumes that evangelism is a spiritual gift. As we have already covered, it isn't. The office of the evangelist is the only thing mentioned in scripture that comes close.

Second, this list promotes the idea that our relative level of comfort concerning evangelism determines our effectiveness and giftedness in that area. This is both ludicrous and infuriating. If this were true, I never would have shared the Gospel with a single person. Anyone who tells you that they have always been comfortable or "at ease" sharing the Gospel is not telling the truth. It is true that one can *become* more comfortable and effective at sharing the Gospel over time, but it comes through practice. It takes stretching yourself beyond your comfort level.

The third and perhaps most frustrating problem about this kind of thinking is the implication that if you haven't led anyone to Jesus, it is because you are not gifted in that area.

Question six asks if you have been instrumental in leading others to Jesus and implies that this is a sign of your giftedness in evangelism. In reality, it could mean many different things, one of which might simply be the sin of lack of action.

> Anyone who tells you that they have always been comfortable or "*at ease*" sharing the Gospel is not telling the truth.

This statement alone implies that people haven't been instrumental in leading people to Jesus because they are not gifted, which might lead some to give up on their efforts. This, of course, renders them entirely impotent in sharing the Gospel at all. It is a self-fulfilling prophecy that says, *"I am not gifted in reaching people; therefore, I will not reach people."* This, of course, leads people to believe even further that they are not gifted in the area of evangelism. It is a circular thought pattern that is inflicting major damage on the Kingdom of God.

The list also asks, *"Do you get frustrated when others do not seem to share their faith with unbelievers as much as you do?"*

That is like saying to an upright person, *"Do you get frustrated when you see people in the church who live like the devil on Saturday night and then try to pass themselves off as righteous on Sunday morning?"* If the answer is yes, it doesn't mean the person has some kind of *"gift of purity"* or *"gift of holiness."* It simply means they are living normal Christianity. In the same way, Christianity, as it was meant to be, teaches every individual to share the Gospel. It requires no special gift.

In the prologue I shared my experiences of being utterly terrified of the concept of sharing the Gospel with people. If I had read this list back then, I might have become convinced that evangelism just wasn't for me and given up on stretching myself, putting myself out on a limb, taking courage, and sharing Jesus, even when I wasn't comfortable. Had that happened, you could chalk it up as a major victory for the enemy over my life and my life's purpose. I am so thankful that I had never heard any of this when I began sharing my faith with others.

> It takes giving your life entirely.

Every Christian believer is privileged with the responsibility of sharing the Good News of the Gospel with others. I confess that it comes more naturally for some than it does for others. I admit that some are naturally gifted public speakers and that some can articulate their thoughts better than others. Just a casual observation of people will prove that. But, coming from a person who was terrified and felt helpless, I can attest that the ability to share one's faith effectively and naturally is something that can be learned. It takes dedication, patience, and effort. It takes stepping out of your comfort zone into unfamiliar territory. It takes consistency and study. It takes finding the methods that you are capable of utilizing and using them often – and many times the methods you are capable of are not the methods that you are initially most comfortable with. It takes giving your life entirely.

You can be a soulwinner. Don't let anyone tell you otherwise. It is in you to be used of God. Don't let the idea that some have a special gift and others don't rob you of the potential that is in you to make a difference in the lives of people for God's Kingdom. I challenge you to put those thoughts aside and pursue a lifestyle of bringing people to our Savior.

> You can be a soulwinner. Don't let anyone tell you otherwise.

4. I just want to "let my light shine": For many Christians, the extent of their Christian witness and evangelistic efforts goes like this: Make some friends . . . live a good life around them . . . hope they catch on.

It is not uncommon at all for Christians today to walk a fine line. They try to be just normal enough, just cool enough, to fit in so that they can develop relationships that are so important to the spread of the Gospel. And then they try to be just different enough that people will "notice" and hopefully come to faith in Jesus. This lifestyle can be a very difficult line to walk, and we must be careful. We must make sure not only that our lifestyles reflect the Gospel of Jesus but also that our words declare Him and what He has done in our lives.

The last thing we want in terms of our witness is an attitude that says, *"Look only to my lifestyle and you will figure this whole thing out."* The idea of outreach is to have people place their eyes, not on us or our lifestyles, but on Jesus, the *"Author and Perfecter of our faith."* For this to happen, someone must point them in the right direction. Lifestyle evangelism without a verbal witness of some sort is both arrogant and dangerous.

As long as we are setting ourselves up as the example to look to, we are missing the point of evangelism entirely.

We must be very careful not to think that our personal morality has anything to do with our salvation. It can be tempting to think that just because we don't drink, don't smoke, don't cuss, or don't watch certain

> Lifestyle evangelism without a verbal witness of some sort is both arrogant and dangerous.

movies, somehow this makes us right with God. It does not. Only the grace of God acting in our lives makes us right with God.

Often, Christians think that because they don't tell dirty jokes or engage in certain behavior they are being an effective witness. The truth is, without an explanation of the Gospel, behavior that is *"different from the world"* only comes across as foreign at best and haughty at worst. A clear explanation of the Gospel is necessary.

Of course, as we have already covered, good behavior and moral standing are musts in reaching the world. Christians shouldn't cuss. They shouldn't smoke. They shouldn't tell dirty jokes. They should come across as radically different from the rest of the world. But we must be very careful not to forget what is truly important in the Gospel – the grace of the Lord Jesus Christ. In addition to our lifestyles, people must see that it is the Lord Jesus who has made the difference. The emphasis must be on Jesus, not our behavior. Good behavior can certainly be the starting point for the presentation of the Gospel, but it is only that, a starting point. Good behavior is not a Gospel presentation in and of itself.

No one has ever received Jesus just by seeing someone else living a moral life. It may have been a factor in showing the person he or she had a need, or it may have drawn attention to the fact that a changed life is truly possible. If a person has

> No one has ever received Jesus just by seeing someone else living a moral life.

received Jesus, however, it is because, without exception, that person heard the Gospel message and responded. We must make sure that our lifestyles are characterized not only by good living but also by the proclamation of the Gospel of Jesus. Proclaiming the Gospel without living a Godly lifestyle is not enough. In the same way, living the life of a Christian without proclaiming the Gospel is greatly missing the mark. Our lives must have both.

In Matthew 5:16, Jesus says, *"Let your light shine before men, that they may see your good deeds and praise your Father in Heaven."* There is no doubt that our lifestyles are designed to be a part of our witness. The people around us should most definitely notice that there is something different about the way we live our lives. Let us remember, though, that the light that is within us is not a light of our own making. It is Jesus. Jesus is the light. 1 John 1:5 says that *"God is light,"* and Jesus says in John 8:12, *"I am the light of the world. Whoever walks in me will never walk in darkness, but will have the light of life."* So when Jesus says that we should let our light shine before men, He is effectively saying, *"Let Me shine before men."*

182

When we live rightly before people, it draws attention to God and His ways. It shows that His ways are best and opens people's eyes to the fact that a Godly life is a realistic possibility. It causes them to praise God in the fact that, like it or not, God truly can transform a life. Even if they choose to deny it, inwardly every person can recognize what is right, and something deep inside them must acknowledge light when they see it. When people see good works, God is glorified, whether they choose to respond or not. It is like a genius placing his artwork on display. Some people may have a personal hatred for the artist. When they see his work however, whether they admit it or not, the artist receives glory. Even those who dislike the artist are able to recognize the genius of his creation. It is the same with God. Good works show off the wonder and glory of His ways. However, recognizing the genius of an artist's creation and choosing to follow the artist are two totally different things.

As followers of Christ, we mustn't stop at bringing God glory through our good works. We must press toward the goal that all men everywhere might follow the Artist and emulate His ideals. For that to happen we must do our best to introduce

> We must do our best to introduce them, not only to the Artist's work, but to the Artist Himself.

them, not only to the Artist's work, but to the Artist Himself. We must go beyond displaying His work to displaying Him.

In addition, when Jesus says that people will see our good works, He is talking about things that we *do*, not things that we *don't do*. He is not addressing all of the things we do not do as Christians, like sleeping around, getting drunk, stealing, talking ourselves up, or putting people down. He is talking about the things that we *do*. For people to see our good works, we must have good works to demonstrate. We must be people who encourage others. We must be people who give our time and resources to the poor and suffering. We must give ourselves over to serving others and doing what we can to help other people. Good works is something that we *do*. Many people cannot comprehend a Christian who remains a virgin until marriage or who chooses not to watch certain television shows, but every person everywhere can connect with the importance of giving oneself to helping others. Whether it is teaching impoverished children how to read, taking time out of our busy schedules to help a neighbor who is struggling, or stocking shelves at the local food dispensary, people most definitely recognize good works when they see them.

> Every person, everywhere can connect with the importance of giving oneself to helping others.

> The Gospel must shine through, not only in our actions but also in our words.

Letting our light shine is one step in the evangelism process, but we need to guard ourselves against the idea that it alone is enough. Our lifestyles must be tied to our speech. The Gospel must shine through, not only in our actions but also in our words. It is still the Word of God that shows people the way to salvation, and that Word must be proclaimed. We need both proclamation and demonstration for a complete Gospel witness.

Discussion Questions:

-What is the gift of evangelism as found in Ephesians 4?

-What are some of the gifts God has given you that you can use to reach people for Him?

-Is it possible to learn how to do things that at one time you felt extremely "ungifted" and uncomfortable doing? How so?

-Why is living a Godly lifestyle without a verbal witness not enough to win people to Jesus?

-Why is it important to live a moral lifestyle?

-What kind of good deeds should people see us doing?

"Oh, that I had a thousand lives, and a thousand bodies! All of them should be devoted to no other employment but to preach Christ."   -Robert Moffat

Thinking Clearly III

"How shall I feel at the judgment, if multitudes of missed opportunities pass before me in full review, and all my excuses prove to be disguises of my cowardice and pride?"

-Dr. W. E. Sangster

5. If I can't disciple a person, I shouldn't lead that person to Jesus: Christians who share their faith regularly, especially with strangers, are often accused of *"hit and run"* evangelism – sharing Jesus with people, leading them in some kind of a prayer, and then leaving them out in the cold with no help in growing.

Because people believe (and rightly so) that evangelism (and salvation, for that matter) is a process, they sometimes believe that, in order to effectively reach someone for Jesus, the person doing the outreach must be involved in every step of that process. In other words, I shouldn't lead people to Jesus unless I am also willing and able to follow up with them and make sure that they are adequately discipled. While it is true that, whenever possible, we should do all that we can to help people grow in their relationship with Jesus, it is important that we dispel the idea that evangelism should only happen in the context of a long-term relationship. We are each limited in how many people we can effectively "disciple" in Jesus. God would not have us limit our evangelistic efforts to the number of people we can actively invest our lives in. Instead, He would have us disciple some, but share the Gospel with many.

> God would not have us limit our evangelistic efforts to the number of people we can actively invest our lives in.

Jesus preached the Gospel to multitudes of people in His lifetime, calling them to surrender their lives to the Kingdom of God. The people He personally invested in and discipled formed a much smaller group. Clearly, Jesus did not believe that evangelism should only occur in the context of discipleship. It is also important to remember that at this time there was not even an established church for the people to attend. Christian churches were not established until several years later. Even so, Jesus considered it important to preach to the masses. Regardless of whether they received follow-up, Jesus preached the Kingdom of God, calling people to surrender their lives and hearts to God. He practiced both discipleship and evangelism. He invested His life heavily into a few people and yet took time regularly to minister the truths of scripture to people He would more than likely never encounter again.

In Acts 8 we see another of the many examples in scripture that illustrate this truth concerning evangelism and follow-up. In this passage, we find that the Holy Spirit leads the apostle Philip to a desert road between Jerusalem and Gaza. When he arrives he finds an Ethiopian riding in a chariot, reading from the prophet Isaiah. Philip starts up a conversation, and, after hearing the Gospel, the Ethiopian indicates a desire to become a Christian. He and Philip exit the chariot so that he might be baptized in a nearby body of water. This is where the relevant part of the passage comes in: Philip baptizes the man, but, when he comes up out of the water, verse 39 tells us, *"The Spirit of the Lord suddenly took Philip away, and* **the eunuch did not see him again***, but went on his way rejoicing."*

> The Holy Spirit took this man where he needed to go from there.

Can there be any more clear indication that God Himself believes in evangelism even when follow-up is impossible? Not only did Philip have no part in discipling this man, he never even saw him again. God physically removed him from the situation. Without a doubt, God desires the Gospel to be preached, regardless of what follow-up is or is not available. Again, at that time there was probably no formal network of Christians available to the new convert. There was no church to refer him to and quite possibly no other believers in the area to whom he could relate. He was, for all intents and purposes, left "out in the cold." He did, however, now have the Spirit of God living inside of Him, and he *"went on his way rejoicing."* I am convinced that we will see this man in Heaven and that, in the months and years after his conversion, he sought out and found ways to grow in the knowledge of Christ. I am confident that he took the burden upon himself. I trust that the Holy Spirit took this man where he needed to go from there. Do you agree?

One passage of scripture that will help us greatly in understanding God's view on discipleship and follow-up is Acts 2:41-47: *"Those who accepted his message were baptized, and **about three thousand were added to their number** that day.* ***They devoted themselves to the apostles' teaching and to the fellowship****, to the breaking of bread and to prayer . . . . All the believers were together and had everything in common. Selling their possessions and goods, they gave to anyone as he had need. Every day they continued to meet together in the temple courts. They broke bread in their homes and ate together with glad and sincere hearts."*

The most important part of this passage, where our topic is concerned, is in verse 42. In verse 41 we see that three thousand people became believers that day (which may or may not include women and children). Verse 42 says that *"they"* (the three thousand new Christians) devoted *"themselves"* to the teachings of the apostles and the fellowship of believers. In other words, the burden of entering into discipleship, training, and follow-up was on the new believers. The believers (as we see in the verses that follow), continued to meet together, continued to study together, and continued to share with one another. The new believers simply entered into the fellowship that had been established. The task would have been insurmountable if the responsibility had been left to the one hundred twenty believers to disciple the thousands who had been saved and the many more who were added to their number daily. Instead, they continued to serve God to the best of their ability. The new believers came alongside them and did so as well.

There is no doubt that follow-up and discipleship are indispensable in God's Kingdom. Our churches and our personal lives must make room for helping other believers grow in their faith and experience God more richly. We must make ourselves available to others to equip them and train them to be effective in serving Jesus. But we mustn't let this need override our primary mission, which is to reach unsaved people with the Good News of the Gospel.

The Biblical example of the correlation between evangelism and discipleship seems to be this: God has established His church on Earth – bodies of believers who meet together to encourage one another, worship together, and study the Word of God together. It is the responsibility of new

> It is actually a part of the salvation process.

believers to enter in to that body and become a part of it. It is actually a part of the salvation process. When people become subservient to Christ and declare Him Lord of their lives, entering in to Christian fellowship and becoming a part of His body becomes very much a tenet of life. This is a huge part of passing from self-sufficiency to sufficiency in God and His Spirit.

There are numerous Bible passages that seem to indicate this responsibility.

2 Peter 1:10-11 - *"Be all the more eager to **make your calling and election sure**. For if you do these things, you will never fall, and you will receive a rich welcome into the eternal kingdom of our Lord and Savior Jesus Christ."*

Ephesians 4:1 - *"I urge you to live a life worthy of the calling you have received."*

Philippians 2:12-13 - *"Continue to work out your salvation with fear and trembling, for it is God who works in you to will and to act according to his good purpose."*

This last verse is especially important, as it points out the crux of the matter. It is God who works in people. By His Word, God changes lives. When we think that our participation is an essential ingredient in the life of a new believer, we are saying that we don't fully trust that God, by His Spirit, can prompt, lead, and guide new believers into the path that they need to go down. Please, please don't misunderstand me. We should help them as much as we possibly can, certainly, but to think that they are doomed to failure without our help shows both personal arrogance and a lack of trust in what God can do in a person's life.

It is very important that we realize this and that we realize that God can change a person's life in an instant! A person really can be born again and changed forever in a moment's time when that person receives Jesus into his or her life. It is an instantaneous event that begins a lifelong term of service. Salvation is a process, but it is also an instant. Even a very brief Gospel presentation or a single Bible verse can result in total spiritual transformation in the life of a person.

Dr. D. James Kennedy tells a story of visiting a home and sharing the Gospel with a man who, throughout the entire conversation, seemed completely unengaged and uninterested. Upon leaving the man's house,

Dr. Kennedy turned to his wife and said, *"If anything ever comes of that, I'll eat my hat."*

Over the years that followed, that man's life was entirely changed. He became an active soulwinner and led many others to faith in Jesus – possibly more than one thousand people.

> *"If anything ever comes of that, I'll eat my hat."*

One never knows what even the smallest seed of the Gospel planted in the life of a person can do. It is absolutely impossible for us to gauge the effect. Some (as we see in the parable of the sower) receive the Gospel immediately with joy but fall away when the troubles and cares of the world overtake them. They cry when they pray, they get excited about church, and they seem to be doing well, but over time they return to their life before Jesus. Others seem not to listen, not to care, and may even seem irritated or angry. Sometimes these people are the very ones who eventually respond to the message and surrender to Jesus. You simply can't tell by a person's reaction, or even lifestyle, what is

> The power is in the seed. The receptiveness is in the soil.

really happening spiritually. That is why God has established things the way He has. We are called to scatter the seed of the Word of God. The power is in the seed, the receptiveness is in the soil.

Sometimes we can be so caught up in trying to disciple people who are only halfheartedly interested in the Gospel that we neglect our duty of introducing others to Jesus. It seems a shame that some people hear the Gospel over and over when others have yet to hear it for the first time.

Luke 12:48 tells us, *"From everyone who has been given much, much will be demanded; and from the one who has been entrusted with much, much more will be asked."* Some versions phrase it like this: *"To whom much is given, much is required."* When people hear the Gospel of Jesus, they are personally responsible for their response. The Gospel of Jesus is the greatest gift a person could ever receive. When a person hears of the Gospel, he or she has been given much. At that point, much is required. It shouldn't always require compulsion, babying, or coddling. We should do all that we can to help the person, with patience and sacrifice, but we must never forget that our responsibility is to share the Gospel with people, even if follow-up is impossible or unlikely.

We should be available to people. We should compassionately help people break down the walls that hold them back in their spiritual life. The church should gently and carefully instruct

> Discipleship is a two-way street.

people in the Word of God. We absolutely must, as God's church, disciple the believers. However, a person who has recognized and received the Spirit of God into his life must take personal responsibility for his spiritual life. Discipleship is a two-way street requiring both the availability of the church and the willingness of the believer.

When I am sharing Jesus with a person and that person indicates a desire to receive Him into his or her life, it is a great privilege to lead the person in a prayer of repentance and acceptance. Afterwards, it is a good idea to talk through what needs to happen next. I explain that salvation is a process and that receiving Jesus into one's life is just the beginning of that process. I tell the person that, just like any relationship, it begins with an introduction, and growing in that relationship requires time spent together, intimacy, and sacrifice. I outline a few steps that will help a Christian grow as close to Jesus as possible.

Studying the Word of God: I usually will point out John 1:1-14, which indicates that to know Jesus intimately requires an intimate knowledge of the Word of God. I encourage people to begin in the New Testament (usually with the book of John because it is the basics of the life and teachings of Jesus) and to read at least a chapter a day. I also encourage them to apply what they read to their life and will relate James 1:22-24, which says, *"Anyone who listens to the word but does not do what it says is like a man who looks at his face in a mirror and, after looking at himself, goes away and immediately forgets what he looks like."* I usually will elaborate on this and explain that when we look in a mirror, we do so in order to correct anything that may be wrong with our appearance. It is the same with God's Word. When His Word reveals that something in our life doesn't match up with God's desire for us, it is important that we correct whatever is wrong. When Jesus says that we are to love our enemies, we should then do our best to begin loving our enemies. When the Word of God points out that we should encourage others with our speech, we should begin to do so. Whatever the Word says, we should do.

> Whatever the Word says, we should do.

Prayer: Just as the Word of God is one of the ways God communicates with us, prayer is the way that we communicate back with God. Any strong relationship requires communication, and our relationship with Jesus is no different.

> Many people don't really know how to pray.

Many people don't really know how to pray. I will usually encourage them that prayer is actually very simple. (Of course, mastering prayer is a lifelong pursuit.) It simply means talking with God. I will encourage new believers to take time every day to get alone and talk with God. Sometimes that will mean going for a walk. Sometimes it will mean shutting yourself up in your bedroom and crying to Him on your knees. Either way, it is important that we tell Him what we feel, what we want, and what our worries and concerns are. Prayer is one of the quickest ways to know that God is a friend who sticks closer than a brother.

Church attendance/Christian fellowship: I will always point out to a new believer that it is simply a fact that people become like the people with whom they spend the majority of their time. If they spend time with people who care nothing about the things of God, it will be very difficult for them to live for Jesus with all of their heart. If they will surround themselves with other believers who are doing their best to please God and walk with Him, it is going to be much easier. If I know of a good church in the area, I will do my best to refer new believers there. If I don't, I will encourage them to find a good church that believes the Bible and start attending. It is important to mention that a good church isn't always necessarily the one that makes them feel comfortable. I will also point out the need that they be water baptized and encourage them to do so.

Telling someone: Just like a person who is going on a diet, trying to save money, or setting life goals, people are far more successful if they let others know what is going on. I will mention to new believers that the Bible teaches that opening your mouth and confessing Jesus is one of the things necessary on the road to

> People are far more successful if they let others know what is going on.

salvation. It is also much easier for others to help us in our walks if they know where we are coming from and where we are headed. I always encourage new believers not only to find a good church, but also to make sure the pastor knows about their decision to follow Christ. I will often talk about the fact that each person makes a difference in the lives of many other people. We are all either influencing people toward God or away from God. I will encourage them that, now that they have made a commitment to Jesus, it is up to them to start influencing people toward God. Opening their mouth and telling people is a great start.

There are many other things that a person should incorporate into their life in order to live fully committed to Jesus, but the four items above are the basics from which all the others spring forth. And these four items can be shared with a new believer in less than a couple of minutes. They are the bedrock principles of discipleship, and if people will take the responsibility upon themselves, these principles will lead them down the road that God has for them. It is very much like the old saying, *"Give a man a fish and he will eat for a day, but teach a man to fish and he will eat for a lifetime."* If we will, from the beginning, help people understand what they can do personally to reach God, and stress the importance of seeking Him on their own, we will be doing them a great service.

For those who desire to disciple people, understand that living the life of an active soulwinner is the single most effective way to disciple and train those around you. A good teacher leads by example and through repetition. As we have already discussed, living life as a soulwinner is the fastest way to grow into Christian maturity. It embodies the heart of Jesus on every level. Likewise, if we want to help others grow, the best way to do this is to equip them and train them to share their faith with others. We must lead a life of example and show them how it is done. There is a desperate need for men and women of God who will set the example in this area and disciple others through their words and their lifestyles so that every Christian, everywhere, will share Jesus with those around them.

> It embodies the heart of Jesus on every level.

Pastors, Sunday School teachers, and others who are called by God to teach His Word, I challenge you. Emphasize the need for evangelism from your pulpit and in the classroom. Many don't because they realize that to do so places responsibility on their own shoulders. As I mentioned in an earlier chapter, I have heard of pastoral conferences where, when the time came to go out and share Jesus, pastors literally would climb out their hotel room windows, sneak to their cars, and drive away in order to avoid evangelism.

It is certain that Jesus has commanded us to go and make disciples. This means that we are required to go out into the world and do our best to produce followers of Christ. If we are to produce followers of Christ, then we must understand the need for training people to follow His mission and to give their lives over to the pursuit of the souls of men and women everywhere. The following chapters of this book will be dedicated to that purpose: practical training. From here on you will see practical ideas and methods that will help you share the Gospel on a regular basis.

Discussion Questions:

-What does it mean that discipleship is a two-way street?
-How can we help new believers and also teach them to take responsibility for their own personal growth in Jesus?
-What do the scripture passages in this chapter say about God's view of evangelism and discipleship?
-How could stressing the need for outreach help our congregations and classes grow in Christian maturity?

"Brethren, do something; do something, do something! While societies and unions make constitutions, let us win souls. I pray you, be men of action all of you. Get to work and quit yourselves like men. Old Suvarov's idea of war is mine: 'Forward and strike! No theory! Attack! Form a column! Charge bayonets! Plunge into the center of the enemy!' Our one aim is to win souls; and this we are not to talk about, but do in the power of God!"

-Charles Spurgeon

Do Something

"Being an extrovert isn't essential to evangelism -- obedience and love are."

-Rebecca M. Pippert

Eva Young said, *"To think too long about doing a thing often becomes its undoing."* Benjamin Franklin once said, *"You may delay, but time will not."*

My suggestion to you is this: Start right now.

I don't mean tomorrow. I don't even mean when you are finished reading this chapter.

I really mean it. Start now. Right now.

If you are on a plane, put this book down and start up a conversation with the person sitting next to you. If you are at home, go grab the phone, call your pastor and tell him that you are interested in teaching a

Sunday school class. If you are at the library, do a quick Google search, find someplace that sells Gospel tracts, and place an order. Go to your computer and type out an email to a family member who doesn't know Jesus. Call friends and invite them to church with you this weekend. Do something and do it now. You can finish the book later.

There will more than likely be many people who read this book, agree with its contents, and still do absolutely nothing. Don't let yourself be one of those people.

> Don't let yourself be one of those people.

Jesus described the kind of people who hear about His teachings but do not allow it to change their behavior. Matthew 7:26-27 says, *"But everyone who hears these words of mine and does not put them into practice is like a foolish man who built his house on sand. The rain came down, the streams rose, and the winds blew and beat against that house, and it fell with a great crash."* And of course, we have all heard the expression, *"The road to Hell is paved with good intentions."* It is one thing to hear about evangelism and to respond with emotional and intellectual consent that says, *"Yes, I agree. That seems like a good idea."* It is another thing entirely actually to go out and make a difference in the world with the Gospel of Jesus.

> It is another thing entirely to go out and make a difference.

Jesus says some very challenging words in Luke 11:23: *"He who is not with me is against me, and he who does not gather with me, scatters."*

202

Jesus is in the business of gathering. He is gathering all people who will respond to His call. He makes it clear in this passage that those who are not gathering alongside Him are actually working against Him. He isn't addressing people's thoughts, motives, or conceptions here. He is addressing people's actions.

Later in the same chapter, Jesus makes a statement that contributes a great deal of clarity to this teaching. He says in verse 33, *"No one lights a lamp and puts it in a place where it will be hidden, or under a bowl. Instead he puts it on its stand, so that those who come in may see the light."* This is, of course, fairly straightforward and easy to understand. Later, though, in verse 35, He says the following, which may not come across so clearly: *"See to it, then, that the light within you is not darkness."*

What in the world does that mean? How can the light within us be darkness?

> If the light that is in you isn't let out, it ceases to be light.

The explanation is fairly simple. Light that is hidden isn't light at all. It is darkness. If the light that is in you isn't let out, it ceases to be light. Think about it this way: If you enter a pitch-black room with a lit flashlight, but the flashlight is completely wrapped in towels and then placed in a sealed container, is darkness pushed back? Have you introduced light into the room?

Christians who fail to let their light (and Jesus is our light) shine are actually propagating darkness. Light that is contained is no light at all. Containing light is advancing darkness.

The Kingdom of Darkness is not always a kingdom of rape, murder, hatred, strife, war, and disease. It also can be a kingdom of laziness, inactivity, uncaring, unhelpfulness, and procrastination. Getting out of our *"comfort zone"* doesn't just mean conquering our fears. It also means conquering our apathy and laziness. Typically, a comfort zone is a place where we kick back, relax, and enjoy inactivity. (A Lazyboy recliner is a good example of a comfort zone.) God's Kingdom is a kingdom of action, and the time for action is now.

> Containing light is advancing darkness.

Matthew 9:36-37 says, *"**When he [Jesus] saw the crowds**, he had compassion on them, because they were harassed and helpless, like sheep without a shepherd. Then **he said to his disciples, 'The harvest is plentiful but the workers are few.'"** Proverbs 10:5 tells us, *"He who gathers crops in summer is a wise son, but **he who sleeps during harvest is a disgraceful son."***

When Jesus said that the harvest was plentiful, He was saying that those who go out and work the fields will see great results because there are many people who will respond to the Gospel. The missing link is this: There aren't enough people who will faithfully work the fields while they are ripe. They are ripe right now, even as you read this.

The goal here is not to condemn a lack of action but to allow the Holy Spirit to convict us into action. There is a big difference between condemnation and conviction. Condemnation causes people to despair and give up. Conviction causes people to press onward and do great things. Condemnation tells you that you can't do it, that you have been a failure thus far, and you will continue to be a failure in the future. Conviction tells you that up until now, something hasn't been quite right, but it challenges you to change and to grow. Jesus wants to spur you on to action. The devil wants you to be complacent and defeated. If nothing else, he wants to delay change in your life for as long as possible, knowing that every moment that goes by leads you closer to no change at all. Putting off action leaves us in inaction and threatens to keep us there. An object at rest tends to stay at rest.

> Draw a line in the sand and, with God's help, decide once and for all.

Don't let yourself be condemned. Rather, receive the conviction of the Holy Spirit and make a quality decision that beginning now (not later), evangelism, in one shape or another, is going to be an everyday occurrence in your life. Draw a line in the sand and, with God's help, decide once and for all that your life from now on will be dedicated to reaching people with the Gospel of Jesus Christ. Never look back. Begin now and consistently do something to spread the Word of God. Make it your life's ambition. Every single day, you are presented with opportunities and situations where you can share the Word of God with those around you. Decide now that you will begin to take advantage of those situations more and more often.

Years ago, I boarded a plane after a long trip out of town. I was tired and quite ready to return home. I distinctly remember thinking, *"I hope I don't have to talk to anybody."* I found my seat, said *"hello,"* and introduced myself to the person next to me, but, in order to keep from having to talk to anyone, as soon as the captain gave the signal, I donned my headphones and turned on some music. I kicked back and reveled in what seemed like was going to be a comfortable and uneventful flight.

I was listening to an underground band named Red Letter Print that had recently played at a small coffeehouse in Louisville, Kentucky, and, to my knowledge, is no longer making music. I don't know the name of the song, and I will need to paraphrase the lyrics, but I distinctly remember the impact they had on me.

Hello, my name is (this and that).

It's good to meet you (this and that).

I know your name, and you know my name, but

I sit right beside you; you cannot see me.

I am speaking; you cannot hear me.

I reach out to touch you, but you cannot feel me,

and I cannot feel you.

The lyrics continue later in the song:

Hello, my name is (you don't care).

It's good to meet you (I don't care).

I know your name, and you know my name, but

I sit right beside you; you cannot see me.

I am speaking; you cannot hear me.

I reach out to touch you, but you cannot feel me,

And I cannot feel you.

We never feel.

Needless to say, I ditched the headphones and struck up a conversation with the person seated next to me. The time passed quickly, and I was able to share my testimony with him and talk with him about spiritual things. I don't remember all of the details, but I remember afterwards thinking about how glad I was that the Lord had chosen to convict me and challenge me.

My prayer for you is that you will take the headphones off, so to speak, and begin talking with the people next to you in every place you find yourself.

With that said, it is finally time to get down to business. In 1 Corinthians 9:22, Paul says, *"I have become all things to all men so **that by all possible means I might save some**."* My goal is to present many different methods so that everyone reading will have something to work with regardless of their particular situation.

Some of the methods are going to be very simple and straightforward and can be accomplished pretty much anywhere at any time. Others will require more of an investment and will work better with some planning. Some methods will require tremendous courage to step out and accomplish. Others will require no courage whatsoever and can even be accomplished completely undercover. My encouragement and advice to you is this: Don't automatically disqualify any of the methods. They all work, and chances are good that even if you don't feel comfortable or capable, you can learn to become so.

Discussion Questions:

-What are three ways that you could be used to spread the Gospel right now if you were willing?

-Are you willing?

-What is stopping you?

Get Em' Talking

"It sure is easier to talk to God about men than it is to talk to men about God. We must put legs to our prayers."
                                                                        -Ray Comfort

Joe Marlar's grandfather could talk to anyone.

At his funeral, the story was related about one time when he had been standing in line at a grocery store. A young girl was standing in front of him buying a pack of M and M's. He tapped her on the shoulder, leaned forward, and whispered, *"Hey, you're not going to buy those, are you?"*

With a questioning look on her face she responded, *"Uhm, yeah. Why?"*

Still whispering, he said, *"There's ants in them."*

"Do what?"

"Oh yeah, ants in the M and M's. Hadn't you heard?"

At this point his face broke into a huge winning smile, and she realized that he had just been pulling her leg. She smiled back and laughed. He had connected with her and won her over in just one moment of friendliness and humor. From there it was easy. *"I'm Paul. What's your name?"*

Apparently, this kind of thing was completely normal in his life. He would talk to just about anyone, anywhere, and his efforts at being friendly often turned into conversations about spiritual matters. Not only was he an active soulwinner, but he was just flat out a nice guy. He was extremely bold in his witness and frequently challenged people to receive Jesus, but he also walked away from almost every encounter with a new friend.

As Christians, one of the greatest tools we can have in our belts is the ability to converse with people. Even more important perhaps is the ability to transition from a non-spiritual conversation to one with spiritual implications. Learning how to open and maintain conversations with people equips us more effectively to reach out on a daily basis. No matter where we go, we are constantly interacting with people. Good communication skills allow us to connect with people in ways that nothing else can. Those skills make it possible for us to learn where people are coming from and then help us tailor what we say in order to meet them where they are. In short, learning the art of conversation is an indispensable asset in reaching the world for Jesus.

Over the years I have talked with countless people who sincerely desire to share Jesus but are not sure what to say or how to go about initiating a conversation. They are confident in what they believe and feel that they could adequately relate those beliefs to others, but they are not sure how to get around to the point of sharing. They want to know how to talk about spiritual matters in a way that is natural and real instead of forced and phony. In this chapter we are going to discuss several tips that will help us in our ability to talk with people. Whether it is with our friends and coworkers or a stranger on a bus, it is essential that we learn to talk with people.

> Talk about spiritual matters in a way that is natural and real instead of forced and phony.

Start talking: It seems obvious, but in order to regularly talk with people about Jesus, we must be in the habit of initiating conversations. In order to talk to people, we have to talk to people. It's that simple. There are a thousand different ways to strike up a conversation. For friends, family, coworkers, and the like, this is usually pretty straightforward and simple. We do it every day. Things like, *"How was the ballgame last night?"* or *"You said your mom was sick last week; how is she feeling now?"* or *"So, what did you do this weekend?"* are all great examples that work well. Initiating conversation just takes a little effort. Often even these types of conversations can make a difference for God's Kingdom if we are diligent and faithful to take advantage of them.

Initiating a conversation with a stranger is something different, but, in most cases, it really can be just as simple.

"I like your necklace. I've never seen one like it. Where did it come from?"

"I notice your shirt is from a volleyball competition. Do you play?"

"Excuse me. We are only in town for the evening and don't know the area but want a decent restaurant . . . maybe something that we can't find anywhere else. Any suggestions?"

Of course, this list could go on and on. The point is, in order to talk with people, it is important to break the ice.

I was recently in Denver, Colorado, for a Broncos football game (Go Broncos!). While I was standing in line waiting for a train, surrounded by a swarm of people in orange and blue, I noticed a husband and wife who were wearing clothing that supported the opposing team. I made my way through the crowd to stand near them, smiled, and said, *"Hey, guys, I'm sorry to have to tell you this, but when you weren't looking, somebody snuck some Baltimore Ravens sweatshirts into your luggage."* They immediately smiled back, laughed and said something about how they had to support their team, even in the hard years. At that point, continuing a conversation was easy: *"So, you guys are from Baltimore?" "How many games do you go to each year?" "How long will you be in Denver?"* This brings us to our next point.

Learn the art of asking questions: Once a conversation is started, carrying it on is easy. Learn to ask questions about the person you are meeting. Every good conversationalist will tell you – people love to talk about themselves. So, when in doubt, ask them something about themselves. Remember, awkward silences remain awkward silences only until someone speaks. A well-placed question is a great way to get people talking. If one question seems to fail, try another.

Where are you from?

What do you do for a living?

What do you do for fun? If you had a weekend off to yourself, what would you do with your time?

Your children are adorable. How old are they?

At this point, the idea is just to keep the conversation going. Looking for an inroad into spiritual discussion is another skill entirely.

Watch for an opportunity and take it: I am convinced that if Christians will be faithful to initiate conversations with people and expect great things to happen, then great things will happen. If we will begin each day prayerfully expecting opportunities to develop, and then do what we can to create a situation for those opportunities, we will see the hand of God. Bill Bright, the founder of Campus Crusade for Christ, had a personal policy that if he were alone with any individual for more than a few moments, he considered it a divine encounter and did his best to share the Gospel. We need to be the same way.

There are many ways to create a transition from a non-spiritual conversation to one with spiritual meaning.

> There are many ways to create a transition from a non-spiritual conversation to one with spiritual meaning.

"Really? You are from Seattle? I have some friends who work with a ministry there. It's called (ministry name). Have you ever heard of it?"

"So you ride motorcycles? There is a ministry at our church that works with bikers. Man, it is unbelievable what has happened in some of their lives. There's this one guy who . . . ." (Tell someone's story.)

Perhaps the easiest transitions come when the person begins to ask about you. If that happens, take the opportunity to make a transition.

"I teach high school English, and I head up one of the Christian groups on campus, so some of my free time is spent organizing meetings and that sort of thing. Do you have a Christian background?"

"Wow, I'm glad you asked. My life has changed a lot over the last few years. Do you mind if I share some of the great things that have happened?" (Share your testimony.)

"I work with a company that (does this or that) and in my off time I am actively involved in my church doing (whatever it is you do at church). Do you have a church you go to in town?" (If they don't, be sure to invite them.)

From here, the idea is to ask leading questions that have the potential to enter into more spiritual areas. There are many good questions that can lead in this direction. A couple of my personal favorites are, *"Do you have a church you go to in the area?"* or *"Do you have a spiritual background?"* Both of these are generally inoffensive questions that will tell the person that you would like to talk about spiritual things and create an opportunity in a way that is natural and comfortable. A very large percentage of time I have found that when confronted with one of these two questions the average person will go into much greater depth about what they believe or where they stand spiritually. I can't emphasize enough the value of these two questions in creating an opportunity for spiritual dialogue. If you didn't catch them, go back and read this paragraph again.

> I can't emphasize enough the value of these two questions.

Decide how far to go: At some point you are going to have to decide just how far to take a conversation. Some people, as soon as you ask a question with any kind of spiritual implications, are going to make it very clear that they have no interest in talking about it. At this point you may decide to transition back to normal conversation. In each situation, be as sensitive as you can be to the Holy Spirit and love people with a sincere love that cares nothing for self, and you cannot go wrong.

My good friend Mark, whom I mentioned in the prologue, was once on a shuttle while traveling. Another friend he was with struck up a conversation with the driver and eventually asked him about something concerning his faith. The bus driver gruffly replied, *"I don't talk about religion with people."* At this point, the person doing the asking sat back in his seat and was silent.

A minute or two later, after total silence, Mark leaned forward in his seat and asked the driver, *"So, how come you don't talk about religion with people?"* The driver replied that he thought religion was between a person and God and it was a *"private thing."* Mark continued to ask him questions about his reasoning, and the conversation went on for about 30 minutes. Ultimately, the Gospel of Jesus came out, and the man was very thankful that they had talked. They were even able to pray with him that he might experience God. Sometimes, the best thing to do is hang in there, even when the opening seems rough, and great things will result.

On the other hand, I believe there is clear scriptural teaching that says it is acceptable to move on when someone refuses to respond or listen.

Matthew 7:6 - *"Do not give dogs what is sacred; do not throw your pearls to pigs. If you do, they may trample them under their feet, and then turn and tear you to pieces."*

Mark 6:11 - *"And if any place will not welcome you or listen to you, shake the dust off your feet when you leave, as a testimony against them."*

When a person seems unresponsive to your efforts to engage them in spiritual dialogue, it is going to be up to you to make the decision whether or not to continue. Some of the best witnessing opportunities I have experienced have been ones in which a person didn't want to talk with me initially, but I hung in there anyway. On the other hand, there have been situations when it seems my time would be best spent talking with someone else. Still other times I have walked away but left the person with something to think about. I believe every situation is different, and this is one area where we especially need the leading and direction of the Holy Spirit. Remember this, though: Even the smallest seed can grow into something great. If you ask someone about his or her beliefs, the person becomes irritated, and you decide to walk away, that alone may be enough to cause the person to question his or her beliefs later and begin to contemplate matters of faith. Just making an effort to talk with someone may have lasting spiritual implications.

> Even the smallest seed can grow into something great.

Dig deeper: Digging deeper into conversation involves more of the same – asking questions. The key is knowing what kind of questions to ask.

Sometimes it is best to ask more questions that will help you understand where the person is coming from. If the conversation began with, *"Do you have a church you attend here in town?"* and the person responds with, *"No, I don't believe in organized religion,"* you might ask him why he feels that way or ask him if he grew up in church as a child. If you initially asked her if she has a spiritual background, and she tells you she grew up Baptist but in college became Buddhist, you might ask her what it was about Buddhism that attracted her. The idea here is to get to know more about where the person is spiritually before you begin to ask some of the most important questions. As we will discuss later in this chapter, we are not trying to confront issues here. We are simply trying to get a feel for what the person believes. The following is a list of questions that are absolutely excellent for taking conversations to a deeper level.

"Who do you think Jesus is?" *"Do you believe He was God in the flesh?"*

"What would happen to you if you died today?"

"If I were to ask you how to get to Heaven, what would you tell me?"

"Do you consider yourself a good person?"

"Do you believe you have a need for a Savior?"

All of these are great leading questions that can segue into a direct presentation of the Gospel.

We have already covered what the Gospel is, but, for the sake of conversation, we will sum it up here in a few points that can be explained easily:

-We are all sinners.

-The end result of our sin is destruction (Hell).

-God doesn't want us to go to Hell, but, because He is just, He must punish sin.

-Jesus came to take our punishment upon Himself.

-By calling out to Jesus and receiving Him into our lives, we receive forgiveness of sins, are declared right before God, and receive a new spirit that allows us to begin living for God.

-Receiving Jesus is the beginning of a process of walking out our new relationship with God. Some things that will help with that are prayer, Bible reading, church attendance (fellowship), and telling others what we have experienced.

Obviously, every conversation is going to be different, and we must be careful not ever to think of sharing the Gospel as a formula in which we go through a list of bullet points and put another notch on our belt.

> People are people to be reached, not mountains to be conquered.

People are people to be reached, not mountains to be conquered. On the other hand, having a general idea of what to say in some kind of straightforward way is beneficial in helping us present the Gospel. Just as a minister is typically more effective when he comes to the pulpit prepared, with at least a sermon outline in hand, so also we are usually more effective when we are prepared with points that people can understand.

The Gospel never was intended to be complicated or even varying. It is straightforward and can connect, as-is, with every person on the planet. No matter whether they are male or female, black, white, Hispanic, or Asian, the Gospel itself applies to them. Getting around to sharing the Gospel may be different with every person, and presenting it in such a way that people will listen may change from time to time, but the core message will always remain the same. Our goal is to present that message and give people the opportunity to receive Jesus.

Don't make issues the main issue: When you begin sharing your faith regularly, you are going to see it frequently: People are going to want to debate the issues with you. Whether it is abortion, creation/evolution, or the cause of suffering in the world, people are going to want to talk about issues. Sometimes this will be out of a desire to skirt the most important issues, but at other times it will be because these issues are of great importance in determining the decisions the person will make about his or her spiritual life. It will be up to you to discern which is the case, but, in general, it is always a good idea to try to get back to the main points of the Gospel.

It is extremely important that Christians become adept at answering the difficult questions that challenge Christianity, but we must also become adept at keeping people on target and challenging them concerning their own spiritual lives. Our conversations may stray toward politics, Bible inerrancy, or hypocrisy in the church, but we always need to do our best to return to the Gospel message as it pertains to the people with whom we are sharing. If you find yourself getting off topic, feel free to say something along the lines of, *"That is an important thing to talk about, but it still leaves the most important question unanswered. What do you think about Jesus?* (Or, depending on the conversation thus far, *"Do you see your personal need for Jesus?")"*

Whenever possible – pray: This will be the most difficult part for many people, but we must remember that it is not hearing the Gospel or even mentally recognizing the truth of the Gospel that saves us. It is embracing Jesus. It takes a response.

When we share the Gospel with others, whenever the situation warrants, we should give them a chance to respond. This, of course, will be different for every conversation, but, in most cases, leading the

> Give them a chance to respond.

person in a prayer is a great start. Of course, *"just praying a prayer"* is not enough, but the truth is that prayer is the starting point of salvation. When a person calls out to God, He answers.

Often, when I am sharing the Gospel with someone, I will conclude by asking the person a question: *"So the real question is, have you received Jesus to the point where He has come into your life and made you a new person?"* If the answer is yes, depending on the situation, I will try to encourage the person in some other area that may have come up in our conversation. *"That's great. Let me encourage you in another area. You mentioned earlier that you don't read the Bible very often (or you rarely attend church, or whatever else might be relevant). It made a very big difference in my walk with Jesus when I began reading it daily."* If the answer is no, I will follow up by asking the person, *"Do you want to?"* and then offer to lead him or her in a prayer.

If the person does want to call out to Jesus, I will explain that it is not a prayer that saves us, but it is receiving Jesus, turning away from selfishness, and surrendering to Him. In order to be in a relationship with someone, however, it is important to be introduced.

> In order to be in a relationship with someone it is important to be introduced.

Praying a prayer is that introduction. At that point, I will invite the person to repeat after me – *"not because my words are anything special,"* I tell the person, *"but because at first it might help for someone else to give you an idea of what to say."*

Typically, the prayer will go something like this: *"Lord Jesus, I recognize my need for You in my life. I have sinned against You and been selfish. I don't want to be selfish anymore. I ask You right now to come into my life and change me. I ask You to forgive my sins and help me to walk with You. If You will show me what to do, and You'll help me, I will live for You the rest of my life. In Jesus' name. Amen"*

After the prayer, as we discussed in a previous chapter, I will typically run through a few quick ideas that will help the person grow from there. Please see Chapter 17 - Thinking Clearly III - for more details.

If a person indicates a desire to know Jesus but, for whatever reason, does not want to be led in a prayer, encourage the person that he or she can call out to Him anytime, anywhere, even immediately after your conversation or that night lying in bed. Make it clear that it is something between that person and God and that he or she should take care of it as soon as possible. At times, people will indicate

> Offer to pray, but keep your eyes open.

a desire to respond but say that they are uncomfortable praying publicly. In those times it can be a good idea to offer to pray, but to keep your eyes open. Say something along the lines of, *"I'll tell you what. I'll lead you in a prayer, but we will both keep our eyes open. We can pray, but no one will know the difference. We will just look like we are having a conversation."* Not only have I prayed like this with several people in my lifetime, but each time there is something special about looking a person in the eye as he or she prays to receive Jesus.

Of course, regardless of the person's decision to pray or not to pray, it is always a good idea to offer to pray for him or her. Ask if the person has any prayer requests and then pray on the spot. When you pray, pray for those requests, but also pray that God will reveal Himself to the person with whom you are talking. Pray that this person will seek Him and find Him. There have also been many times in my life when a person, at first, was not willing to pray to Jesus but changed his or her mind after I prayed for him or her. Prayer works!

Put it all together: I have heard it said that not only should Christians go out to witness, but they also should witness as they go out. In other words, not only should we have particular times and places that we go out into the *"highway and byways"* to share the Gospel, but we also should share the Gospel in our everyday life: as we go to the grocery store, as we wait for our car to be fixed, and even as we walk down the street. Starting conversations with people and doing our best to talk about matters of eternity is one of the most important skills that we can learn as Christians. Even one conversation can go a long way toward changing the world. Will you play your part?

Discussion Questions:

-What are some examples of questions that you might use to initiate conversations with people?

-What are some examples of a situation in which it is best to walk away?

-Describe a time when it would appear that walking away would be the best idea, but in reality sticking around is the right choice.

-How could you use *"Do you have a church in the area?"* or *"Do you have a spiritual background?"* as good questions for transitioning to the Gospel?

-What are some responses that might result from the above questions?

-What is the main issue?

-What are some reasons why it is important to pray with people when possible?

The Big, Big Question

"The most pressing question on the problem of faith is whether a man as a civilized being can believe in the divinity of the Son of God, Jesus Christ."

-Fyodor Dostoevski

Imagine yourself in attendance at the 1st Church of the Holy Brethren. It is the first time you have been here.

The service has been going along quite nicely. The music is good, the people seem nice, and the message has been absolutely excellent. The minister, Pastor A.J. Wilson*, has been sharing about the need for service, the excellence of showing love, the importance of showing forgiveness, and the fact that God is personally interested in the lives of people. You are feeling particularly challenged to go out and make a difference in the world. Then, suddenly, the pastor says something that just doesn't quite sit right with you.

*No relation to any real person.

He says, *"Listen carefully, folks. One of these days, this church is going to burn up in flames. In fact, the whole earth – no, the whole universe is going to melt away. But my words, the words of Reverend A.J. Wilson, are going to live on forever. So make sure you are listening."*

> A short time later he makes another, even more outrageous claim.

You look at the person to your left to see if that struck her as odd, but she is intently focused on the message and doesn't seem to notice. You turn to the right and see the same lack of a reaction.

It gets worse. A short time later he makes another, even more outrageous claim.

He says, *"I am the road to salvation. Forget everything that you have ever heard because without the effect of A.J. Wilson in your life you are condemned to wander around aimlessly. I am your light. Follow me."*

Whoa! Now that is just a bit too much. You begin looking around the room. You see a couple of raised eyebrows and weird looks that indicate that others, too, are shocked. Many, however, are smiling. One person even begins to applaud.

He continues. *"If you want to know God, there is only one way: Me! I am the only way you can get to Him. If you don't follow me, you can forget this whole God thing altogether. In fact, God and me, we are the same. He's me and I'm Him. Can you receive that?"*

Many at this point stand to their feet cheering and applauding. A few begin running down the aisles and throwing themselves prostrate in front of the platform. Others, however, begin yelling at him and shaking their fists. A few throw their hymnals and cry out in anger.

> Others, however, begin yelling at him and shaking their fists.

You make your way to the aisle and walk toward the back door, amazed at what you have seen and heard. Then, as you are leaving, the preacher is really flipping out. He is saying something about the need to eat his flesh and drink his blood to obtain salvation. It is way too much for you. You're out of there – you and many others who leave with you.

I think you probably know where I am heading with this. The example above isn't entirely accurate because Jesus' message was spread out over a three-year period. He didn't teach everything to people at the same time, but the point remains the same. Jesus made some pretty outrageous, even shocking claims. The ideas that A.J. Wilson was preaching are paraphrases of the exact teachings of our Lord Jesus. At that time, they were just as revolutionary and weird as we would consider them now if a person taught them today. Perhaps even more so. Consider the following passages. It may help to think of how you might respond to a person today who claimed such things.

Matthew 9:6 - *"The Son of Man has authority on earth to forgive sins."*

Matthew 11:29 - *"Take my yoke upon you and learn from me, for I am gentle and humble in heart, and you will find rest for your souls."*

Mark 8:38 - *"If anyone is ashamed of me and my words in this adulterous and sinful generation, the Son of Man will be ashamed of him when he comes in his Father's glory with the holy angels."*

Luke 22:29 - *"I confer on you a kingdom, just as my Father conferred one on me."*

John 6:35 - *"I am the bread of life. He who comes to me will never go hungry, and he who believes in me will never be thirsty."*

John 14:6 - *"I am the way and the truth and the life. No one comes to the Father except through me."*

> He claimed to be the ultimate judge of all mankind.

It would be easy to fill page after page with the radical claims of Jesus. He claimed that all things had been given to Him by God (Matthew 11:27). He claimed to be the One who sends prophets into the land (Matthew 23:34). He claimed that children should believe in Him as an object of religious worship (Mark 9:42). He claimed to be the ultimate judge of all mankind

(Matthew 25:17-46). He claimed that He would speak from Heaven and give people wisdom and words to say in times of trial (Luke 21:14-15). He even claimed the ability to forgive sins (Mark 2:5, Luke 5:20 and 7:48). And, perhaps most importantly, He received worship from other people, despite the fact that He also taught that God is One and that only God is to be worshiped (Matthew 4:10 and 28:9, John 20:28).

So, the big, big question is this: *Who was Jesus?*

It is the most important question a person can ever answer, and it should be a question that we commonly use to challenge people in their spiritual walks. Anytime you encounter a non-Christian, whether an atheist, agnostic, Hindu, or Buddhist, this is a good question to ask.

A few years ago, I was on a short-term missions trip to Brussels, Belgium, and during that trip, while doing surveys in La Grand Place de Bruxelles, I met an atheist gentleman from Norway. It only took a few questions from the survey before he wanted to make it very clear where he stood. He said, *"I'll be honest with you. I think Christians are idiots."* He continued to say, *"Christianity is just a religion that weak people use as a crutch for something to lean on. It is a fairy tale."* He went on to elaborate on his opinion of Christianity and Christians in general, but the gist of it was that he had an intense dislike for everything Christian. As far as his treatment of me was concerned, he was actually quite nice, or at least as nice as a person can be when he calls you an idiot, but he most definitely was not

> *"I'll be honest with you. I think Christians are idiots."*

an advocate of my faith. He was clearly intelligent, however, and I enjoyed talking with him.

At the end of the survey, after he answered all of the questions, I said to him, *"So, I know what you think of Christianity at this point. What do you think about Jesus? What is your take on Him?"* He explained to me what he thought, and I responded with something like, *"The reason I ask is that, even though I grew up in church, I didn't want to believe the whole thing just because my mom and dad said I should or the preacher said I should. But I also figured if there was even the possibility, even the remotest possibility, that there might be a Heaven and a Hell, I'd better figure this whole thing out. Make sense?"* He indicated he understood my view, and I continued. *"So, for about the last thirteen years, I have dedicated myself to studying this stuff, and I found out some pretty amazing things about Jesus, the Bible, and Christianity. Can I share with you a few things that I discovered? It will only take a few minutes."* He said that it would be fine, so I began to talk with him about a few of the things that we are going to discuss in the next two chapters – ideas concerning the identity of Jesus.

> *"I guess I am going to have to go home and rethink my position."*

After just a few minutes of sharing with him, I asked him what he thought, and I loved his response. He said, *"Hmmmm. Well, I had never heard any of that before. I guess I am going to have to go home and rethink my position."*

I concluded by asking him if he would consider reading the Bible, and he said he might consider that. At that point, we shook hands and parted ways. I have had many such conversations over the years. The arguments that will be presented in the next couple of chapters are strong. In my opinion, they are overwhelmingly conclusive. In 1 Peter 3:15, Christians are instructed, *"Always be prepared to give an answer to everyone who asks you to give the reason for the hope that you have."* The reason for our hope is Jesus. As Christians, then, we need to become skilled at sharing with others why we follow Jesus – what it is that sets Him apart from every other person, philosophy, and religion.

I am convinced that the reason more people don't actively share their faith with others is that they are afraid of running into someone like this Norwegian atheist. They are afraid they will encounter someone who makes comments or asks questions that they don't

> Because there are people like that out there, many Christians don't talk to anyone.

know how to answer. And, even though the average person isn't nearly that skeptical, because there are people like that out there, many Christians don't talk to anyone. Even though a person like the skeptic above might be one in a hundred, Christians don't share with the other ninety-nine for fear of an encounter with the one. For that reason, learning some of the evidence behind the Christian faith is absolutely essential for us to reach our potential in God's Kingdom. Of course, beyond that, when we know the evidence ourselves, it encourages us, builds us up, and strengthens our own beliefs.

C.S. Lewis is often quoted as saying, *"My heart cannot rejoice in what my mind accepts as false."* The sad truth is, many Christians walk around with nagging doubts in the back of their heads because of their own personal concerns pertaining to the veracity of the Bible, the historicity of Jesus, and so on. Often, these nagging doubts are catered to rather than the truths that we embrace. Because of this, many Christians are rendered completely impotent when it comes to their witness. How can a Christian stir deep-seeded passion in the life of another when in reality the Christian himself is somewhat passionless? Studying the evidence behind Christianity can help us dispel some of those doubts, which in turn can open doors for God to increase our faith as we continue in obedience to Him. Of course, knowledge of the truth and actual faith are two completely different things.

I have heard stories centered on Niagara Falls that will help illustrate this point.

On June 30, 1859, tightrope walker Jean Francois Gravelet, the great Blondin, was the first man ever to cross Niagara Falls on a tightrope, and the crowd loved it. He was amazing. On some trips he would turn backward somersaults to excite the crowd. At other times he would lower a rope to a boat below, pull up a bottle, and sit down for a refreshment. On still other occasions he would walk blindfolded, ride a bike, push a wheelbarrow, make an omelet, and make the trips with his hands and feet manacled. His greatest stunt, however, was that of carrying his manager, Harry Colcord, on his back.

I want you to imagine what could have happened next.

What if, as the crowd was still cheering, excited about what they had seen him do, the Great Blondin had raised his hands to hush them. After a few moments, the crowd had become silent and the Great Blondin addressed them.

"I know what you have seen today has been amazing, but I have saved my best trick for last. Today, you will be a witness to history as I not only carry my manager back across the falls on my back but I also put another person in a wheelbarrow and push him in front of me!"

At this announcement the crowd would go wild, cheering, screaming, and whistling. Some would be yelling, *"You can do it, Blondin!"* Others would scream, *"You've got this! Piece of cake."* The crowd might continue to cheer for a couple of minutes as Jean Francois readied himself on the platform with his wheelbarrow and his manager.

Then, as the crowd continued to yell, cheer, and push him on, he would turn to the crowd, raise his hands in the air and yell, *"Who is going to be my volunteer?"* And then . . .

Silence.

Nothing.

Not a sound.

Somewhere in the background a baby might begin to cry, a young man would clear his throat, and a few people would shift from one leg to another as they stared at the ground, avoiding eye contact. A few proud souls might manage to smile politely, but not one of the thousands of people gathered would step forward.

This crowd would have seen the evidence. They would know, almost without the slightest doubt, that this daredevil could do what he said he could do. They would have seen with their own eyes that he was reliable and trustworthy. There will always be a difference, however, between knowing someone is trustworthy and placing your trust in that person. It would be one thing to acknowledge the safety of the wheelbarrow. It would be another thing entirely to climb aboard.

When it comes to Jesus, the evidence is available. I believe it is overwhelmingly conclusive and convincing. But not all will choose to respond to it. I can hear what it would have been like for some as they left Niagara Falls that day. Grown men would have remarked casually to their families, *"The wind seemed to be picking up a bit, don't you think? Seemed a little more risky to me than before."* Others would say, *"He looked a little wobbly to me on the last trip. Did he look wobbly to you?"*

> All the evidence in the world will not convince some people of the truth of Jesus Christ.

All the evidence in the world will not convince some people of the truth of Jesus Christ – not because the evidence isn't good, but because acknowledging the evidence demands something from them that they are not willing to give. It demands their life. For many, the battle for faith is not a battle of the mind, it is a battle of the will.

So, who is Jesus?

The bottom line is this: About 2000 years ago, a radical new religion sprang up centered on the life and teachings of a man called Jesus. Many people came to worship Him as God. Today, it is the largest religion on the planet with more than two billion people who call themselves Christian. There are only a few possibilities:

He was a legend or myth: He may or may not have been a real historical figure, but through word-of-mouth testimony (or deliberate lies) His story became blown way out of proportion. He never intended to be worshiped as God.

He was a liar: He knew He wasn't God, but He convinced others that He was. This would make Him a vicious liar.

He was a lunatic: He thought He was God, but He wasn't. He was insane.

He was the Lord God: He was who His followers claimed He was – the Son of God, sent to Earth to redeem man from his sins; God in the flesh.

There are a very few other possibilities that exist in the world, specifically when talking with Muslims (Jesus was a prophet of God) or Mormons (Jesus was one god in a series of many gods, and we can become like Him.) For the purposes of our discussion here, however, we will restrict ourselves to the four possibilities listed above. In the vast majority of situations Christians are likely to encounter while sharing their faith, these arguments should prove sufficient. Typically, if you

> The next time you encounter someone who doesn't believe Jesus is the Son of God, you will be equipped.

ask a group of average non-Christians on the street who they think Jesus was, about 7 to 9 out of 10 are going to say something along the lines of this: He was a great teacher, a good person, or a great moral reformer. A very small portion are going to say He was a myth and that He may or may not have been a real historical entity, but they will say that, either way, His story was blown up beyond reality. Still another small percentage will say that they aren't sure, they don't really care, or they never really think about it. We will address these issues in the next two chapters. Hopefully, the next time you encounter a person who doesn't believe Jesus is the Son of God, you will be equipped to rationally and intelligently give reasons for why you believe what you believe. But remember, getting there begins by asking them the big, big question: *"Who was Jesus?"*

So, the next time you encounter a person and are not sure what to say, make sure to ask the big, big question. It has amazing potential to change people's lives forever.

Discussion Questions:

-What are some things that Jesus said that would be considered very outrageous if you heard them today?

-Why is the identity of Jesus important?

-What is the difference between recognizing something as trustworthy and placing your trust in that something?

-What are some common answers when people are addressed with the question "Who was (is) Jesus?"

-Who is Jesus to you?

"I am an historian, I am not a believer, but I must confess as an historian that this penniless preacher from Nazareth is irrevocably the very center of history. Jesus Christ is easily the most dominant figure in all history."

-H.G. Wells

Jesus and the Pink Little Bunny

"As the centuries pass, the evidence is accumulating that, measured by His effect on history, Jesus is the most influential life ever lived on this planet."

-Kenneth Scott Latourette

I can think of only one time that I have ever lost my cool with someone when I was sharing my faith.

We had taken a team of college students to London, England, for a short-term missions trip and were out on the streets one evening talking with people about Jesus when we met two men in their early thirties who were quite hateful. The reason I was upset is that one of them had gotten in my wife's face, said some derogatory things that were unrelated to anything spiritual, and upset her quite a bit. They had pointed their fingers in her face and yelled at her. I think the two never suspected that I was upset – I only lost my cool inwardly – but I remember thinking that I needed to keep my mouth shut and listen for awhile to avoid any major confrontation.

One of the two men went on and on about his imaginary "pink little bunny." He pretended he was cradling his imaginary bunny in his arms and would mime as if he were petting its fur. My friend Bill couldn't get a word in edgewise. Anytime he tried to make a point about Jesus or even bring the

> He kept yelling, *"Why won't you put your trust in my pink little bunny?! Huh?"*

conversation around to Jesus, the man would turn it around and apply the same point to his pink little bunny. For example, if Bill expressed the need to put our trust in Jesus for salvation, the man would say that he had placed his trust in the pink little bunny. He put his face right up in Bill's face and yelled, saying he couldn't believe that Bill wouldn't accept his pink little bunny into his heart. He kept yelling, *"Why won't you put your trust in my pink little bunny?! Huh? Ask him into your heart!"* He would act as if he were trying to place his bunny into Bill's arms. Essentially, he was trying to get his point across that he saw as much evidence for Jesus as he did for an imaginary pink little bunny. He considered Christians fools and believed we were narrow-minded idiots for believing what we believe.

So, the question is this: *Is* there any difference between Jesus Christ and this man's imaginary pink little bunny? Is the Gospel a fairy tale that someone concocted a couple thousand years ago that happened to catch on and spread around the world? Is there a difference between Jesus and Santa Claus or Jesus and the Tooth Fairy, or is Jesus just another myth that people believe in to comfort themselves? These are very important questions that need to be addressed.

Christianity is not a blind faith. It is a faith based on evidence. It is not a philosophy or a self-help religion. If the basic facts that Christianity is founded on – namely, the life, death, and resurrection of Jesus – are not true, the whole thing falls apart. If the events are not historically accurate, the religion itself is a sham, a myth, and a lie. It is important that we are able to articulate why we believe what we believe.

Concerning the resurrection of Jesus, the Bible says in 1 Corinthians 15:14, *"And if Christ has not been raised, our preaching is useless and so is your faith."* In other words, if the actual event of the resurrection didn't take

Is there a difference between Jesus and Santa Claus or Jesus and the Tooth Fairy?

place in history, you can forget Christianity altogether; the whole religion is worthless.

The remainder of this chapter will be dedicated to arguments that show that Jesus was not a myth. For the sake of our purposes here, they will be broken down into manageable chunks that can be readily absorbed and remembered. Of course, entire encyclopedias could be written on this topic. In this book, however, we will focus on ideas and arguments that can be understood easily and that are practical in terms of our witness on a daily basis. For a more detailed examination, see *"additional reading"* at the end of the next chapter.

Remember, though, that there will be some people who are not interested in the evidence or who, for whatever reason, are predisposed to believe something else. The evidence presented in this chapter does, in my opinion, logically eliminate the possibility that Jesus was a mere myth. However, some people will believe what they choose *in spite of* the evidence. There are many people today who believe that Elvis is still alive. As mentioned in the last chapter, just because the facts say otherwise doesn't mean that people will stop believing what they want to believe.

The Minimal Facts: In *The Case for the Resurrection of Jesus*, authors Gary Habermas and Mike Licona present evidence using what they call a *"minimal facts"* approach. I will let them describe this approach in their own words: *"This approach considers only those data that are so strongly attested historically that they are granted by nearly every scholar who studies the subject, even the rather skeptical ones."* (1)

Dr. Habermas' research included more than 1400 modern-day sources (from 1975 to the present) in three different languages (English, German, and French). The following facts were part of what he concluded were the minimal facts, or the facts on which nearly every scholar in the field would agree.

> The minimal facts are the facts on which nearly every scholar in the field would agree.

1. **Jesus died due to crucifixion.**

2. **Jesus' disciples sincerely believed Jesus rose from the dead and appeared to them.**

3. The church persecutor Paul was changed suddenly.

4. The skeptic James, brother of Jesus, was changed suddenly.

(The evidence for these minimal facts can be examined, not only as recorded in the Gospels and the Epistles, but also in the non-biblical works of Josephus, Tacitus, Lucian of Samosata, Mara Bar-Serapion, Clement, Polycarp, Ignatius, Tertullian, Origen, The Talmud, and more. Again, it is unfortunate that a discussion of each of these is inappropriate in the scope of this text. I urge each reader to continue further reading as detailed in the following chapter.)

> These four facts indicate the clear truth that Jesus was a real and historical individual.

These four facts, on which nearly every scholar would agree, imply much more than they themselves state. Specifically, these four facts indicate the clear truth that Jesus was a real and historical individual. To have died by crucifixion, for others to believe He was resurrected, and even to have a brother at all, indicate that His existence as a historical being is not even under question by nearly all scholars who study the field.

Of course, the consensus of these facts does not prove the historicity of Jesus with absolute certainty. In fact, in terms of history, scholars can never use phrases like "absolute certainty" or "100% sure." Because the events occurred in the past, we must rely on evidence which supports "strength of probability" instead. In other words, we cannot be 100%

certain about any facts in history, but we can study the evidence and determine with great certainty whether an event or events actually transpired. This is the case with Jesus. Based on the information that we have today, the evidence is overwhelmingly in favor of the facts described above. Is it possible to believe that Jesus never existed? Yes, but to believe so puts a person at odds with facts that nearly every scholar who has studied the issue finds to be true. Is it possible that all of the scholars who believe these facts are incorrect? Of course it's possible, but we must admit that it is unlikely. In other words, given the evidence, it takes more faith to believe in Jesus as a fairy tale than it does to believe in Him as a real, historical entity.

> It takes more faith to believe in Jesus as a fairy tale than it does to believe in Him as a real, historical entity.

Compare this to my English friend's pink little bunny. Obviously, there is no comparison at all. History leans strongly in favor of Jesus as a real historical figure who drew a following of believers and began a religion that changed the world. There is no evidence whatsoever for the pink little bunny. Trusting in his bunny would be blind faith. Trusting in Jesus is not.

Did the Myth Arise from the Minimal Facts? The basic facts of Jesus as a historical being can be shown with relative certainty, but this doesn't establish the truth of Christianity as a whole. To do so requires still further investigation of the facts.

Some skeptics argue that Jesus was a real, historical entity but that *Christianity* arose from myth. In essence, they might say that the traditions of Christianity were passed on for quite some time through word-of-mouth testimony and stories told to children. Eventually, they were written down, but by that time they had been blown greatly out of proportion and exaggerated. These traditions are sometimes compared to the telephone game played by children, in which a message is whispered in the ear of a child and then passed around the room from child to child until, at the end, the message has been distorted greatly.

> Is it possible He never meant to be worshiped as God?

Is this fair? Is it possible that the stories we have now pertaining to Jesus are highly exaggerated stories that have no basis in reality? Is it possible that Jesus never said many of the things that are attributed to Him? Is it possible that He never meant to be worshiped as God? These, too, are important questions that demand answers. The following points will help.

There was very little time for myth to arise: Somewhere in your home you more than likely have copies of three letters that were written very close to the middle of the first century A.D. You may not have recognized them as such, but chances are good that you own them. They are called 1 Thessalonians, Galatians, and 1 Corinthians.

For the sake of our discussion here, it is not important that we treat these books as the inspired Word of God (although I firmly believe they are). Instead, we will treat them as what virtually every skeptic must admit that they are: letters that were passed back and forth among real individuals, and real churches, sometime in or around the middle of the first century. By the vast majority of scholars, these books are dated AD 49-52 (1 Thessalonians), AD 48-57 (Galatians), and AD 54-58 (1 Corinthians). (2)

Why are these dates important? They are important because these letters tell us a great deal about what people believed concerning Jesus at these times.

The content of 1 Thessalonians makes it clear that as early as AD 49-52, a church had already been established in Thessalonica, which in turn had already (at that time) influenced other congregations of believers in Macedonia and Achaia (1:7). It shows that they believed Jesus had been raised from the dead and was returning (1:10,3:13, & 4:13-18), that they were imitating churches that had already been established in Judea (2:14), that there were Christians throughout Macedonia (4:10), and that they believed salvation was received through Jesus (5:9-10). All of this was within the time frame of approximately sixteen to twenty-two years following the crucifixion.

The writing in Galatians also shows that by the time it was written, there was already an established church in the area. It clearly had been there for some time because Paul had had enough time to go away after helping found the church, and corrupting influences had begun to infiltrate (1:6-9). It also shows that this established early church believed that Jesus Christ had been raised from the dead (1:1). It documents Paul's travels throughout the land and his interaction with Peter, James, Titus, and Barnabas (1:13 – 2:14). It, too, shows the church's belief that salvation comes through Jesus Christ (3:10-14). It establishes that Paul had been teaching the Gospel for about seventeen years prior to this writing (1:18 & 2:1). These things were written between seventeen and twenty-seven years after the crucifixion (keeping in mind that most scholars place the crucifixion around AD 30 – 33).

And finally, 1 Corinthians is invaluable to us for the same reasons and even more. Namely, the earliest known Christian creed is found in Chapter 15:3-7, which says, *"For what I received I passed on to you as of first importance: that Christ died for our sins according to the Scriptures, that he was buried, that he was raised on the third day according to the Scriptures, and that he appeared to Peter, and then to the Twelve. After that, he appeared to more than five hundred of the brothers at the same time, most of whom are still living, though some have fallen asleep. Then he appeared to James, then to all the apostles, and last of all he appeared to me also, as to one abnormally born."*

This creed makes it clear that the church at that time believed in the literal death, burial, and resurrection of Jesus Christ. It claims that this creed was passed on to Paul at an early date (some scholars argue within three to seven years of the crucifixion). At the very latest, these things were clearly believed and embraced by many within about twenty-five years of the events as they happened.

Perhaps the most compelling evidence as far as this point is concerned is found in the writings of the ancient historian Cornelius Tacitus, who has been referred to as the greatest historian of ancient Rome. Writing in approximately AD 109, Tacitus, a non-Christian, says the following concerning the burning of Rome in AD 64:

*"Nero fastened the guilt and inflicted the most exquisite tortures on a class hated for their abominations, called Christians by the populace. Christus, from whom the name had its origin, suffered the extreme penalty during the reign of Tiberius at the hands of one of our procurators, Pontius Pilatus, and a most mischievous superstition, thus checked for the moment, again broke out not only in Judaea, the first source of the evil, but even in Rome, where all things hideous and shameful from every part of the world find their centre and become popular. Accordingly, an arrest was first made of all who pleaded guilty; then, upon their information, **an immense multitude was convicted**, not so much of the crime of firing the city, as of hatred against mankind. Mockery of every sort was added to their deaths. Covered with the skins of beasts, they were torn by dogs and perished, or were nailed to crosses, or were doomed to the flames and burnt, to serve as a nightly illumination, when daylight had expired."* (3)

In this non-Biblical passage we have ample proof that there was not enough time for myth to arise.

In this non-Biblical passage we have ample proof that there was not enough time for myth to arise. This non-Christian historian, who is known as a man who wrote with accuracy and integrity, affirms that by the year AD 64 there was an *"immense multitude"* (*multitudo ingens*) of Christians who were convicted and sentenced to torture and death. This immense multitude only accounts for the Christians who were sentenced to die. It says nothing of the others who went on to propagate the Christian faith.

In conclusion, we have documented evidence in the form of letters and even a non-Christian, well-recognized ancient historian that makes it very clear that, at a minimum, within a couple of decades of

> Within approximately thirty years an immense multitude could be found.

the events themselves, people were worshiping Jesus as God. They believed that He had died and risen again, they believed that He was returning soon, and they were establishing churches throughout the land to reach people with the message of the Gospel. Within approximately thirty years, there were enough Christians in just the area of Rome that an *"immense multitude"* could be found. They were willing to die for their faith. And this does not account for the Christians spread throughout other parts of the world or Christians in the area of Rome who were not captured and put to death. Clearly, it seems, there was not enough time for myth to arise.

The New Testament was written by people who claimed to have firsthand knowledge: As mentioned before, Luke 1:1-4 says, *"Many have undertaken to draw up an account of **the things that have been fulfilled among us**, just as they were **handed down to us by those who from the first were eyewitnesses** and servants of the word. Therefore, since **I myself have carefully investigated everything from the beginning**, it seemed good also to me to write an orderly account for you, most excellent Theophilus, so that you may know the certainty of the things you have been taught."*

Essentially, what we have here is the introduction of a letter written from one man (Luke) to another man (Theophilus). It is no different than my beginning a letter by writing, *"Hey John, H.L. here. I've got some more information for you that I collected from the people who saw what went down."* These were real people in real human history.

The author of this letter claimed to have collected the information firsthand by talking with the people involved. Either he had or he hadn't. It is either the truth or a lie. Someone at some point wrote this letter. Suggesting that this arose from highly exaggerated word-of-mouth testimony is simply foolishness. The possibility that time destroyed the reality of the evidence does not exist. Either the author really did interview the people involved or he didn't. If he didn't, who did? When? Why did they lie – not exaggerate, but blatantly lie? What was their motive? How did they convince people it was true? Why would someone blatantly lie to create a document that has done so much to propagate honesty? The idea creates far more complications and questions than it answers. It makes a great deal of sense to accept the authorship at face value. This was written by the person who signed the document.

1 John 1 is chock full of references declaring that the author was involved personally with the people and events about which he wrote: *"That which was from the beginning,* **which we have heard, which we have seen with our eyes, which we have looked at and our hands have touched—this we proclaim** *concerning the Word of life. The life appeared;* **we have seen it and testify to it**, *and we proclaim to you the eternal life, which was with the Father and* **has appeared to us.** **We proclaim to you what we have seen and heard**, *so that you also may have fellowship with us. And*

*our fellowship is with the Father and with his Son, Jesus Christ. We write this to make our joy complete. **This is the message we have heard from him** and declare to you."*

Again, for this and many other references in the New Testament, the arguments are the same. These documents were written by those who claimed personal involvement. It comes down to a matter not of myth or non-

> These documents were written by those who claimed personal involvement.

myth, but rather of truth or non-truth. Someone at some point sat down and wrote the words of Luke 1:1-4, which claims he had carefully investigated the matters personally. Either the author was telling the truth or he was lying. Someone at some point wrote the words, *"This is the disciple who testifies to these things and who wrote them down."* (John 21:24) It is either the truth or a lie. Either it was actually the disciple who saw these events with his own eyes, or it was an impostor and a liar. If these are lies, who wrote them? When did they write them? Why? How did they convince people of their truth? There is no room for myth or exaggeration here. Instead, the skeptic is faced with two choices, and neither seems very appealing. Either these people were eyewitnesses when they wrote these things, or they were liars. If they were liars, they were part of a group of liars who more than likely must have come together at some point to coordinate their lies with one another. They would have had to have done so quite some time before the middle of the first century AD (which, by the way, destroys forever the possibilities presented in the *fictional* work *The Da Vinci Code*.) These letters were written at different times throughout the years in very different geographic locations, far separated from the other authors. If the basics of Christianity are not true, there must have been a conspiracy among people to deceive others into believing – a conspiracy of geniuses who executed their plan so perfectly that after two thousand years, billions of people follow the religion they concocted. After two thousand years of emperors trying to squash it and some of the most brilliant minds in history trying to discredit it, the New Testament message is still going strong. If these men were liars, they were liars with an intellect and a plan that also could be considered even supernaturally brilliant. And, of course, we must also ask the question: Why did they lie? If the letters are based on lies, what caused these men to lie in such a way? What was their motive? The skeptic has a great many questions to answer in order to substantiate arguments that the Gospel arose from myth.

They don't sound like myth: The Gospels and Epistles do not use language like, *"A long time ago, in a galaxy far, far away."* Instead, they name actual dates, times, and places.

Have you ever been reading along in the New Testament and found yourself skimming, or skipping entirely, passages that say something along the lines of, *"In the region of such-and-such, during the reign of so-and-so, there was a man named (choose a name). This was during the festival of (choose a festival)"*?

We skim these passages because they come across as boring or impractical. But have you ever considered why all of these passages are in the Bible? It is because these were real events that happened in real history in real places and at real times. In the Gospel of Luke alone,

Luke mentions thirty-two countries, fifty-four cities, and nine islands without a single error. (4) And we must remember that Luke had no Internet to refer to or even libraries with vast numbers of maps and books that he could skim. In such circumstances, the author of Luke must be considered startlingly accurate. This was a man who had done his homework.

Another way the New Testament comes across as non-myth is in its inclusion of material that is distinctly *"non-spiritual."* For example, in 1 Corinthians 9 we find Paul arguing that, in spite of the fact that he has chosen not to do so, he and Barnabas have the same right to take a believing wife along with them as the other apostles do. He says, basically, *"Barnabas and I are the same as everyone else where this is concerned. If we wanted to take a wife along with us we could, we just choose not to do so."*

If this book came about by myth and exaggerated word-of-mouth testimony, why is this passage and many more along the same lines included? (See 1 Timothy 5:23, Colossians 4:7-18, and 1 Peter 5:12-14 for other examples.) If one is honest in reading this, it simply sounds like a letter that one real person wrote to another real person (or persons). It doesn't sound like a fairy tale; rather, it comes across as strikingly genuine.

An even bigger miracle happened: In 1928, Phillip Schaff, in his seven-volume set titled *History of the Christian Church*, estimated that by AD 100, the total number of Christians living in the world was approximately 500,000. (5) More recently, however, research by the Center for the

Study of Global Christianity, which is now at Gordon-Conwell Theological Seminary, indicates that this number is closer to 800,000. (6) If the rise of Christianity can be attributed to myth alone, how can these numbers be possible?

> This creates a very difficult situation for the skeptic of Christianity.

This creates a very difficult situation for the skeptic of Christianity because the stories were fabricated either early on in the first century or much later (as most skeptics would have us believe).

If the stories were created early on, how were people convinced that events were happening right there among them – among their friends, neighbors, parents, and grandparents – if these events never happened at all? They not only were convinced, but they were convinced to the point that an *"immense multitude"* was willing to die for what they believed? What accounts for this?

If the stories were created much later, what accounts for our earlier report from Tacitus? If the stories were created much later, how were thousands and even hundreds of thousands of people convinced in such a brief period that they were genuine?

We are faced with a paradox if the stories are simply stories with no factual basis. Either the basic truths of Christianity were invented early on, which runs contrary to the way myths develop – no skeptic would want to admit this as a possibility – or they were invented and greatly embellished at a much later date, in which case we must ask how it is possible to convince *"multitudes"* that they are true. Which is easier: to convince a few hundred people something happened in their midst that never really happened, or to convince multitudes of people to convert to a new and radical religion that did not exist before and do so in a very short period of time? Both are exceedingly improbable possibilities. The more probable possibility is that the events actually did happen in the lives of these people and that the religion began to grow from there.

This can be summed up best by Thomas Aquinas, who said, *"If the incarnation didn't happen, a bigger miracle happened: the conversion of the world by the world's biggest lie, and moral transformation of lives by mere myth."*

Considering the facts discussed above, it is still possible to believe that Jesus never actually existed. It is possible to think that perhaps He did exist but that His story was highly embellished and exaggerated. However, to do so, as we mentioned before, requires more faith than it does scholarship. Rest assured, if you choose to believe the basic truths of Christianity, you have good grounds to do so. You can also feel confident that, after studying this material, you can share your faith effectively with all but the most hardened skeptics. I challenge you, study this material until it becomes second nature to you. Keep this information at your disposal and draw on it when the situation warrants.

> To do so requires more faith than it does scholarship.

Discussion Questions:

-Is it important to share the facts with a person who believes Jesus was just a fairy tale? Why or why not?

-Consider the quote from Tacitus that was cited in this chapter (p.250). What does this quote say about the rise of the early church?

-What are some fairy tales or legends that you have read? How do they compare with the New Testament?

-In what ways does Jesus stand out as a perfect role model?

1. Habermas, G. & Licona, M. (2004). *The Case for the Resurrection of Jesus*. Grand Rapids: Kregel Publications

2. For a current list (at time of publication) of New Testament dates by various authors and scholars, both conservative and liberal, see: http://www.errantskeptics.org/Dating_the_NT.htm

3. Tacitus, *Annals*. 15.44

4. Geisler, N. (1999). *Baker Encyclopedia of Apologetics*. Grand Rapids: Baker Books

5. Schaff, P. (1928). *History of the Christian Church* (7 vols.). New York: Charles Scribner's Sons, Vol 1

6. Barrett, D. & Johnson, T. (2001). *World Christian Trends AD 30 - AD 2200: Interpreting the Annual Christian Megacensus*. Pasadena: William Carey Library. p 934

Identity Crisis

"Christ is the only religious leader who has ever claimed to be deity, and the only individual ever who has convinced a great portion of the world that He is God."

-Robert H. Stein

A psychiatrist at an insane asylum was examining a new patient for the first time.

The moment the psychiatrist walked in the room, the patient stood up from his bed, tucked his right hand inside his robe, and stood at attention with his head held high and a stern expression on his face. The psychiatrist took a seat in a nearby chair and began his interview. *"Name, please."*

The man continued to stand rigidly and stated emphatically, *"I am Napoleon Bonaparte."*

"Hmmm, interesting," the psychiatrist replied. *"And just why do you believe that you are Napoleon Bonaparte?"*

Without hesitation, the patient replied, *"Because God told me."*

Then, without warning, the patient across the hall yelled through his door, *"Don't listen to him, Doc. He's crazy! I never told him any such thing!"*

In a previous chapter, we covered many of the radical claims of Jesus. He claimed the ability to forgive sins, He received worship from others, He claimed to be the one who sends prophets into the land, and much more. He even claimed to be in existence before Abraham was born (John 8:38). In this chapter we are going to talk about the implications of these claims. We have already established that the evidence leans strongly in favor of Jesus as a real historical figure who convinced many that He was divine. In this chapter we will build on this even further and show that, not only did He convince people of His deity, but also, in all likelihood, He truly was who He claimed to be.

As I mentioned before, when asked about the identity of Jesus, the vast majority of non-Christians today will claim that He was a good teacher, a great moral reformer, or the like. When they claim this, they are admitting a couple of things. They are admitting that He was a real historical figure. They are also claiming, whether they realize it or not, that, in general, they believe at least a portion of the Gospel texts to be accurate. Without these texts it would be difficult for is to establish much about His teachings at all. In other words, when they claim that His teachings were good, they are saying that, at least in general, they agree that we have some kind of accurate knowledge as to what His teachings were. The majority of this knowledge comes from a basic understanding of the Gospels. However, if we consider the Gospels to be generally reliable, the idea that Jesus was just a good teacher is completely thrown out the window.

When I meet people who claim they believe that Jesus was simply a good teacher, I typically ask them if they have ever heard of C.S. Lewis. If not, I ask them if they have heard of *The Chronicles of Narnia* (of which Lewis was the author). If they have not heard of *The Chronicles of Narnia,* I ask them if they are familiar with J.R.R. Tolkien, author of the *Lord of the Rings* series. (Usually I will receive an affirmative reply to at least one of these questions.) I will then explain to them that Lewis, a professor at Cambridge, was a good friend of Tolkien and that he for some time considered himself an atheist, but, after reviewing the facts and studying the evidence behind Christianity, he became a Christian.

> The idea that Jesus was just a good teacher is completely thrown out the window.

C.S. Lewis gave his opinion on the issue of Jesus' having been only a great teacher in *Mere Christianity*, saying, *"I am trying here to prevent anyone saying the really foolish thing that people often say about Him: 'I'm ready to accept Jesus as a great moral teacher, but I don't accept His claim to be God.' That is the one thing we must not say. A man who said the sort of things Jesus said would not be a great moral teacher. He would either be a lunatic – on a level with the man who says he is a poached egg – or else he would be the Devil of Hell. You must make your choice. Either this man was, and is, the Son of God; or else a madman or something worse. You can shut Him up for a fool, you can spit at Him and kill Him as a demon; or you can fall at His feet and call Him Lord and God. But let us not come with any patronizing nonsense about His being a great human teacher. He has not left that open to us. He did not intend to.* " (1)

Lewis' argument essentially went like this:

1.   **Jesus claimed to be God. Either He was or He wasn't.**

2.   **If He wasn't and He knew He wasn't, He was a liar.**

3.   **If He wasn't and He thought He was, He was a lunatic.**

4.   **If He was God, each person must decide whether to worship Him or not.**

Once again, it is impossible to cover these points completely in this book, but the following ideas and thoughts should be sufficient in nearly all witnessing situations.

Jesus convinced others that He was divine, but He knew that He was not. He was a liar: This idea is immediately repugnant to most people. Those who consider Him a great moral teacher do so because they believe that, in general, the life and teachings of Jesus were marked by love, integrity, and self-sacrifice. They view Him as one of the greatest examples of morality the world has ever seen. Most people, even non-believers, tend to consider Jesus as one of the greatest moral figures of all time, if not the greatest of all time. Most people would place Him on a level above even figures such as Mahatma Gandhi or Mother Teresa, and rightly so. Jesus and His teachings have done more for the human race in terms of ethics, integrity, and morality than any hundred other individuals combined.

Jesus began a movement that transformed the world in terms of morality and integrity. Are we to believe the same person was Himself a great liar?

In John 8:44, Jesus says, *"You belong to your father, the devil, and you want to carry out your father's desire. He was a murderer from the beginning, not holding to the truth, for there is no truth in him. When he lies, he speaks his native language, for he is a liar and the father of lies."* In this passage He says, essentially, *"Lies find their root in the devil."* Many other times (more than seventy-five times in the Gospels) we see

> Jesus began a movement that transformed the world in terms of morality and integrity.

Jesus preceding His statements with *"I tell you the truth."* When Jesus taught, He taught as one who spoke only truth. In essence, He would say, *"I am going to teach you something right now. You can trust what I have to say because it comes from me, and I only speak truth. Truth is the only thing that comes out of my mouth."*

Can you imagine Jesus teaching such things, knowing that He Himself was a terrible liar? The depth of His hypocrisy would have been unimaginable. Remember this: If Jesus taught that He was God but knew that He wasn't, He wasn't just a person who lied occasionally or told *"white lies"*; He was a person who lied *constantly* about issues that absolutely and radically changed people's lives. Based on the teachings of Jesus about His own identity, people have left riches and families behind. They have endured unthinkable persecutions and torture in order to live their lives in a way they thought would please Him. If Jesus lied about His identity, He was not only a liar but also a terrible hypocrite and a wicked man. To any honest thinker, this doesn't fit the picture of the Jesus we know.

Jesus thought He was God, but He wasn't. He was a lunatic: Professor of philosophy at Boston College Peter Kreeft wrote, *"A measure of your insanity is the size of the gap between what you think you are and what you really are."*

When I am lecturing, I often borrow Kreeft's idea, using myself as an illustration. When I stand before a group of people, if I were to introduce myself saying, *"Hi, I'm H.L. Hussmann, former Engineering Physics student at Murray State, and I am a Bible teacher,"* I am nowhere near insanity because that is precisely who I am. If I were to say, *"Hi, my name is H.L. Hussmann, and I am the best Bible teacher you will ever hear,"* I still would not be considered insane. I might be considered proud and arrogant, but I have not strayed into the area of lunacy. The identity I have given myself may or may not be true, subject to one's opinion. However, if I introduce myself as Genghis Khan, it could be said rightfully that I am dealing with issues of insanity. If I say that I am a caterpillar, it could be assessed fairly that

I am even more insane than in thinking I am Genghis Khan. Again, the measure of my insanity would be the measure between what I think I am and what I actually am. When I claim I am Genghis Kahn, at least I am claiming to be human. A caterpillar is another thing entirely. If I claim to be God, however, I have stepped into heights of insanity that are rarely seen. I have actually made myself out to be the one thing that is most extreme: the most powerful force in the universe that is in all and through all.

> If I claim to be God, however, I have stepped into heights of insanity that are rarely seen.

With this in mind, we must realize that to place the label of lunatic on Jesus we cannot merely think of Him as a person who was a bit confused, or as someone who had in some ways lost touch with reality; rather, we must consider Him as having totally gone over the deep end. If He was not divine but thought He was, He was not a great moral teacher – He was a basket case. Of course, the label of basket case is one of the last that we ever would want to place on Jesus.

> Jesus was the perfect combination of genius, practicality, compassion, and realism.

Those who study the teachings of Jesus (from which the idea that He was a great teacher rightly extends) will see a sharp mind, unparalleled depth of thought, and incomparable wisdom. The fact is, Jesus was the perfect combination of genius, practicality, compassion, and realism. His teachings are universal and cross every boundary of race, sex, and culture. His advice has a depth that continues to baffle scholars and yet can be embraced by small children and simpleminded people. His expressions avoid the trivial and the nonsensical and still manage to penetrate every factor of human living to the most practical level – shaping everyday decisions around the world. Jesus was not only a great teacher, He was history's greatest teacher. An examination of His teaching will reflect a heart, wisdom, and intellect that could only be that of God. Are we to believe that the man who gave the human race such perfection in teaching was also a raving lunatic? As always, if people choose to believe such, it is their prerogative, but to do so, in my opinion, is intellectual suicide.

> They didn't just trust Him; they worshiped Him as God.

In addition to the above information, if we are going to embrace either the lunacy or the liar theory, we must also ask ourselves this: If Jesus was a consistent liar or a lunatic, why is it that His disciples never seemed to pick up on it? We all know that when we are around a person who lies regularly, we tend to notice. We would also suspect that a person insane enough to believe He is God would also show signs of lunacy in other areas. Is it possible to think that Jesus fooled His followers so completely that not only did they consider Him a very honest, trustworthy, and stable person, but they also saw His level of integrity and the words of His mouth as equal to God's? They didn't just trust Him; they worshiped Him as God, attributing to Him not only goodness but also perfection. If we are going to believe that Jesus was a liar or lunatic, we must also believe that His disciples were gullible, foolish, and unobservant. This, too, creates difficulties for the skeptic.

He was the Lord God: All of the evidence points in this direction: Jesus Christ was God in the flesh. The question does not have to be one of His identity; the question becomes one of our identity. Are we identified with Him and surrendered to His Lordship, building His Kingdom, or are we identified with ourselves and serving our own interests?

> All of the evidence points in this direction: Jesus Christ was God in the flesh.

Jesus was the greatest teacher the world has ever seen. His teachings were perfection and His morality was of a level where even His enemies could find no fault in Him (John 18:38; Luke 23:39-42, 47). His deity was constantly affirmed by the miraculous signs and wonders that followed Him, including healings, resurrections, miraculous provisions, command of the elements, and much more. The same writings that have brought us the great teachings of Jesus are also chock full of stories about His miracles. The conclusions of the New Testament authors were based not only on the upright moral lifestyle and the defining wisdom of Jesus' teachings, but they rise or fall based on the claims of miraculous signs that followed Him. Any theories that claim Jesus was just a great teacher must skirt the issue of supernaturalism entirely. When a person claims that Jesus was *"just a great teacher,"* ask him or her, *"Do you believe miracles occurred in His life?"* Based on His life, teachings, and the miracles that surrounded Him, He is the only human candidate for divinity.

Jesus is worthy to be followed and worthy of our worship. He is worthy of our giving our lives to Him and worthy of our dedicating ourselves to

His mission. Can you say that you have given your life to Him and worshiped Him as Lord? Is your life a sacrifice that you have laid down before Him and continue to lay at His feet? If you have not given your life to Him, you can do so right now as you read this book. Simply call out to Him and invite Him to take control. He will do it, and, as you continue to surrender to Him more and more completely, you will see His hand in your life more and more clearly. He is the real deal, and you can trust Him. Turn away from yourself and turn toward Jesus. You can call out to Him today. If you haven't, will you? I pray that you will.

Discussion Questions:

-Is it possible Jesus was a liar? Why or why not?

-Is it possible Jesus was a lunatic? Why or why not?

-Even if logic says otherwise, what are some reasons people might dismiss Jesus as "just a great teacher" or "a moral reformer"?

-Who do you say Jesus was? What does that mean to your life?

1. Lewis, C.S. (1952). *Mere Christianity*, revised edition, New York, Macmillan/Collier. p. 55 ff

2. Kreeft, P. (1988). *Fundamentals of the Faith:Essays in Christian Apologetics.* San Francisco: Ignatius Press. p. 60

Further Reading:*

The following books and websites are some of my personal favorites and have proved invaluable for learning more about apologetics (defending the faith.)

Josh McDowell – *The New Evidence that Demands a Verdict* (Thomas Nelson – 1999)

Dr. Gregory A. Boyd & Edward K. Boyd – *Letters From a Skeptic* (Chariot Victor – 1994)

Lee Strobel – *The Case for Christ* (Zondervan – 1998) (See *The Case for Faith* and *The Case for a Creator* as well.)

Gary R. Habermas & Michael R. Licona – *The Case for the Resurrection of Jesus* (Kregel – 2004)

And websites: www.carm.org   and   www.tektonics.org

*The views and opinions expressed in these books and websites are not necessarily the views and opinions of the author.

"The concern for world evangelization is not something tacked on to a man's personal Christianity, which he may take or leave as he chooses; it is rooted indefeasibly in the character of the God who has come to us in Christ Jesus. Thus it can never be the province of a few enthusiasts, a sideline or a specialty of those who happen to have a bent that way. It is the distinctive mark of being a Christian."

- Dr. James S. Stewart

Tell Em' Your Story

"Here is a test to find whether your mission on earth is finished: If you are alive, it isn't."

– Richard Bach

In World War II, a US soldier was staring down the sights of his M1 Garand rifle.

He had been waiting for eight hours, hunkered down in a small ditch, surrounded by weeds. It was nearly dusk. He was hungry, tired, and at times his muscles had cramped. But his patience had been rewarded. There, in the cross hairs of his rifle, was the first of four enemy soldiers who had entered his area.

He waited patiently, allowing them to close the distance. Two hundred yards, then 150, then 100; finally, they were within 50 yards. At this point, he couldn't miss. With a little luck he could down all four before they even knew where he was. He was confident his rear sights were adjusted perfectly. His clip contained eight shots. It was more than he would need. His heart was racing.

Taking a bead on the lead soldier, he inhaled slowly, exhaled even more slowly, and gently pulled back on the trigger.

Click

. . . and nothing.

He tried the trigger again. Still nothing. By now the soldiers were only thirty yards away, and even at their slow pace, they were closing quickly. There was no time to determine why the rifle had misfired. It had never happened before. Even the slightest movement might give away his location, but it didn't matter. Within a matter of seconds, they were going to find him anyway. He had only a moment to react.

> They were going to find him. He had only a moment to react.

Breathing heavily but moving as slowly as possible, he reached down toward his belt for his sidearm. Carefully slipping it out of its holster and silently clicking off the safety, he raised it up and leveled it on the men, now within only a few steps of his location.

He fired.

As a soldier for Jesus, there are going to be times when it seems like your weapons misfire. People will ask questions that you have no idea how to answer. You will go to share Jesus with someone, and suddenly your mind will go blank. This might happen more at first than later. After years of sharing your faith you will have encountered many different types of people and heard virtually every question there is to ask. But at first it might seem that every time you *"go into battle"* something goes wrong. When those times come, reach for your sidearm: your testimony.

When you don't
know what to say,
tell your story.

Our testimony is one of the most effective weapons in our arsenal and the one that we reach for when we are not sure what else to do. When in doubt, share your story. I want to say it again so that it gets down deep inside of you. When you don't know what to say, tell your story.

Revelation 12:11 says, *"They overcame him by the blood of the Lamb and by the word of their testimony."*

There are many reasons that it is important to share your testimony with others.

People respond to testimonies: If you pick up nearly any best-selling book, chances are good that you will see testimonies from other people about how great they think the book is. If you watch commercials for a while, it won't take long for you to see testimonies of others: *"This item is the greatest! It works! Take my word for it."* It would be very foolish for someone to try to market a new dieting plan without showing both before and after pictures of people who have been successful. In fact, anyone in marketing knows that testimonies work. People respond to the experiences and successes of others because they can relate to them.

Your testimony is *evidence* for the Gospel: At some point, someone is probably going to ask you a question that you don't know how to answer. Remember this: There is no shame in saying, *"I don't know. I'll try to find out for you."* But do your best to follow this up with, *"May I share something with you that I do know?"* and then share your testimony.

The Gospel works! It does what it says it will do. If you are born again, you are living proof – proof in the flesh that God is real, that Jesus was who He claimed to be, and that the message of the Bible is truth. When God transforms a life it declares His reality. The transformation of a life is a miracle as real as the parting of the Red Sea. Every time you share your testimony with others you are declaring the fact that the Gospel is the truth. It works.

> If you are born again, you are living proof that Jesus was who He claimed to be.

Your testimony equips you in every situation: When you have a testimony, you can be ready at a moment's notice in any circumstances to share your faith with others. As mentioned earlier, your testimony is your sidearm. It is the weapon that you always carry with you. You can reach for it at any time. Whether you are talking to a Buddhist, an atheist, a Mormon, or a nominal "Christian," your testimony can be very effective in reaching a person. It requires no special knowledge or training. You don't need a degree in theology or an understanding of Greek or Hebrew to share your testimony. In short, using our testimonies allows any Christian to share the Gospel with any other person on the planet in a way that is effective, natural, and reliable. If you have a testimony, you have all that you need to be an effective witness.

> If you have a testimony, you have all that you need.

In the fourth chapter of John, a woman has an encounter with Jesus that touches her deeply. Her response to this encounter is extremely valuable in a discussion about testimonies.

Verses 28 – 30 tell us of the woman's response to her meeting with Jesus: *"The woman went back to the town and said to the people, 'Come, see a man who told me everything I ever did. Could this be the Christ?' They came out of the town and made their way toward him."* Perhaps even more importantly, verse 39 tells us how the people responded: *"Many of the Samaritans from that town believed in him **because of the woman's testimony**."*

It would be fair to say that this woman had virtually no spiritual training. She wasn't trained in the effective use of the Romans Road. In fact, the New Testament would not be written for several more years. She didn't know what redemption or sanctification was. She had probably never heard about the concept of being born again. What she did know is that she had encountered Jesus, the living Christ, and it had changed her. She wanted to tell people. More importantly, she had all she needed to bring people to Jesus. She had a testimony.

Sharing your testimony follows in the path of the early Christians: Reading the New Testament shows us very quickly that the early Christians believed in sharing their testimonies as an effective witness. (Of course, even the word *"witness"* implies sharing what we have seen and heard.)

John 1:34 shows John the Baptist testifying that he has *"seen"* and he *"testifies"* that Jesus is the Christ. Acts 4:33 tells us that the apostles were active in *"testifying"* concerning the resurrection of Jesus. In 2 Timothy 1:8 we see Paul instructing the young evangelist Timothy not to be ashamed to *"testify"* concerning the Lord Jesus. Of course, Paul, perhaps the leading evangelist and greatest proponent of the Christian faith, shared his testimony regularly before crowds of people and kings. (Acts 22 and 26 are examples.) Even a large portion of the New Testament was written directly as testimony to what the authors had seen and heard.

John 20:24 - *"This is the disciple who testifies to these things and who wrote them down. We know that his testimony is true."*

Luke 1:1-4 - *"Many have undertaken to draw up an account of the things that have been fulfilled among us, just as **they were handed down to us by those who from the first***

*were **eyewitnesses** and servants of the word. Therefore, since **I myself have carefully investigated everything from the beginning**, it seemed good also to me to write an orderly account for you . . . so that you may know the certainty of the things you have been taught."*

1 John 1:1-3 - *"That which was from the beginning, which **we have heard**, which **we have seen with our eyes**, which **we have looked at and our hands have touched – this we proclaim concerning the Word of life**. The life appeared; **we have seen it and testify to it**, and we proclaim to you the eternal life, which was with the Father and has appeared to us. **We proclaim to you what we have seen and heard**, so that you also may have fellowship with us."*

From Genesis to Revelation, the Bible is one continuous story of what people have seen, heard, and learned concerning God. It is one continuous testimony.

For these and many other reasons, we need to learn how to share our testimonies with others. Following are several tips to help do this effectively.

Have a testimony: The first step to sharing your testimony is to have a testimony. If you cannot look back on your life and see that the Lord Jesus has come into your life and made you a new person, it is time. Right now, where you are, you can call out to Him. Admit to Him that you have broken His law and sinned against Him. Give your life over to Him. Ask Him to come into your life, forgive you, and cleanse you. He will do it, and this is the starting point for a lifetime of sharing your testimony. In order to share the power of the Lord Jesus in your life, it is important that you experience that power firsthand.

Stick to what's important: Telling your life story can take forever and can easily bog someone down in trivial details if we are not careful to trim it down to the important and relevant facts. For that reason, every Christian should develop his or her testimony and be able to share the important parts in just a couple of minutes. Every conversation is going to be different, and some facts of your testimony may relate to some people and not to others, but, in general, our testimonies should contain a few key points:

> Be able to share the important parts in just a couple of minutes.

a. **What was your life like (or what were you like) before Jesus?**

b. **How did you realize that you needed Jesus in your life?**

c. **What did you do to receive Jesus?**

d. **How are you different now?**

A simplified sample testimony might be something along the lines of the following (taken from my own testimony):

"I grew up in church and thought I was a pretty good person, but around my junior year of high school I began reading the Bible and found out that the lifestyle I was living and

the lifestyle the Bible expected were two totally different things. I remember in particular reading Matthew 7:21, which said something like, 'Not everyone who says unto me 'Lord, Lord' will enter the Kingdom of Heaven, but only he who does the will of my Father who is in Heaven.' That really shook me up because until that time I pretty much believed that anyone who believed in God and believed that Jesus was His Son was going to Heaven, but here was a verse that said you couldn't just call Him Lord but that you had to do what He says, or something like that. At that time I was partying and getting drunk sometimes, I had a filthy mouth, and pretty much my every thought was centered on girls. The more I read the Bible, the more I found out I was probably in trouble. I knew I didn't want to stand before God on Judgment Day. I was scared.

"I can remember many times being on my knees, crying and praying and telling God that I wanted to live for Him and that I needed Him in my life. I'm not sure when it happened exactly, but I know for sure that at some point, God changed me. I've never

> *"I knew I didn't want to stand before God on Judgment Day. I was scared."*

been the same. I met some amazing people during my first year of college who helped me see that it really is possible to live the lifestyle that Jesus demands. I began making better decisions and did my best to surrender every area of my life to Him. I think the biggest change, though, was that when I realized how important Jesus is, it changed me from being a totally self-centered individual to a person who genuinely is concerned about other people. That's why I am talking to you today."

Relate your story to the listener: The idea in sharing your testimony is to create a bridge between your experiences and the life of the person you are talking with. In the above example, the follow-up questions might be, *"How about you? Have you ever read the Bible much?"* or, if you know that the person is familiar with the Bible, *"How about you? Have you ever* *surrendered your life to Jesus like that?"* The important thing is that we don't only share our testimony, but we also use our testimony as a tool to encourage and challenge others in their spiritual lives. Make it a habit not ever to share your testimony without some kind of follow-up question that will bring it home and minister to the person.

Borrow someone else's sidearm: Not only is your testimony a powerful tool, but the testimonies of others can be extremely effective in relaying the Gospel.

One of my favorite testimonies is that of Frank Turner, an Emmy award-winning investigative journalist and anchor on the *"Action News"* in Detroit, Michigan.

> He was smoking nearly two thousand dollars worth of cocaine every week.

For twenty-two years of his life, Frank was hopelessly addicted to smoking pure cocaine, possibly the most addictive substance available. He was smoking nearly two thousand dollars worth of cocaine every week. His lifestyle had finally caught up with him, and he was exposed after racking up hundreds of dollars in phone sex charges on his girlfriend's credit card. He eventually was fired from his job and put to shame in front of millions of viewers who had invited him into their homes night after night on the evening news. His life degenerated to one of depression, divorce, suicide, and bankruptcy – that is, until he met Jesus.

A short while after receiving Jesus, Frank was water baptized, and at that very moment he was completely and permanently set free. His addiction had held him in bondage for more than two decades and had destroyed his life, but in an instant he was transformed.

After some time, because his life had been so drastically changed, Frank was reinstated on the evening news and to this day is known as "America's First Evangelical Anchorman" because of his openness about his conversion and commitment to the Lord Jesus Christ, even during a public news broadcast on a major network affiliate. He is proof that Jesus is alive and still works miraculously in the lives of people. Anyone who knows the power of cocaine knows that what Frank experienced was a miracle. He is also a living, breathing person whom people can investigate for themselves if they desire to do so. (You can see his entire testimony at frankturner.org.)

When I am sharing with people who indicate that drugs are a problem for them, I will often tell Frank's story. When someone asks me, *"Why doesn't God work miracles today?"* I will tell them Frank's story and the stories of other people I have met personally. His story is an excellent tool to have in my belt for sharing the love of Jesus.

The important point is this: Memorize other people's stories as well as your own. It is best to share stories that you know of personally, people whom you know well, or stories you have investigated yourself. Make sure the stories are true. (Great stories that you have received through email chain letters usually should be disqualified.)

I know people who were sex addicts but were instantly changed by the Spirit of Jesus in their life. I have met a woman who had multiple sclerosis, was blind in one eye, had a withered arm, and had to use a walker or a wheelchair to get around, and over the course of a few hours was completely healed. I know the people who were involved with the whole situation. I know a man who was so violent that he attacked another man with a baseball bat out of jealousy. Today he is one of the most gentle people I know. All of their stories are tools that I carry with me to aid in sharing the Gospel. In the same way, do your best to remember testimonies that you hear in order to pass them on to others.

Your testimony and the testimonies of others are essential keys in the expansion of God's Kingdom. Your story can be shared with and recognized by any person you encounter and can help bring the Gospel to people in a meaningful way. I challenge you in the name of Jesus to begin today. Tell your story to others on a regular basis. Be a *"witness"* for the Lord Jesus Christ.

Discussion Questions:

-Why is sharing your testimony effective?

-What is your personal testimony?

-What are some ways that you could transition from talking about your own testimony to applying it to the lives of others?

-What are some other people's testimonies that you know of?

Give Em' A Sign

"I would rather die now than to live a life of oblivious ease in so sick a world."
-Nate Saint

David Anderson is about five feet, eight inches tall.

The sign he is holding is about five feet tall.

Pretty much all you can see of David when he holds his sign are his nose, his sunglasses, and his hair.

His sign, which is black with bold yellow text, reads simply, *HONK IF YOU LOVE JESUS. HE LOVES YOU.*

He is standing at a major intersection in his hometown, stationed between three drugstores and a bank. Hundreds of cars drive by, and it doesn't take long for things to begin to happen. Many people honk and wave and give him the thumbs up. When semi trucks lumber by, the horn blast is loud . . . really loud. Others sit at the intersection and try to make it very clear they are ignoring him.

Rarely, someone might yell at him, *"Get a job!"* or something else not fit for print. Even more rarely, he might be shown someone's middle finger. It is not uncommon for others to stop at the intersection, roll down their windows, and encourage him by saying, *"Keep up the good work"* or *"God bless you."* In still other cars, a passenger might reach over to honk the horn while the driver slaps his or her hand away. A person in the back seat asks the driver, *"Well, aren't you going to honk?"* The driver pretends not to hear the question.

> There can be no doubt: people are noticing.

Regardless of the reaction, there can be no doubt: People are noticing, and that is the idea. Some people might think about Jesus who otherwise would have gone days or even weeks without a spiritual thought in their heads. Others may engage passengers in their cars in conversation about spiritual things. Still others will stop and talk.

Public sign holding can be a remarkably valuable way of getting the Word of God or the name of Jesus out into the world around us. It is a great way to stretch us in the area of boldness but is so simple that anyone can do it. It doesn't require a theological degree, the ability to prepare an effective sermon, or even great conversational skills. Young children can do it (and many have). And the truth is, it can most definitely be a whole lot of fun.

The first time I ever held signs publicly, I had been feeling kind of down for a couple of weeks. I had a minor case of the blues and was sort of feeling sorry for myself. During my prayer times, I really felt the Lord urging me to go out and do something to get my mind off of myself and onto other people. I had thought briefly before about holding signs publicly but had never seriously considered it. If nothing else, I was worried about what people would think of me. I thought about my bank loan manager who would probably drive by. I thought about my former physics professors who would more than likely see me. I even thought about how strange it would be just to stand out in public and try to get people's attention. Regardless of my concerns at that time, I really felt like the Lord wanted me to go for it. So eventually I decided I would do it. I made a commitment to the Lord that on that Thursday, from 10 a.m. to 11 a.m., I would go hold a sign near a busy street.

> I was worried about what people would think of me.

I showed up in front of my bank at 9:50 a.m. and refused to get out of my truck until the bank clock ticked over to exactly 10 a.m. I was nervous, and I wasn't going to stand out there a single minute beyond what I had committed to do. At precisely 10 a.m., I stepped out of my truck, grabbed my sign that said, *TALK TO JESUS TODAY – HE WILL ANSWER,* and planted myself at the intersection. As soon as I got there, a minivan rolled up and stopped not three feet in front of me. The driver, a brunette lady in her mid-thirties, looked over, smiled a huge grin, laid on her horn and gave me a thumbs up. Somehow, that was all the encouragement I needed. Nearly all of my fears disappeared, and I have been holding signs fairly regularly ever since.

In the time that I have been holding signs, I have seen people honk and wave, I have seen people stop and talk, and I have seen people purposefully ignore me. At one point, I was holding a sign that said, *JESUS GIVES HOPE.* I saw a woman staring at it with tears rolling down her face. I have seen others look at signs, get a very serious expression on their face and then look me in the eye as

> I saw a woman staring at it with tears rolling down her face.

if to thank me or somehow say, *"Yes, that's what I need."* I have seen children point and ask their parents questions. My physics professors and bank loan officer have driven by as well as many other people I know in my community. Many friends have joined me from time to time. The real truth is this: At this point, I love holding signs. It is a blast.

I encourage you to try it. You just might like it. Here are a few tips that I have learned about holding signs that might help you along the way:

Buy the right materials: The first time I ever tried this, I bought flimsy, run-of-the-mill poster board. Every time a truck or a stiff breeze blew by, the sign would flap in the wind like a flag, and it seemed like I was constantly working to keep the sign together (using both hands in the process). This also limited me to having a message on only one side of my sign.

Make sure to buy good, thick presentation board. It is inexpensive, easily available, and durable. It is both lightweight and solid, which makes it easy to hold with one hand. Also, make sure to use a big dark magic marker for the writing.

Choose your message: There are countless ideas for what could go on a sign that might minister to someone. Some are confrontational; some are gentle. Some are

> Some are confrontational; some are gentle. Some are challenging; others are encouraging.

challenging; others are encouraging. While it is impossible to say everything that needs to be said on one sign, it is very possible to touch a person's life with a simple phrase.

As a general rule, do your best to make sure that your message is simple, straightforward, relevant, and clearly communicated. Do your best to avoid Christian lingo and instead speak in language that non-churchgoers would understand. A sign that says, *ARE YOU WASHED IN THE BLOOD OF THE LAMB?* is only going to weird people out. *HAVE YOU GONE TO JESUS FOR FORGIVENESS?* probably

> Speak in language that non-churchgoers would understand.

would be a better choice of wording that says the same thing.

The following are several examples of signs that are some of my favorites:

FOLLOW THE WAY OF LOVE. FOLLOW JESUS. (Or simply, *FOLLOW JESUS.*)

"I CAME INTO THE WORLD AS A LIGHT." ¬JESUS (John 12:46)

CHRISTIANS - SHARE YOUR FAITH.

GIVE UP SELFISHNESS – FOLLOW JESUS.

TALK TO JESUS TODAY. HE WILL ANSWER.

JESUS GIVES HOPE.

JESUS FORGIVES THE PAST. ASK HIM.

JESUS WANTS ALL OF YOU.

WHAT IF YOU STOOD BEFORE GOD TODAY?

READ THE BIBLE.

GOD SAYS, "SEEK ME AND YOU WILL FIND ME" – (Jeremiah 29:12)

With a bit of creativity and the direction of the Holy Spirit, there are limitless ideas for messages that can be used. So, decide what you want to say, grab your marker, and write legibly. If you can't write legibly, ask a friend who can.

Grab a friend: Bringing a friend along will help in several ways. First, it will hold you accountable and help make sure you go through with it. Second, it will encourage you and give you strength. Third, having an extra person along allows people to see a couple of different messages at a time. Sometimes two sentences can say a great deal more than one. And finally, it is just more fun to go with a friend.

> Now is when the rush comes.

Get started: Making the sign is the easy part. Now (for some) is when the rush comes. Find a place where there are a lot of people and go there with your sign. It's that simple. A major intersection, an outside park, outside a busy mall; all are great places for sign holding. Make sure, however, that the place you choose is a public area. It is perfectly legal to hold signs on any public sidewalk in America. It also may be a good idea to choose a spot that is not too close to any area businesses. Be careful not to look like you are picketing or to impose yourself in such a way as to hurt someone's business. A spot fifty or a hundred feet away from any business should suffice.

Intersections are ideal because it is possible to show your sign to both directions of traffic at once. With hard poster board it is possible, as mentioned before, to hold your sign with one hand and allow people coming from both directions to see your message. With two boards it is possible to switch messages around so that up to four messages can be seen by simply flipping them over and exchanging them. At one sitting at a stoplight, a person could see a series of messages:

WHAT IF YOU STOOD BEFORE GOD TODAY? . . . GIVE UP SELFISHNESS – FOLLOW JESUS . . . JESUS GIVES HOPE . . . TALK TO JESUS TODAY. HE WILL ANSWER.

Be prepared to talk with people: If you hold signs, it is going to happen. Someone is going to stop and want to talk. In fact, talking to others should be one of your goals. Some people will stop just to encourage you and let you know that they appreciate what

> If you hold signs, it is going to happen. Someone is going to stop and want to talk.

you are doing. Some will stop and ask you about your sign, why you are doing what you are doing, or other matters that can lead into great conversations. It is also not uncommon for local newspapers to stop by for a picture and an interview. Remember, when in doubt, share your testimony.

In the fall of 2004 a couple of friends of mine and I had decided to go to Memphis and preach, hold signs, and pass out tracts on Beale Street. At one point one of my friends, Bill, was holding a sign that said JESUS WANTS ALL OF YOU. I was standing about a half a block away when I saw a very large, rough-looking man approaching Bill from behind with a couple of buddies. Bill had no idea that he was there. The man, who looked like a football linebacker, was walking toward him with his hands at his sides and his fists clenched. I thought Bill was about to get decked, so I began walking quickly toward him.

At the last minute, right before the man reached him, Bill turned around. The man looked up at Bill's sign, looked Bill right in the eye, and pointed, saying,

> *"That's what I need, man! That's what I need!"*

"That's what I need, man! That's what I need!" I drew a sigh of relief as Bill began sharing the Gospel with him and his friends.

It is not uncommon at all for great conversations to occur as the result of holding signs. Plus, the conversations are usually initiated by the other person, which helps you avoid the awkwardness of trying to initiate conversation yourself. In reality, one of the goals of holding signs is to create an opportunity for conversation. As we have already covered, conversations are one of the best ways not only to sow seeds in a person's life but to really delve into the Gospel of Jesus.

Maximize your time: When you are holding signs, pray. Pray that the right people come by at the right time. Pray that people's hearts and minds will be open to your message. Pray specifically for the people that you see. Pray that the Spirit of God touches them. Pray also that people will stop and talk with you and that you will have wisdom when the time comes to share the Gospel. Sing songs of worship to Jesus. (Be careful, though, about singing or praying out loud unless you do it loudly and clearly for people to hear, on purpose. The last thing you want is to stand there mumbling to yourself. If you do, go ahead and wear a t-shirt that says, *"I am a crazy person"* as well, just to make sure the point is clear.)

Another way to maximize your time is to memorize scripture. It is very easy to lightly pencil in a memory verse on the inside of your sign and memorize it while you are standing there. Again, though, try not to mouth it to yourself over and over lest people think you are a bit off your rocker.

> Don't just do it once and consider yourself a graduate.

As far as the amount of time you should spend holding signs is concerned, that is up to you and between you and God. For your first experience, I would suggest limiting yourself to forty-five minutes or even a half an hour so that it doesn't seem quite so overwhelming. Remember that even if you only have a short period of time, even five or ten minutes can make a very big difference, both in the lives of others and in your own life as you increase in boldness. My challenge to you is this: Right now, before you have too much time to think about it, decide when you are going to do this. Call a friend and ask him or her to join you. If that friend refuses, call another friend. Set a time, buy the materials, and go for it. I am confident that you will be glad you did. After that, make it your goal to hold signs regularly. Don't just do it once and consider yourself a graduate. Make it a regular part of your outreach efforts.

Discussion Questions:

-What are some of the advantages of holding signs to proclaim the Gospel?

-How might seeing a sign affect a person's life?

-What are some possible messages that might be effective? What would you like to place on your sign?

-How would it help to bring along a friend?

-Where would be a good place to hold signs in your community?

"I will place no value on anything I have or possess except in relation to the Kingdom of Christ. If anything I have will advance that Kingdom, it shall be given or kept, whichever will best promote the glory of Him to whom I owe all my hopes, both for time and eternity."

-David Livingstone

Checkbook Evangelism

"Priority number one for too many of us is not the glory of God but the blessing of ourselves."

-David Shibley

Your bank account is one of the most powerful tools you have in reaching the world for Jesus Christ. As individuals, we can be limited in our ability to reach the world. In general, our direct influence extends to a very small number of people. Through financial partnership and faithfulness with the resources that God gives us, however, we are able to reach out to people worldwide.

> We are able to reach people worldwide.

You may not be called by God to minister directly to the people of Korea, South Africa, or Afghanistan, but through your financial giving you can play a major part in reaching these people groups and others around the world. You may not feel equipped for or capable of preaching to masses of people, but through your faithful giving you can help enable those whom God has called to do so.

We looked at Romans 10:13-15 in a previous chapter. It says, *"Everyone who calls on the name of the Lord will be saved. How, then, can they call on the one they have not believed in? And how can they believe in the one of whom they have not heard? And how can they hear without someone preaching to them? And **how can they preach unless they are sent?**"*

In the Kingdom of God, there are two kinds of people:

A. Full-time ministers: Christians who receive their living from the Gospel and consider ministry to be their primary occupation.

B. Senders: Christians who receive their living from something other than the Gospel and consider *sending* other ministers to be one of their primary occupations.

"How can they preach unless they are sent?"

The two categories above are the only categories that exist. Some people exist in a combination of both (the apostle Paul is an example of this), but all believers, everywhere, fit somewhere in those two categories. To which do you belong? If you find that currently you are not living in either category, something needs to change.

Several passages of scripture seem to indicate this point:

Numbers 18:21 - *"I give to the Levites all the tithes in Israel as their inheritance in return for the work they do while serving at the Tent of Meeting."* (The Levites were the priests who received their living from the tithes of the Israelites.)

Luke 8:1-3 - *"Jesus traveled about from one town and village to another, proclaiming the good news of the kingdom of God. The Twelve were with him, and also some women . . . Mary (called Magdalene) . . . ; Joanna the wife of Cuza, the manager of Herod's household; Susanna; and many others. These women were helping to support them out of their own means."*

Matthew 10:5-10 - *"These twelve Jesus sent out with the following instructions . . . . Go rather to the lost sheep of Israel. As you go, preach this message: 'The kingdom of heaven is near.' Heal the sick, raise the dead, cleanse those who have leprosy, drive out demons. Freely you have received, freely give. Do not take along any gold or silver or copper in your belts; take no bag for the journey, or extra tunic, or sandals or a staff; for the worker is worth his keep."*

Acts 18:4-5 - *"Because he was a tentmaker as they were, he stayed and worked with them. Every Sabbath he reasoned in the synagogue, trying to persuade Jews and Greeks. When Silas and Timothy came from Macedonia, Paul devoted himself exclusively to preaching."* (The implication is that Paul, at times, would work to support his own ministry, sending himself. At other times he seemed to rely on others as sending agents in his life.)

1 Corinthians 9:13-14 - *"Don't you know that those who work in the temple get their food from the temple, and those who serve at the altar share in what is offered on the altar? In the same way,* **the Lord has commanded that those who preach the gospel should receive their living from the gospel.** *"*

> Every Christian is called to live well below his or her means.

I am convinced that every Christian is called to live well below his or her means financially in order to reach the world with the Gospel of Jesus Christ. For category A, the full-time minister, living below their means frequently comes with the job. It is often not a choice. I know preachers who opted out of medical school and left behind lucrative careers in medicine in order to pastor churches. I know very gifted businessmen who have given up the potential for great wealth in order to minister as missionaries. There are many future (or practicing) engineers, journalists, business managers, and contractors out there who have laid down their career plans and pursued the spreading of God's Kingdom on Earth instead. For them, living below their means comes with the territory. It is part of the job. There are exceptions, but, in general, entering full-time ministry means living below your means. Of course, every minister must be faithful where money matters are concerned, and, just like everyone else, they must use the money that comes into their hands to do the work of God's Kingdom with integrity and sacrifice. Interestingly enough, some of the most generous people around are missionaries who are already living below their means in order to advance the Gospel, but they still support other works around the world out of the finances that God places in their hands. In the same way, ministers are responsible for their own personal finances, making sure they are faithful with the money that God gives them.

Category B is where things become more difficult. For people who are not full-time ministers, living below their means often does not come with the territory but rather is a matter of daily choices.

> It is actually a mentality that is severely undermining God's work in the world.

Many times, because this is so ingrained into our minds as a result of our culture, Christians believe the following axiom – *income equals lifestyle.* In other words, if I make $60,000 a year, then I am able to (and should) have a lifestyle that reflects my income. If I make $60,000, I live like I make $60,000. If I make $100,000, I live like I make $100,000. This is, of course, not how it should be. It is actually a mentality that is severely undermining God's work in the world. Worse still perhaps is the idea that if my financial situation increases, my lifestyle should increase to match it.

College students make an excellent example of how this can work.

Many college students survive for years on nothing but Beanie Weenies and Ramen noodles. They work part-time jobs at fast-food joints in order to make some gas money, and they shop at thrift stores to save on clothing. It is not uncommon for college students to live on next to nothing in order to make it through school. And then it happens.

When many college students graduate and get their first full-time salaried position, they go flat-out hog wild. All of a sudden, they have gone from living on $2,000 a year to $42,000 a year, and boy do they take advantage of it. They rent a better apartment, buy a new car, fill their place with new furniture (that they pay no interest on for the first five years), and eat out every day. They buy new computers, new phones, new

> They go flat-out hog wild.

electronics, and new clothes. They are living large. Not only does their spending increase to match their income, it often exceeds their income, and within months they find themselves drowning in debt and struggling even to stay afloat. Somehow, they managed to get by when they were making $2,000 a year, but they can't seem to make ends meet now that they are making $42,000 a year. How much better would it be if they would learn how to manage their money, place their priorities in God's Kingdom, and learn to live a moderate lifestyle? It would be possible at this point for the same college student to live very comfortably on $32,000 a year (which still would be a tremendous financial increase) and give the other $10,000 toward the work of God's Kingdom. Is there any doubt that this is the kind of lifestyle that Jesus would have us lead?

Billy Graham once said, *"Give me five minutes with a person's checkbook, and I will tell you where their heart is."* It is definitely true. You can tell a great deal about people's priorities by examining the way they spend their money.

How about you? If you take a good look at your bank account, what does it say about your dedication to missions and the advance of God's

Kingdom in the world? Does it show that you are firmly committed to laying down your own life and making sacrifices in order that people around the world might be saved, that the homeless will find shelter, that the hungry will be fed, and that the captives will be set free? Or does it say that you are firmly committed to your own kingdom and the expansion of your own territories? Does a look at your check register show that media, sports, travel, clothing, cars, and other worldly things are taking priority over the love of Jesus being spread worldwide?

The church today desperately needs people who are passionate about living for God in the secular marketplace. There is a tremendous need for more Godly doctors, lawyers, teachers, and engineers. We need Godly people in the military, in the classroom, and in big businesses around the world.

There seems to be a mentality in Christianity today that people in the marketplace are second-class citizens in God's Kingdom and that people who are really serious about spreading God's Kingdom are destined to be preachers, missionaries, or evangelists. This is not only incorrect, but it creates an unhealthy imbalance in the Body of Christ.

The Word of God says that we are all part of one body and that there are many parts. Just as in the human body, there are some parts that are in the forefront: the eyes, mouth, hands, and feet. There are also parts that are unseen: the cardiovascular system, the skeletal structure, and the nervous system. Of course, all of these parts must exist, must work together, and must work properly in order for the body to function. Just as in the theater – there are actors and directors, but there are also stage managers, props people, and set designers. There are people in the forefront and people behind the scenes. In order for the show to go on, everyone involved needs to know their job and do it well. The key is for each believer to find out personally where God would have him or her and then work at it with great passion.

If God has called you into the secular workplace, He has placed you there for two reasons. One is so that you can reach the people who work with you. The second is so that you can make money that will accomplish two things: supporting you and your family and helping to promote the Gospel around the world.

> God expects just as much out of the man who works on an assembly line as He does one who works behind a pulpit.

Make no mistake about it – if you are not called to be a full-time minister, you are called to live sacrificially and use your resources to send people who are. It can be very simple for a Christian to use a life in the secular workforce as a place of hiding, building a personal kingdom and giving God just a portion of life. It is important that we understand that God expects just as much out of the man who works on an assembly line as He does one who works behind a pulpit. Both have a responsibility to reach the world with the Gospel using the resources, gifts, and positions that God has given them. Their responsibility is the same. Their parts in the grand scheme are simply different.

A couple of points need to be made clear concerning God's global mission and personal finances.

1. Every person's giving is different: It's an old Christian cliché, but it still rings true: God doesn't expect equal giving; He just expects equal sacrifice. God does not expect a person who works at McDonald's to give the same amount as a person who works for McDonnell-Douglas. However, He does expect both people to make sacrifices financially in order that the Gospel might go forward.

> What impresses Jesus is your amount of faith, and faith is shown by obedience.

I talked with a young lady recently who said she has a hard time putting money in the offering because she is embarrassed by the small amount she is able to give. I reminded her of the passage in Mark 12 where Jesus was watching people place their offerings in the temple treasury. A poor widow placed a couple of copper coins in the offering that were worth just a fraction of a penny, but this caught Jesus' attention more than all of the others who had thrown in large amounts. He pointed her out to His disciples, saying, *"They all gave out of their wealth; but she, out of her poverty, put in everything – all she had to live on."*

Jesus is not impressed with the *amount* of your financial giving. What impresses Jesus is your amount of faith, and faith is shown by obedience. When you give sacrificially, it shows that you trust God and that your highest priorities are tied to His highest priorities. It shows that you are investing, not only in this life, but also in the life to come.

2. The amount of giving is between each believer and God: By the end of his life, John D. Rockefeller Sr. was giving away 90% of his income and keeping only 10%. At the time of his death, he had *given away more money than any other individual had ever been worth* – an amount well over 500 million dollars! (That's the equivalent of about 6.8 *billion* dollars today.)

He didn't start out giving away that much money, but over his lifetime he came to that point gradually. He began by giving away 10% and keeping 90%. Eventually he moved up to giving away 20% and keeping 80%. And so on, until near the end of his life he kept only a very small percentage for himself (which was still more money than most of us will ever see in our lifetimes).

> 100% of your money came from God, and 100% of it should still belong to Him.

God may not, at this point, expect you to give away 90% of your money, but He does expect you to live sacrificially. It is up to you to seek God for what percentage He expects from you. But remember this: 100% of your money came from God, and 100% of it should still belong to Him and His mission. You are simply an account that He has placed His money in. He trusts you to do what He wants with it. It is also important that you figure this out for yourself and don't become overly concerned with what amount He expects from other people.

A couple of years ago I had a friend who sold boats for a living. They were big, expensive boats, and he had a lot of money coming in. He also drove a Mercedes and wore a Rolex watch. Some people might look at him and think to themselves, *"Why would a Christian need a Mercedes and a Rolex watch?"* Some would consider it excessive. In my opinion, however, he *should* wear a Rolex and drive a nice car. When people fly 1500 miles to look at a boat, they don't want to talk to a guy driving a Metro and wearing a Casio (not that these aren't fine items). The kind of people who buy $300,000 boats want to talk to a guy who wears a Rolex and drives a Mercedes. To me, it was very clear that having money helped him make money. Wearing a Rolex equipped him to give away even more money than not wearing one.

On the other hand, God calls some people to live very simple lives in order that the Gospel might go forth. In her lifetime, Mother Teresa saw millions of dollars pass through her hands, and all of it went toward ministering to the poor. In fact, when she died, it is my understanding that the only things she owned were a couple of inexpensive robes. Today she is a household name because of the great work she did for the Kingdom of God.

The point is this: People's situations are different, and it is up to every believer to seek God and find what level of financial giving He has for them. We must prayerfully determine what God would have us do and then be faithful to do it. We must be willing to do anything God asks of us. We must lay our finances down on the altar of sacrifice.

There is no doubt that lowering your lifestyle and living sacrificially can be difficult. I have heard it said, however, that the minute your worship ceases to be sacrificial, it ceases to be worship. God expects your giving to be sacrificial. It means giving up things that you want in exchange for things that you think are important.

Giving of your finances toward the work of God on Earth is an act of worship toward God. It shows that you trust Him. It shows that you believe in the importance of the Gospel. It shows that you are attached to the Kingdom of Heaven and separated from the kingdom of the world.

It is not my intention in this chapter to tell you precisely what to do with your money. There are thousands of great places in the world that will make good use of finances:

> It does not take a long search at all to find great places to invest.

missionary organizations, ministries dedicated to saving young girls out of human trafficking situations, homeless shelters, disaster recovery organizations, churches, campus ministries, and many, many more. There are countless young people going on short-term missions trips. (The next time your youth group has a bake sale, look at it as an opportunity and give them a couple hundred bucks for that burnt cookie.) It does not take a long search at all to find great places to invest in God's Kingdom.

My challenge to you is this: Take a serious look at your finances and determine if you are where you need to be. Is your money being used to fulfill the mission of Jesus on Earth? Give generously to your church consistently. Find missionaries and organizations that you know are faithful to God's Word and begin supporting them regularly. If you have been irregular in your giving, repent and take the steps necessary to be faithful. Find people you know are pursuing a life in missions and become a part of their education, training, and travel. Find some areas that you can sacrifice what you want and use the money for the Gospel. Basically, do something!

God loves a generous giver. He desires that you be unattached to the things of this world. He has a mission on the Earth that requires the diligence and faithfulness of every believer to accomplish. He has a plan, and your checkbook is a part of that plan. Will you submit it to Him?

Discussion Questions:

-Currently, how do you honor God with your money?

-When has God proven Himself faithful to you in the area of finances?

-What are some great places that you could be investing your money in for God's Kingdom? Will you begin today?

"God is a missionary God. The Bible is a missionary book. The Gospel is a missionary message. The church is a missionary institution. And when the church ceases to be missionary minded, it has denied its faith and betrayed its trust."   -J. Herbert Kane

Gospel Literature

"Nothing surpasses a tract for sowing the seed of the Good News."

-Billy Graham

Mac Gober's life had degenerated to the breaking point.

In his lifetime he had brutalized people to the point of biting off one person's finger and knocking another's eye out of its socket, leaving the person permanently blind in one eye. He had beaten one young man into unconsciousness and left him lying in a ditch. The young man was later hospitalized for a concussion, severe lacerations, and head contusions. Mac was strung out on drugs so much that his body would shake constantly. He was both a user and an active dealer. His personal hygiene had deteriorated to the level that he would stand in line at a store and relieve himself right where he stood, allowing the urine to puddle into his motorcycle boots and onto the floor without a concern. Even under such circumstances, he might go weeks without bathing.

As a child, he had been beaten and abandoned by his father, who at one point had choked Mac to the edge of death. He had experienced violence and hatred on the streets as a teenager and as a young adult came to know the cruelty of war in the Vietnam conflict. After Vietnam, he entered the horrible world of America's biker gangs, where his life fell even further into drugs, sex, and brutal violence. He had barely escaped death many times. Most people would have considered him beyond reach. He testifies that Jesus was nothing but a profanity to him, and at times, to get laughs from his friends, he would even mock Jesus on the cross while the group was partying together, getting stoned out of their minds. His life seemed to be a one-way trip toward destruction – that is, until a man handed him a Gospel tract.

> Jesus was nothing but a profanity to him.

Mac was standing in line at Western Union one day when a man came in and began passing out literature. He walked down the line and eventually put a small piece of paper into Mac's hand. The paper said on the front, *"Just as I am."*

Mac watched as others in the line made faces and wadded up the tracts to throw them away. His first impression was to do the same, but when he went to throw the tract on the ground it stuck to his filthy fingers. He was so dirty that the paper stuck to him like glue. He tried several times to get rid of the annoying paper, but even in switching hands it clung to him. After trying several times, he finally gave up and examined it further. The tract explained that God could love people just as they are and that even though we are sinners, God had made a way for us to be saved. He would later testify that those words literally seemed to jump off the page at him as he read. For perhaps the first time, he really considered the possibility that God could forgive him after all of the terrible things that he had done.

Two weeks later, when visiting the home of another drug addict, Mac walked into the house to find another Gospel tract sitting on the floor, just inside the door. It referred to the amazing prophecies contained in the Bible, and Mac began to read it, thinking how strange it was running into so much *"God stuff."*

When his friend came into the room, he explained to Mac that earlier that morning, a lady had come to his door passing out tracts, and he had hit her in the mouth and slammed the door on her. The tract had fallen out of her hand and onto his floor. Mac left his

> He had hit her in the mouth and slammed the door.

friend's house shaken up, and for two weeks he could not get that precious woman out of his mind. He couldn't stop wondering what would prompt a woman like that to go into such a bad neighborhood just to tell people about Jesus. The words that were written in both tracts also weighed heavily on his mind.

It was shortly thereafter that Mac Gober gave his life to Jesus. Alone in his dark apartment, with no one there to help him, he called out to God and asked for His forgiveness. God answered.

Today Mac is a changed man. He has ministered to thousands, both in the pulpit and on the streets. He founded Canaan Land Ministries, which has helped hundreds of men, much like Mac, with drug and alcohol addictions, broken home lives, and violent backgrounds. A man who was once an absolute menace to society has been changed so completely that now judges, district attorneys, and probation officers work with him regularly to help other men with similar lives. And his change happened shortly after two faithful Christians used Gospel literature to get the Word of God into his hands.

Gospel literature is one of the most effective and most neglected methods of spreading the Word of God (barna.org lists it as one of the *"least widely used methods"*). Tracts are extremely simple to hand out, they require absolutely zero courage to distribute in many cases (anyone can leave a tract on a

> Gospel literature is one of the most effective and most neglected methods of spreading the Word of God.

table somewhere), and they have the potential to change a person's life forever. I have even heard a story of a scuba diver who found a Gospel tract while diving and later gave his life to Jesus as a result.

If our goal is to get the Word of God into the eyes and ears of people everywhere, it is a self-evident truth that using tracts works. In other words, if, theoretically, our goal is the distribution of the Gospel around the world, then, practically, it is the literal distribution of the Word that will go a long way toward accomplishing that goal. Handing out Gospel literature equals spreading the Word.

Here are several tips to help make it a point to distribute the Gospel in paper form:

Acquire Gospel literature: When I teach seminars on evangelism, I often ask the question, *"Who here regularly purchases Christian books to read?"* When I ask that question, about ninety to ninety-five percent of the hands usually go up. I then follow up with the question, *"Who here regularly purchases Gospel tracts and literature to distribute?"* At that point nearly every hand goes down. On occasion, one or two hands might remain up. This, of course, re-emphasizes the tragedy of spiritual gluttony that is so alive and well in our lives today. We spend a great deal of money on Christian books for ourselves, and very little on Christian literature for distribution.

There are many great places where Gospel tracts can be acquired both locally and online. I suggest beginning today by stopping at your local Christian bookstore and grabbing a handful of tracts that you can distribute in the coming weeks. If they don't carry tracts, request that they do. Beyond that, do a search online for the phrase *"Gospel tracts,"* and there will be no end to the resources available. Some of my personal favorites are The American Tract Society (actsociety.org) and Living Waters Ministries (livingwaters.com), but there are countless resources out there.

Also, consider shopping at thrift stores in your area for Bibles and other Gospel books that you can distribute. Thrift stores like the Salvation Army, Goodwill, or DAV almost always have dozens of Bibles, booklets, and other Christian books available for about a quarter or fifty cents each. It is not only a great way to stock your own personal library, but it is a fantastic way to acquire literature that you can give away. I have found literally dozens of copies of Frank Peretti's *This Present Darkness* and *Piercing the Darkness* that I can give away to people. They are fantastic reads that both Christians and non-Christians will find riveting. Then, after giving them to a friend and giving him or her a chance to read them, there is an open door to talk with the person about the book's content, which can easily segue to the Gospel.

"Aha! Finally I've got you. I want my twenty dollars."

Carry tracts with you: Years ago, I had the privilege of accompanying Ray Comfort in downtown Dallas, Texas, as we went out and talked with people about Jesus. He related at that time that he always carried at least one Gospel tract with him and had even made a deal with his friends that he would give them twenty dollars if they could ever catch him without a Gospel tract on his person. At one point he had gone swimming with a friend, and when he was in the water, wearing swimming trunks, his friend pointed his finger at him and said, *"Aha! Finally, I've got you. You don't have a Gospel tract on you now. I want my twenty dollars."* Ray then proceeded to reach into his swim trunks, peel away a soaking Gospel tract, and hand it to his friend. This was clearly a man committed to carrying tracts. (Since then I have found out that he now offers $1000 to anyone who can catch him, in public, without a tract.) My challenge to you is this: Make it a similar priority in life to carry tracts with you. If you don't have them with you, you can't distribute them. It is that simple. Put a stack of them in your car, in your purse or backpack, in your desk at work, or wherever you might need access to them. Carrying the Gospel with you in paper form always leaves you ready at a moment's notice to share Jesus with someone. Even if you only have two seconds in a person's presence, if you are equipped with Gospel literature, you are equipped to share the Gospel in a way that may have eternal implications.

There are tons of great tracts out there. Some are seasonal and should be used when appropriate (Christmas or Halloween, for example.) Some are confrontational, pointing out that we will all be judged by God someday and that the time to prepare is now. Others are more mercy-oriented and emphasize that there is a God out there who loves people and cares about their eternal destiny. Some are educationally oriented, talking about science and religion. Others argue the existence of God, the legitimacy of the Bible, or the historicity of Jesus.

One of my favorite tracts is produced by Living Waters Ministries. It is a small, multi-page booklet that features on the cover the face of an attractive woman and has the following words: *Everything man has learned about women.*

The inside is, of course, empty. On the back cover is a small Gospel presentation that begins with *"Man doesn't even know much about man"* and goes on from there. I have passed out that tract many, many times, and it never fails to elicit a great response. When I see a man and a woman walking down the street, hand in hand, I might walk up to the guy, hand him the tract, and say, *"Hey, man, you might need this."* Almost without fail, he will walk just a little farther, laugh, and then turn around with a big grin on his face. He will then usually show it to the woman with him. I have had many people come up to me, even an hour later, and ask me if I have any more copies of that tract so that they can give them to their friends. Creative tracts like that (and there are several out there) will be passed from hand to hand, person to person, and have the potential to impact many lives.

Another possibility for acquiring tracts would be to create your own. Whether it is a note written on the back of a napkin or a full-color glossy brochure, it can be used to reach people with the Gospel. Why not type up your testimony and give it to your friends and family? Why not pick a favorite joke, find some kind of connection to the Gospel, type it up, and print out a couple dozen copies to distribute? If you will use your imagination, the possibilities are limitless.

Distribute them: It should go without saying that in order for tracts to be effective they need to be distributed. Having libraries full of books and mounds of tracts that go unread helps no one.

There are many ways to get tracts and literature into the hands of people. Some methods require very little or no courage at all. Information kiosks on university campuses are a great place to put tracts. Leaving tracts in public restrooms is a possibility. (But please, avoid unnecessary litter and please, please don't ever consider writing or carving Gospel messages into bathroom walls. We are looking for evangelism here, not *evandalism*.) When you eat at a sit-down restaurant, leave a very generous tip (Christians are notorious for under-tipping. A generous tip is 20% or more) and leave a Gospel tract. Don't leave a tract without a good tip. Use your imagination. There are lots of places that you can leave tracts where people will find them and read them.

One of the most effective ways to get tracts into the hands of people is literally to place them there. In other words, you hand them to people directly. This can be accomplished anywhere you find people: relaxing at the park, walking on the street, or waiting for a bus. Carry tracts with you in your car, and every time you go through a drive-through restaurant, make it a point to give the worker a tract of some sort. Many times, when I drive through at a restaurant, I will tell the worker something along the lines of, *"Hey, I've got good news for you."* When the person asks me what the good news is I will say, *"Jesus knows your potential, and He is excited about it,"* or *"Jesus is pursuing you and He knows what is going on in your life."* I usually will then hand the person a Gospel tract to read later. Or I might hand the person a tract with some kind of illusion on it, or a list of one-liners with a Gospel message. In that case I might just say, *"Here, you might get a kick out of this"* and leave it at that. The point is this: Be creative, and you will have no trouble distributing the Gospel of Jesus to people if you will make the effort.

Start conversations: There are a lot of great tracts available that can be instant conversation starters or great visual tools for sharing the Gospel in an already-established conversation. Another set of tracts available through Living Waters Ministries is a series of IQ tests. In order to show you how effective they can be, I am going to include them here.

Basically, these can be used anywhere that a conversation can be started. Simply ask someone, *"Have you ever seen this I.Q. Test?"*

The first test follows. In the image below there are three phrases contained in triangles. Read each one OUT LOUD and then read on further. Don't read further until you have read each triangle.

Now that you have read the phrases, go back and read them one more time carefully. Pay attention to every single word.

You may or may not have noticed that each triangle contains an unnecessary word. It doesn't say, *"Bird in the hand,"* *"Paris in the spring,"* and *"Once in a lifetime."* It actually says, *"Bird in the the hand,"* *"Once in a a lifetime,"* and *"Paris in the the spring."*

Did you get it right? Most people don't. Many don't, even when you ask them two or three times to read it very carefully and check out every word.

Here's the second test. In the following paragraph (the one in the box) how many times do you count the letter *"F"*? Count them now and then read on.

FINISHED FILES ARE THE RESULTS OF YEARS OF SCIEN- TIFIC STUDIES COMBINED WITH THE EXPERIENCE OF YEARS.

Go ahead and read it again to be sure.

You might be surprised to find that there are six *"F's"* in the above paragraph. If you didn't count six, chances are good that you missed the *"F's"* in the word *"of."*

How are you doing so far?

Here we go. Test number three. Read the following out loud and do the math as you go:

ONE THOUSAND plus FORTY.
Now add another THOUSAND.
Add TEN. A THOUSAND more.
Add FORTY. Now add TEN more.
What is your total?

Did you come up with the answer 4000? If you did, you got it wrong. The real answer is 3100. 3090 + 10 will always equal 3100. (This one is a great one to give bank tellers or salesmen. Tell them with a smile that you want to test their math skills before you do business with them. If they fail, you might ask them, *"What school did you go to?"* Then smile and proceed to do business with them anyway. It can be fun.)

Okay, we have made it to the final test, which happens to be our transition to the Gospel. What does the following say?

GODISNOWHERE

There are two ways that a person might read this. One says, *"God is nowhere."* The other says, *"God is now here."* Both of these responses can easily turn into spiritual conversations. Usually, by this point, the people are laughing along with you and enjoying themselves, and when you get to this question, you can follow up with a question. If they say *"God is now here,"* you can respond with, *"Some people think it says, 'God is nowhere.' Which do you believe?"* If they respond with *"God is nowhere,"* you can respond with, *"Some people think it says, 'God is now here.' Which do you believe?"* Either way, the transition into a conversation about spiritual things is very, very easy. Even as I am writing this I have shown this quiz to three people, one of whom was a total stranger. Afterwards I was able to talk with him about his spiritual life, find out what his beliefs are, and encourage him to live for Jesus with all of his heart. These things work, and they are fun. And each of these tracts has a Gospel message on the back. Even if you don't continue talking with the person afterwards, or if the person is in a hurry (the whole thing takes two or three minutes to present), you can leave the cards with him or her to read the back later. Chances are, people will not only read the cards, but they will show them to their friends as well.

The bottom line on the use of Gospel literature is that it is effective and easy. It can reach people who normally would not step foot in a church or have any kind of conversation about spiritual things. It is one of the tools that every Christian should have in his or her belt for reaching the world with the Gospel of Jesus.

So what are you waiting for? Go get some tracts!

Discussion Questions:

-What is it that makes Gospel literature effective?

-Why would some people read a tract who would not normally go to church, listen to a preacher, or have a spiritual conversation?

-What are some creative ways to distribute Gospel literature?

-What are some ideas for creating your own literature for distribution?

-Will you begin to acquire and distribute Gospel literature regularly? Why or why not?

If You Invite Them, They Will Come

"Any church that is not seriously involved in helping fulfill the Great Commission has forfeited its biblical right to exist."   - Oswald J. Smith

Joe Whitis refused to go to church.

His roommate Adam had been hounding him for months. If he had asked him once, he had asked him a thousand times. *"Joe, why don't you come to church with me this week?"* Joe's answer was always the same. *"Not this week. Maybe next time."* But then, the day came.

One evening, after meeting a girl he was interested in, Joe was sitting in his dorm room talking to Adam about her. He was convinced that she liked him and was waiting for her to call. Adam was certain that she wasn't interested and that the phone call was never going to happen. Joe, confident as he was, told Adam, *"Look, man, I can tell when a girl likes me. She'll call before tomorrow morning, guaranteed."* Adam wasn't so sure. *"Tell you what, Joe, if she calls, I'll admit that you are the man. But if she doesn't call, you have to go to church with me this weekend. Deal?"* Joe maintained his confidence and agreed. The girl never called, and a humbled Joe was in church the following Sunday. In fact, he has been in church almost every Sunday since then. He has become actively involved in ministry, and God has completely revolutionized his life. Today, he is the one inviting others to church, and it was all because his college roommate wouldn't take no for an answer.

In my seminars, I often take a brief poll. I ask those in attendance what method God used to reach them with the Gospel. In a room of thirty people, usually one or two will raise their hand saying they gave their life to Jesus

> It was all because his college roomate wouldn't take no for an answer.

as a result of some kind of Gospel literature. Maybe one more might say it happened after seeing something on TV. A couple might say it was through a friend who explained the Gospel to them personally, and a handful more might say it was the influence of their parents. The vast majority, however, will say it is because they attended some kind of Christian service where the Gospel was preached, and they responded. Whether it was a regular church service or some kind of special event or crusade – in my experience, the majority of people who become Christians do so as a result of attending some kind of Christian gathering.

There are two ways of looking at this, and both are true. One way is to say that if this many people are giving their lives to Jesus in some kind of church service, the church isn't doing the job it needs to of reaching people outside church walls. If we are really honest with ourselves, the reason such a high percentage are reached inside the church is that so few people are doing anything for God's Kingdom outside the church. We need to pick up the pace in other methods of reaching people.

However, the second way of looking at this is to say that inviting people to church services is a very effective way of reaching them. The bottom line is, it works. As such, we need to be bringing people to church with us as often as we can.

I have stressed over and over that we need to do something to reach people and that some methods will be easy and others will be difficult. I even considered separating

> The bottom line is, it works.

methods into three categories: *"piece of cake," "life of adventure,"* and *"adrenaline junkie."* The adrenaline junkie category would include street preaching and sign holding. Life of adventure would be relational outreach, service evangelism, and getting people talking. The piece of cake topics would be Gospel literature (most of the time), using your resources, and this one – inviting people to church.

Not everyone is going to get up on a bench and preach or stand on a street corner holding signs, which is perfectly fine. In my opinion, not every person is designed to do so (although there are many who should do so and don't). There are also many others who are just beginning to learn about the Christian faith and do not feel equipped to share it with others effectively. Those people should be continually working toward becoming equipped, but, in the meantime, inviting others to church is an excellent tool. It will remain an excellent tool long after a person begins utilizing other methods. Whether you are currently able to share the Gospel with others is not the point. Hopefully, the environment of your church is such that people who attend will hear the Gospel and will be given a chance to respond.

> This takes a great deal of pressure off the believer.

We have already mentioned several times that it is the Word of God received and planted in our life that saves us. If your church is a good church, then any person who attends your services should hear the Word. In many ways, this takes a great deal of pressure off the believer. The Word is going to be taught at the same time in the same place every week by someone who is trained and knowledgeable. One of the goals of believers should be to get people there to hear the message. In other words, you may feel pretty helpless in reaching others. Don't stress. Simply invite them to church. If you can get them there, they will hear the Word.

Just as we saw in Chapter 2, the Christian faith was never intended to be a religion of self-centered spiritual advancement. It was intended to be outwardly focused. In the same way, we should view our church attendance from that perspective. Our church attendance shouldn't be just about our growing in the faith personally. Of course, it should be a place where our personal needs are met, where we find strength and encouragement from interaction with other believers, and where we are able to let down our guard, so to speak, and relax in the presence of God, worshiping Him. But we must never view church as simply another tool for building our own spirituality – that actually ends up being self-defeating. Church attendance should go beyond that. In addition to being a place for spiritual growth, it should also be a tool we use regularly to help others hear God's Word. The local church is a place for taking our eyes off ourselves, a place for worshiping God, *and* a place for reaching out to others.

Through the years, I have heard people say when changing churches that they were leaving their church because they "just weren't getting fed there." While it is true that our churches should be a place where people grow and mature in the Christian faith, they should also be

> If a pastor wants to *"feed"* the congregation, the best way to do so is to inspire them with a vision for reaching the world.

places dedicated to reaching people who don't know the Gospel. The time to find a different church isn't primarily when we feel we are not being *"fed"* spiritually. The time to find a different church is when our church does not care about winning people to Jesus. A church that does not have outreach as a central focus is a church that has abandoned the teachings of Jesus Christ. As we have already covered, a central focus on outreach is the most important factor in personal growth. If a pastor wants to *"feed"* the congregation, the best way to do so is to inspire them with a vision for reaching the world and then teach them how to do so. A person who wants to be *"fed"* something else is a person whose tastes run contrary to the teachings of the Bible.

Ted Haggard, current president of the National Association of Evangelicals, said, *"The first joint priority of the churches of any city should be that of making it hard for people to go to Hell from that city."* Daniel Bacon, author of *Equipping for Missions*, said, *"Essentially, the church has many responsibilities but only one mission, and that is the evangelization and discipling of all nations."* The great pastor, author, and missions advocate Oswald J. Smith summed the point up succinctly. He said, *"The mission of the church is missions."* We must begin to view our churches not only as places for us to grow personally but also as places we bring people in order for them to come to faith. Our churches are just one more tool (and one of the biggest tools) that Jesus desires to use in reaching the world.

I have heard of many people who actually want their churches to remain small. They think so because they want the personal attention that comes with a smaller group, which is completely understandable, and every church should have a means of both discipling people and attending to their

> A man who wants to keep the church small is a man who has missed the point of the church.

individual needs. Jesus most definitely believed in focusing on a smaller group of disciples, but even then it was a matter of outreach. It was about picking a small group of people and training them to reach the world. All the while, Jesus continued to reach out to the masses. A man who says he wants to keep the church small is a man who has missed the point of the church entirely. When he says, *"I want a small church,"* what he means is, *"I want what I want, and I want it when I want it. Having too many people around here will keep me from getting what I want when I want it. Forget them. This thing is about me."*

Church is not entirely about *"me."* It has always been and always will be primarily about *"Him"* and *"them."* Church will be what it is supposed to be for *"me"* when my focus is elsewhere. I will grow the most through my church attendance when I view church as a place to go and die to myself, glorify God with my life, and lead other people into a saving knowledge of Jesus.

The following are some tips you can use to help you in reaching your community through the power of invitation:

Love your church: Everyone knows that joy and enthusiasm are contagious. If people can tell that you love your church and are excited about going, it is going to influence them in the direction of attendance. If your commitment to your local church seems halfhearted or especially if others hear you

> This is as simple as focusing on what is good and ignoring what is bad.

complaining about the services, the pastor, or any other aspect of the church, you can bet they are not going to be excited about coming. I am convinced that every Christian should have an attitude that says they attend the best church in the world. If you don't love your church, you need to start. Often this is as simple as focusing on what is good and ignoring what is bad – a trait that is helpful in every area of life. With a few exceptions, as long as you are attending a church that teaches the Word of God and challenges people to surrender to Jesus, you should be able to find some traits to be excited about. Focus on the traits that you like and don't think about the traits that you might not like.

Which of the following seems more compelling?

"Man, I love my church. You should check it out sometime. It's made such a difference in my life. The music is great, the pastor is funny, and his teaching is really practical. They take really great care of the kids during the services, and the people are very accepting of others. I can't say enough about how much I like my church. I think you'd love it. Want to come with me this Sunday?"

Or, *"Do you want to come to church with me sometime? I know I've complained a lot about the pastor and how he always seems to want my money, but I guess all in all it's not so bad if you can get past the ugly orange carpet and the 1970's wood grain finish on the walls. My kids seem to like the youth pastor quite a bit even though I personally think he is kind of goofy sometimes. Services are at 10:30 on Sunday mornings. (We don't go to the Sunday school classes – Yawn.) You want to come? Maybe afterwards we can grab some lunch together."*

The first step to successfully bringing people to church with you is being enthusiastic about inviting them.

Invite others regularly and persistently: When we begin to see church as yet another way to reach people with the Gospel, it will change our perspective on bringing people with us. If we are outreach oriented, we will begin to see going to church without someone coming along as an opportunity missed. Make it a point to try your best to always bring someone with you. Consider a service without visitors as a service that is missing one of its most important elements.

The best way to bring people to church with you is to invite people on a regular basis. If you invite a dozen different people throughout the week, chances are good that three or four are going to tell you they "might" come. If three or four people tell you they might come, it is possible that one may actually be willing. If one is willing, there is a slight possibility that he or she will actually be in attendance. Even if no one comes with you on a given week, if you invite enough people consistently over time, someone is going to come eventually. Consistency with invitations is the key. You might even consider going door to door and simply inviting people to go to church with you. The worst that could happen is that people would tell you no. The best that might happen is that some people might come with you, and others will engage you in conversation from which you might share the Gospel with them.

> The worst that could happen is that people would tell you no.

There is also nothing wrong with continually inviting someone to church with you. People will make all kinds of excuses to avoid attendance. If a person makes it clear that he or she doesn't want to come and doesn't want to be asked again, it is perfectly acceptable to leave the person alone and wait. Some people, however, actually would like to attend with you, but they are caught up in so many things that they really are too "busy" to come. Some people need to be invited over and over and over again before they attend for the first time. I have heard many stories of people who were invited dozens of times before they attended a particular church, but after attending just once they became actively involved. (Remember Joe?) You never know – the person you are inviting over and over today may become one of those people if you don't give up.

Invite strangers: In an earlier chapter we talked about using the question, *"Do you have a church that you attend?"* as a means to introduce spiritual conversation. This question serves conversational purposes well, but it is also valuable in and of itself without further conversation. It is obviously an excellent means of inviting people to attend church – even at times when no lengthy conversation is possible. Whether it is a waitress, an auto mechanic, or a bank teller, asking people this question can be done very quickly and usually without coming across as overly abrasive. If they answer, *"Yes, I go to such-and-such church down the road,"* you could respond, *"That's great. May Jesus bless you today."* The

> Asking people this question can be done very quickly.

idea is not to steal people away from their church to start attending yours. But if they say *"no,"* indicating they have no church, feel free to invite them. I have seen it more than once that a person invited cold turkey has shown up at church the next week or even months later.

If people you are engaged in conversation with seem to hem and haw around the topic of church attendance, there are a couple of good questions that can help you know how committed they are to their church. The first is this: *"I've heard of that church. What's the name of the pastor there?"* If people can't tell you the pastor's name, chances are good that they haven't attended there very consistently. The second question is this: *"Did you go last week?"* If the answer is *"no,"* then follow it with this: *"How about the week before that?"* With a few exceptions, if people say they haven't been to church in the last few weeks, you should feel free to invite them. More than likely, you will not be stealing them away from another church.

Exchange contact information and offer to drive: If a person expresses even the slightest interest in coming to church with you, do your best to exchange contact information. Ask if it would be okay for you to email or call. Also, it is usually best to offer to pick someone up the first time. It is much easier for people to sleep in or make other plans if they have to motivate themselves to drive somewhere new. If you are picking them up, chances are good that they will be ready to go.

Without a visitor – show up a little bit early and stay a little bit late: Frequently, church members do just the opposite. They show up late and leave early and thus avoid interaction with others as much as possible. Even if you don't bring anyone with you, it doesn't mean the church service cannot still be outreach oriented. Do your best to look around and find unfamiliar faces. Make it a point to meet those people. Make visitors feel welcome and sincerely take an interest in who they are. Don't be afraid to engage them in conversation about spiritual things. If they are at church, chances are they are at least somewhat open to this. Ask them how they ended up coming to the church. As we saw in Chapter 19, ask them about their spiritual background. Go from there.

Devote some time after services: An excellent way to minister to others is to invite them out to eat after the service (and, of course, offer to pay). Whether the person is a new acquaintance you met at church or a visitor who came with you in the first place, taking the time to talk with people after the meeting is a fantastic way to sow even more seeds of the Gospel into their lives. During lunch, ask how they enjoyed the service. Ask if the experience was different from other church services they have attended. Find out if there was anything they didn't understand. The point is to make yourself available and look for opportunities to minister the Gospel. If possible, swing the conversation toward their current spiritual life. Ask them if they have ever responded to Jesus and received Him. Ask them if He has changed their life. If the answer is no, ask them if they would like to ask Him to do that today. Take the conversation as far as the other person will allow.

If nothing else, remember this: Inviting people to church is a way to change the world. If you will make an effort to invite people with you, some will come, and some may surrender to Jesus. Conversely, if you don't invite them, they probably won't come, and it is possible they may never hear the Gospel. A simple invitation may literally mean the difference between Heaven and Hell for someone. So, the real question is this: Who are you bringing to church this week?

Discussion Questions:

-Why is inviting people to church an effective way of reaching them with the Gospel?

-What are some of the great things about your church that you might focus on when talking with others?

-How has church attendance changed your life?

Hear Ye, Hear Ye

"I believe I never was more acceptable to my Master than when I was standing to teach those hearers in the open fields . . . . I now preach to ten times more people than I should, if I had been confined to the churches."   -George Whitfield

I have a cousin who is considering changing his last name.

His reasoning is this: There are no surviving males in the family line with the same last name as that of his grandparents, whom he loved deeply – Tom and Esma Stephenson.

The last remaining Stephenson male died several years ago, leaving behind no children. Unless someone does something, this branch of the Stephenson name is going to pass on into history with no surviving lineage. To keep this from happening, my cousin is prepared to take action in a way that not very many people would be willing. He will give up his given family name in order to continue the Stephenson name he holds so dear. Because he loves the family, he will take the steps necessary to guarantee the family name goes on.

What if you were the last Christian on the planet?

> What if you were the last Christian on the planet?

If your life were the last hope for the spreading of the Gospel on Earth, would the Gospel die with you, or would it live on and thrive? Are you living your life in such a way that, even if you were the last Christian alive, Christianity would spread throughout the world? Or are you living in such a way that, if you died, Christianity would fade invisibly into history?

The early Christians were faced with a similar situation from the very beginning. There was a very small percentage of Christians at the onset of the faith. If they had not been passionate, bold, and faithful, Christianity would have died in the womb. They had to do something pretty radical if the faith was to survive. And so, they preached. In fact, from Genesis through Revelation, God's people have preached publicly. They have preached on mountains, in cities, near rivers, and in marketplaces. As long as there have been people gathering in crowds, God has sent His followers to preach to them.

You very well may be the next person whom Jesus calls to preach His name publicly. If you do it, you will be in good company. Jeremiah, Isaiah, Jonah, and Noah all preached publicly. Peter, Paul, Timothy, and

Stephen all proclaimed the Gospel in public forums. John the Baptist preached publicly, and Jesus Himself conducted His preaching in highly public places. It can be argued that Jesus' dominant method of evangelism was public proclamation.

> One of God's chosen methods of reaching the world is public proclamation.

It is interesting to note that the word *"preach"* appears in the New Testament (NIV) thirty-six times, and the word *"proclaim"* appears thirty-two times. In contrast, the word *"share"* appears twice, *"minister"* appears five times, and *"testify"* appears fifteen times in the context of sharing Jesus with others (sometimes in conjunction with *"preach"* or *"proclaim"*). Even a cursory study of the Bible (Old and New Testaments) makes it readily apparent: One of God's chosen methods of reaching the world is public proclamation. Consider the following verses, which represent only a very small fraction of the verses on the subject:

Jeremiah 11:6 - *"**Proclaim all these words** in the towns of Judah and in the streets of Jerusalem."*

Psalm 40:9 - *"**I proclaim** righteousness **in the great assembly**."*

Matthew 3:1-3 - *"In those days **John the Baptist came, preaching in the Desert** of Judea and saying, 'Repent, for the kingdom of heaven is near.' This is he who was spoken of through the prophet Isaiah: 'A voice of one calling in the desert.'"*

Mark 1:14-15 - *"Jesus went into Galilee, proclaiming the good news of God. 'The time has come,' he said. 'The kingdom of God is near. Repent and believe the good news!'"*

John 7:28 - *"Then **Jesus**, still **teaching in the temple courts**, cried out, 'Yes, you know me, and you know where I am from. I am not here on my own, but he who sent me is true. You do not know him.'"*

The reason we don't see more Christians publicly proclaiming the Gospel is not that we think it unscriptural or unnecessary. It is because it is difficult. It is uncomfortable, requires effort, and can be downright scary. But should this keep us from doing it anyway?

> So it is uncomfortable. The cross was uncomfortable.

So it is scary. Having courage in the face of fear breeds a life of excitement and adventure. So it requires effort. We can be "Christians" who spend our time reclining and watching *Seinfeld* re-runs, or we can be Christians who get out of the house and make the Gospel known throughout the world. So it is uncomfortable. The cross was uncomfortable, and yet Jesus endured its public humiliation, knowing that greater good would result. He laid down His desires and did what was necessary. We should do the same. John Wesley once said, *"It is no marvel that the devil does not love field preaching! Neither do I; I love a commodious room, a soft cushion, a handsome pulpit. But where is my zeal if I do not trample all these underfoot in order to save one more soul?"*

336

Am I saying that every Christian should be a street preacher? The short answer is, no, I am not. What I am saying is this: Every Christian should be aware that publicly proclaiming the Gospel is one of the foremost ways that God intended us to reach the world. Many of us should do it, and the others should support and encourage those who choose to do so.

I believe there will be some who read this book who, deep down, know that God would have them begin proclaiming His name in public forums. They are confident, courageous, and capable but have never taken the initiative to step out. If that is you, I challenge you in the name of Jesus to go for it. My guess is that you will love it. Chances are, it will be one of the most exciting times of your life, and not only will you see an impact in the lives of others, but you will see your own faith explode as well.

There are others who may think, *"There is no way I could ever do that. It's just not me."* To those I say, you may be wrong. Allow God to shape your thinking and give you strength. Don't automatically disqualify yourself. God is able to do things with people they never thought possible.

> You may be wrong. Allow God to shape your thinking and give you strength.

I remember a time when I was ministering with a group of people in Europe. We were taking turns preaching from a bench near a nightclub where about a hundred people or so were waiting in line to enter.

Hundreds of others were walking by at different times. At one point, a girl in her early twenties approached our group leader and said, *"I really appreciate what you guys are doing. It's awesome. I wish I had the guts to do something like that. I just don't think I could."* There was something about the way the girl carried herself that told our group leader that she was able; she just needed some prompting. He took her by the hand, walked her a few steps to the bench, helped her up, and encouraged her, *"You can do it. Give it a shot."*

What happened next was amazing. The girl didn't hesitate. The best way I know to describe it is like this: She brought the fire! She began by sharing her testimony and then continued on to preach to the crowd about the need for forgiveness and their eternal destiny. From the time she stepped up on the bench, she seemed like she had been preaching publicly her whole life. All it took was a push in the right direction. The passion she needed and the ability to communicate were there. What she needed was to get started.

I can say for certain that the hardest part of street preaching is getting the first sentence out. The first thirty seconds are the roughest. After that, at least for me, it becomes very easy. It is actually getting up and getting started that is difficult. For those who are willing, the following are a few tips to help "get started."

Start somewhere: Public proclamation of the Gospel does not necessarily mean standing on a street corner for hours on end, dueling back and forth with skeptics, hecklers, and antagonists. It can be as simple as jumping up on a park bench, getting everyone's attention, reading a Bible verse out loud, saying "Thank you for listening," and walking away. At other times it might mean sharing your testimony or reading an entire book of the Bible out loud in public. Just like sharing your faith in conversation, public ministry is something you can work toward in manageable chunks.

Come prepared: Whether you are reading from the Bible directly or preaching a sermon, coming prepared helps greatly in getting started. Just because most of the street preachers we see seem to preach without notes and seem to be able to carry on for hours in an improvisational style doesn't mean you have to do the same. There is nothing wrong with bringing a three-point outline with you, preaching your sermon, and then standing down to talk with people or address questions. Try teaching a Sunday school class every Sunday morning (which will help you in public speaking anyway). Then, when you are finished, adapt your lesson for the streets and preach it at your local park. The difference in your message might be minor. It is the audience and the location that will change.

You also don't have to borrow someone else's preaching style when you're on the streets. Be yourself. Be real. Preach on subjects that have relevance in the lives of the people you are addressing. Talk about God's rules and why obedience is necessary. Talk about the forgiveness of God and how we must forgive others to receive forgiveness ourselves. Talk about purity or temperance. There is an endless supply of topics available. Just make sure to show people they have a need (present the law and/or man's lost state) and offer them the solution (the grace and mercy of God through Jesus).

I highly recommend that every Christian take a public speaking course of some sort. Studies show that public speaking is the number one fear of many people, more so than snakes, spiders, closed spaces, and

> Public speaking is the number one fear of many people.

even death. Not only will taking a course in public speaking equip you to minister to others, but conquering such a powerful fear, I believe, will carry over into many other areas of your life as you are filled with greater confidence. Mark Twain once said, *"There are two types of speakers: those that are nervous and those that are liars."* Every great public speaker was probably, at one time, very nervous. It is completely normal. The trick is to conquer your anxiety and take action anyway. Being prepared will help greatly in conquering fear.

It is also important that we prepare ourselves in other areas as we prepare ourselves for public ministry. If I am effective in challenging individuals in spiritual matters and answering their questions in a one-on-one setting, it will go a long way toward helping me do so in a public preaching forum. Your experiences with individuals today may be preparing you for future experiences with crowds of people.

Choose your location: A good location for public preaching must have two factors. There is also a third factor that is helpful but not absolutely necessary.

340

The first factor is that the location must be *public*. The bottom line is this: If your location is not a public place, you may be breaking the law, and you could be arrested. Make sure the place you choose to preach is not privately owned. A K-mart parking lot is privately owned. The sidewalk on the street nearby is probably not. When in doubt, ask. It is not a bad idea to contact the local authorities and let them know what you are planning. As long as the place you choose is public, you should be relatively safe from any legal hassles.

> **When in doubt, ask.**

The second factor is that the place you choose must have *people*. I won't spend too much time here as this is such an obvious point. There are many public places where people are in abundance: parks, state universities, street corners, and more. The idea is to find a place where people gather and go there.

The third factor, which is helpful but not necessary, is that the location you choose should have good acoustics. It can be difficult to talk loudly enough that a crowd of people can hear you, especially for long periods of time. Choosing a poor location acoustically will only compound this problem. Do your best to find a location where you can project your voice toward a wall or a building. The difference in volume level can be amazing. It is also important to make it clear that, under most circumstances, you must rely on your voice alone to be heard. Using an amplification system can be another way of getting yourself arrested. Unless you have sought out the appropriate authorities and secured permission to use a PA system, it is best to go with your voice alone.

Elevate yourself: Nearly every street preacher you see will have some way of elevating himself or herself. Whether it is a milk crate, a stool, or a bench, elevation is very important when proclaiming the Gospel. It is primarily of benefit so that you can be seen and heard effectively. If a crowd gathers, especially if they stand close to you, it is going to be difficult for you to be seen or heard if you don't have elevation. The other benefit is that having elevation carries with it a sense of authority. A simple difference of eighteen inches may mean the difference between a ho-hum sermon and a message that comes across as both powerful and compelling. It is also important to note that it is more difficult for hecklers to be intimidating if they have to look up to talk to you.

> It is more difficult for hecklers to be intimidating if they have to look up to you.

Be engaging: The same rules of public speaking that apply indoors apply outdoors. Use provocative questions. Make eye contact. Don't use verbal pauses like "uh" and "uhm." Try to stick to a few main points, and don't get sidetracked. If possible, use humor. Adapt your message to the audience when applicable.

Questions are an excellent way to get started. As far as gathering a crowd, the first few questions don't even have to be spiritually related. It can be a good idea to give away money or prizes for the first five people who can answer trivia questions – questions like *"Who shot Abraham Lincoln?"* or *"What is the capital of India?"* I once gave away dozens of Christian CDs as *"prizes"* for answering my questions. This was a one-two punch. They listened to me preach and, hopefully, they listened to the CDs later.

Once a crowd begins to gather, it is easy enough to transition into preaching. Your questions might begin to take on a spiritual overtone – *"What religious leader is the only leader to claim to be God and convince a great deal of the world that He was?"* or *"Who here thinks you are a good person?"* You might also try a fairly straightforward approach – *"You might think I am crazy for giving away money, but there is a reason I am doing so. It is because I care about you enough to make personal sacrifices so you will listen to me. I am giving away free gifts today to demonstrate the love of God, who also gives free gifts."* Or even, *"I am giving away gifts today as a bribe for five minutes of your time. Will you listen?"*

Using a drama team or something unusual like sleight-of-hand tricks can be other ways of capturing a crowd's attention. Learn a great trick, announce that you are going to make a rabbit disappear (or whatever your trick is), perform the trick, and, when finished, transition to the

> *"You were tricked. Is it possible you are being tricked in other, more important areas of your life?"*

Gospel – *"You may have thought the hat was empty, but you were wrong. You were tricked. Is it possible you are being tricked in other, more important areas of your life? Is it possible you have been tricked in your priorities (or your lifestyle, your religious beliefs, whatever)?"*

I have heard of a couple different street preachers who will put on mock funerals in the street, complete with pallbearers, a casket, flowers, and the like. When a crowd gathers to see what is going on, they preach. There are endless means of engaging a crowd on the streets. The important idea here is that it can be done effectively with a bit of imagination and effort.

Bring your friends: This point cannot be stressed enough. One reason to bring friends is for encouragement, prayer, and even effectiveness while preaching. Good friends can lift you up in prayer while you preach, nod their heads and smile when you are doing well, and run interference when necessary. Just having other warm bodies can make a difference in drawing a crowd because a few people standing around and listening will encourage others to do so as well.

The most important reason to bring friends, however, is that they can minister to individuals as you preach. Just asking a listener, *"What do you think about this?"* can open doors of conversation that will impact the listener on a more personal level. Often, when I am street preaching, some individuals will remain at a distance and act as though they are not listening. These can be excellent people for your friends to engage while you continue to minister to the crowd as a whole.

Don't be afraid of difficult situations: If you preach the Gospel publicly, it is going to happen. Someone is going to begin heckling you. William Nicholson once humorously described days he had spent street preaching: *"Those were great days, and great victories were won. We always managed a riot or a revival. Sometimes a riot and no revival, but never a revival without a riot."*

A few years ago, the ministry I am involved with at Murray State University decided to read the entire New Testament, Psalms, Proverbs, and Isaiah out loud on the main thoroughfare of campus. We read in one-hour shifts for eight-hour days, five days in a row. While the overwhelming response on campus seemed positive (or, at the least, neutral), we did have our share of hecklers. My personal favorite was a young man who brought a copy of Dr. Seuss' *Horton Hears a Who,* jumped up on a bench across from where we were reading, and began to read at the top of his lungs. The way I figure it, if someone is going to try to distract people, they should at least be creative. He was.

Situations like this are bound to occur. If the person is trying to be funny or entertaining, at times it can be best to let him or her run the course and steal the attention briefly. Then, when the person is finished, resume preaching. In a situation like that, a humorous question from you (*"What class is that book for?"*) might be in order.

Remember this: Often a heckler is just what you need to draw and keep a crowd. Look at hecklers as a blessing, not a curse. Verbal people are exactly what you want to keep things rolling. A dialogue between a preacher and someone on the street can be far more interesting and effective than just the preacher speaking alone.

> Often a heckler is just what you need to draw and keep a crowd.

If hecklers ask questions that you don't know how to answer, be honest. Tell them that you are not sure how to answer, but you would be happy to investigate and find out for them. Think of every street preaching experience as a learning experience. The next time someone asks you the same question, you will be prepared. If you ever become rattled, be honest with people. If you lose your train of thought, pull out your Bible and read a favorite Bible verse to get yourself going again.

In the very rare occasions that a heckler becomes violent or extremely unruly, the best method can be simply to change locations. This can be as simple as walking only twenty yards away. If the heckler follows, move again. If you do it right, eventually the crowd, more than likely, will turn on the heckler and calm him or her down. Having a recording device can also be helpful. If a person becomes angry and outwardly aggressive, having a video recorder or voice recorder visibly available and pointedly asking the person his or her name might be just enough for the heckler to think twice. In fact, I have heard several street preachers recommend always having a recording device in case of any legal troubles that might result. They are rare, but they do happen.

> Some people will imagine a bearded man in army fatigues and combat boots who hasn't had a bath in weeks.

Minimize the distance: I almost titled this section "Minimize the loony factor." If you ask several people what they think of when they hear the words, "street preacher," they probably are going to describe some kind of raving lunatic. Some people will imagine a bearded man in army fatigues and combat boots who hasn't had a bath in weeks. They

346

imagine him holding a banner that says, *"Repent lest ye perish"* while frothing at the mouth and pointing his finger in the faces of passersby.

While that may describe some of the people who preach on the streets, the stereotype is just that: a stereotype. It is not an accurate portrayal of all people who publicly proclaim the Gospel.

I believe that God would love to raise up a generation of Christians who are absolutely bold in sharing their faith, who refuse to compromise the Gospel message, *and* who come across as completely normal people. When you preach, feel free to wear blue jeans and a t-shirt. If you bring a sign, use language people understand. When you preach, preach in the language you use when talking with your friends. The idea is to minimize the walls between you and your listeners. There are exceptions. For example, I know preachers who dress a certain way and act a certain way in order to draw a crowd of curious listeners. For the most part, however, it is best to come across as a normal person who is abnormally courageous, confident, and concerned about the eternal destiny of others.

> Come across as a normal person who is abnormally courageous, confident, and concerned.

Stick around: When you are finished preaching, make yourself available for one-on-one conversation. Offer to pray with anyone who wants prayer. When feasible, take some time before you leave to minister on a more personal level.

Make it a lifestyle: For some who read this, God doesn't just want you to preach publicly every now and then. For many, He would have us make it a lifestyle – something we do regularly.

There are countless people in the world who will never step foot in a church. Our preaching outside church walls may be the only way for them to hear the Gospel. Salvation Army founder William Booth said, *"No sort of defense is needed for preaching outdoors, but it would take a very strong argument to prove that a man who has never preached beyond the walls of his meetinghouse has done his duty."*

We have the great privilege and responsibility of bringing the Gospel outside the church and into the public places of our world. God may be calling you to lead the way in your community. Will you respond?

Discussion Questions:

-What comes to mind when you hear the words "street preacher"?

-In your opinion, why don't more Christians proclaim the Gospel openly in public forums?

-Can you come up with any ideas that might be useful in drawing a crowd?

-What is a location within fifty miles of your home that would be good for a public proclamation of the Gospel?

*Rea*lational Evangelism

"The Gospel is only good news if it gets there in time."
- Carl F. H. Henry

Sharing Jesus with our friends and family is a double-edged sword.

On one hand, sharing the Gospel of Jesus with people we know personally can lend credibility, respect, and trust. When an individual knows us personally and has seen that Jesus has made a real and lasting difference in our lives, we may be able to minister to that person in ways that no other individual ever could.

On the other hand, sharing the Gospel with people we know personally can be incredibly intimidating. Many times it is our friends and family who present the greatest challenge in our lives as far as our personal witness is concerned. For some reason, talking to a stranger on the street may seem to be far easier than it would be to talk to our aunts, uncles, parents, grandparents, classmates, coworkers, and bowling buddies.

Any Christian who is honest would probably agree. Sometimes, having a relationship with an individual makes sharing the Gospel with that person even more difficult. At other times, having a close relationship makes all the difference in the world. The effectiveness of a relational approach varies from situation to situation. Because of this, we need to be careful to keep relational outreach in its proper place – as one way of reaching some people, but certainly not the only way of reaching all people. In this chapter we are going to discuss ways to maximize our relationships and help us become more effective in sharing the Gospel with friends and family.

Interact with people: This should probably go without saying, but touching on it briefly may be important. Interaction with people often requires effort. Whether it is a cousin who lives across town or a buddy whom you haven't seen for a while, sometimes it takes effort to get in touch, and, as Christians, we need to be willing to make that effort. We never know when inviting a friend to lunch may turn into one of the most significant events in that friend's lifetime.

It is also important that Christians learn to place themselves in situations that require interaction with others on a regular basis. More and more, our society is developing into a community of recluses who hide away in our homes, watch television, play video games, and have very little to do with others. Thirty years ago, people typically knew all of their neighbors as close friends; today they hardly even know their neighbors' names. This tendency is a major stumbling block to the advancement of the Gospel. There are many, many opportunities for Christians to interact with others. From PTA to the local rock-climbing gym and from community service centers to political organizations, interaction with people is readily available. For many Christians, one of the first steps in obeying God is getting out of the house and actually making contact with other human beings.

> This tendency is a major stumbling block to the advancement of the Gospel.

Make and/or take the opportunity: The following sentence may be the most important one in this chapter. Read it carefully. Relational evangelism doesn't become evangelism until evangelism is introduced into the relationship. Did you catch that? I want to say it again. Relational evangelism doesn't become evangelism until evangelism is introduced into the relationship.

Richard Bond, the Vice President of Youth EE (Evangelism Explosion), in describing some of the difficulties faced with a relational model of evangelism, said the following: *"I would suggest that the error is not in the approach to the lost but rather in the lack of using opportunities when they present themselves."* In order for our relationships to become effective in reaching people with the Good News about Jesus, at some point we are going to have to share that Good News with them. And the sooner we do this the better. The job of the Christian is not to discern the "best time" for that to be the case. The job of the Christian is simply to look for or create an opportunity, present the Gospel, and go from there. Just like with a stranger, if the person is receptive, give thanks to God and take the person as far toward Jesus as he or she will allow. If someone becomes irritated or even angry, it is acceptable to back off and give the person space. The point is that until you actually talk to the person, it can be very difficult to know how he or she is going to react. Too many times, Christians use relationship as a *substitute* for evangelism rather than as a tool that creates evangelism opportunities.

As a general rule, do your best to make sure that every one of your friends and family members has heard at least one clear Gospel presentation. This might be as simple as inviting your friend to church and talking with him afterward about what he thought. It could be as upfront as sitting your aunt down and asking for fifteen minutes of her time. Tell her that you want to share something with her that you consider very important. If she is unwilling to listen, she is unwilling to listen. There is nothing you can do about it except watch for a future opportunity. If she (or your friend or neighbor or another relative) is willing to listen, be faithful to explain the Gospel. Tell the person your story, ask questions, offer to give him or her a Bible, etc. Take advantage of whatever doors may be opened.

Hurry up: One of the key dangers to a solely relational approach to evangelism is the danger of a lack of urgency. It can be tempting to wait for *"just the right time"* when, in reality, time is not guaranteed. Most

Christians would agree that for every individual, tomorrow is not a guarantee. In fact, in witnessing to people, phrases like, *"What if you died tomorrow?"* or *"You are not guaranteed of your next breath"* might come up, but in our ministry to friends and family, the same urgency is often lacking. We must do our best to share the Gospel in our relationships as soon as we can. In Matthew 24, Jesus spoke with His disciples about the need for urgency.

Matthew 24:37-44 - *"As it was in the days of Noah, so it will be at the coming of the Son of Man. For in the days before the flood, people were eating and drinking, marrying and giving in marriage, up to the day Noah entered the ark; and they knew nothing about what would happen until the flood came and took them all away. That is how it will be at the coming of the Son of Man. Two men will be in the field; one will be taken and the other left. Two women will be grinding with a hand mill; one will be taken and the other left.* **Therefore keep watch, because you do not know on what day your Lord will come.** *But understand this: If the owner of the house had known at what time of night the thief was coming, he would have kept watch and would not have let his house be broken into. So you also must* **be ready, because the Son of Man will come at an hour when you do not expect him."**

> *"Keep watch . . . you do not know on what day your Lord will come."*

Our witness to our friends and family must be accompanied by a sense of urgency, both because the situation actually is urgent (we do not know when they will breathe their last) and because effectiveness requires urgency. If our witness to them is not at least relatively urgent, it actually sends a message that says, *"Don't worry; you have plenty of time."* That is not the message we want to send.

You are in good company: One of the reasons that relational evangelism can be so difficult is that, unlike experiencing rejection from a total stranger, experiencing rejection from a close friend or family member can be crushingly painful. When a stranger says, *"You're a closed-minded bigot,"* it can really hurt. When the same words come from your father or a close friend, it can be devastating.

Some of the hardest people in the world to minister to are the people closest to us. It is not the strangers on the street or casual acquaintances who typically give us the hardest time; it is often the people in our own home, the people at work, and the people we care about the most. Even Jesus experienced this. In Mark 6:4, Jesus declared, *"Only **in his hometown, among his relatives and in his own house is a prophet without honor.**"* In Matthew 10:36 Jesus said, *"**A man's enemies will be the members of his own household.**"* And, in Matthew 13:54-58 we find the following passage: *"**Coming to his hometown**, he began teaching the people in their synagogue, and they were amazed. 'Where did this man get this wisdom and these miraculous powers?' they asked. 'Isn't this the carpenter's son? Isn't his mother's name Mary, and aren't his brothers James, Joseph, Simon and Judas? Aren't all his sisters with us? Where then did this man get all these things?' And **they took offense at him** . . . . **He did not do many miracles there because of their lack of faith.**"*

So we see that even God's Son was limited in His ability to reach the people who knew Him best. If and when you experience rejection from people you care about, realize this: You are in good company. When Jesus was nailed to the cross, the people who were screaming and jeering were probably some of the same people He had been ministering to over the three years prior to that moment. The same people who only days before had welcomed Him into Jerusalem, waving palm branches and placing them at His feet, were the same people screaming, *"Crucify Him! Crucify Him!"* It was His good friend Judas, in whom He had invested His life, who betrayed Him for money. It was one of His closest friends, Peter, who, for fear of being associated with Him, denied on oath even knowing Him.

Jesus knew that His message divided people, and He wanted us to be prepared.

Matthew 10:21-37 - *"**Brother will betray brother to death, and a father his child; children will rebel against their parents** and have them put to death. All men will hate you because of me, but he who stands firm to the end will be saved . . .. For **I have come to turn a man against his father, a daughter against her mother, a daughter-in-law against her mother-in-law – a man's enemies will be the members of his own household.** Anyone who loves his father or mother more than me is not worthy of me; anyone who loves his son or daughter more than me is not worthy of me."*

Matthew 19:29 - *"And everyone who has left houses or brothers or sisters or father or mother or children or fields for my sake will receive a hundred times as much and will inherit eternal life."*

Luke 12:51-53 - *"Do you think I came to bring peace on earth? No, I tell you, but division. From now on there will be five in one family divided against each other, three against two and two against three. They will be divided, father against son and son*

against father, mother against daughter and daughter against mother, mother-in-law
against daughter-in-law and daughter-in-law against mother-in-law."

It is a very hard truth of scripture, but it is truth nonetheless. The Gospel will divide people, even those people who normally would seem inseparable. We must remain faithful to God, however, even at the expense of relationships we hold dear.

An interesting question to ask yourself is this: How do you think that the friends and families of Peter, James, John, and the apostle Paul heard about the Gospel? You can bet that they heard about it because these men shared with them openly. They weren't afraid of the consequences. They knew whose side they were on. Chances are, these men didn't spend their lives fishing, cooking, and eating with their friends and family, looking for that one prime opportunity that might arise so that they could maybe, someday, when the time was right, possibly convince them to become a Christian. I believe it is safe to say that these men were quite open about what they had experienced and sorted out their relationships from there. Should we be any different?

Pray: So, let's assume that at one point or another, you have shared the Gospel with someone you know personally and that person has not responded as positively as you would like. What can you do?

The first step is to pray. We have already discussed in a prior chapter how prayer and outreach go hand in hand. I am convinced that, when it comes to friends and family, prayer plays an even bigger role because, as mentioned earlier, prayer that God honors is persistent, and nothing will keep Christians on their knees longer than knowing their dear friend, son, daughter, or mother has no guarantee of salvation. In truth, no one else is going to pray for your friends like you will pray for your friends. In a great way, the responsibility lies with you.

When people you love reject Christ, there are many ways you can go about praying. Pray that their eyes are opened. Pray that the enemy's plans against them will fail. Pray that, like the prodigal son, the source of their

> No one else is going to pray for your friends like you will.

current affections will dry up and leave them hungry for God. Pray that God will open other doors for you to share with them. Pray they would have unrest and anxiety over their current spiritual state. Use your imagination and pray. Pray often.

Continue to build bridges: If a person rejects your message, it isn't always a rejection of you as a person. Sometimes it will be, but often it is not. Whenever possible, do your best to continue to build bridges. If the bridge between you and another person is to be torn down, let it be the other person who does the destruction. Even then, make it clear that you will always be available to him or her. Whenever possible, continue in your relationships with people for as long as you can without compromising the Gospel and the urgency of the Gospel. If people demand to be left alone, you should probably respect their wishes and leave them alone. However, it is important that you also remain available to them in case sometime in the future they decide that they don't want to be left alone any longer. It is often the people who have rejected you most harshly who later will be the ones who come to you for prayer in a time of need. Continue to love people with devotion, serve people with humility, and patiently respect the walls that they have built around themselves. You never know when a hole in those walls might appear.

Keep on pressin' on: The second way to minister to your friends and family who have not received Jesus is to continue reaching out to others and trust God to minister to your loved ones. God has set a law in effect that gives us hope for our friends and family. It is the law of sowing and reaping.

2 Corinthians 9:6 - *"Remember this: Whoever sows sparingly will also reap sparingly, and whoever sows generously will also reap generously."*

Galatians 6:7-9 - *"Do not be deceived: God cannot be mocked. A man reaps what he sows . . . . **Let us not become weary in doing good, for at the proper time we will reap a harvest if we do not give up.**"*

If we will do what we can do, God will do what we can't do. If we will clearly share the Gospel, God will supernaturally change the hearts of people. If we will work diligently and give generously, God will meet our needs bountifully. If we will study intensely, God will fill our minds with His thoughts and character. Likewise, if we will pursue God's greatest passion – the souls of men, God will passionately pursue those we cherish. Every time we share the Gospel with another person, we are sharing with someone's mother, someone's brother, or someone's coworker. If we will be faithful to share Jesus with the people we encounter, God will be faithful to send a witness to the people we personally care about the most.

Are you concerned about the eternal destiny of the people you love but find that some of them are extremely resistant to your efforts or even to any mention of spiritual things? One of the best things that you can do for those people (in addition to praying) is to do your best to reach others. Place them in God's hands and trust Him to do the work that you can't seem to do yourself. It is only one of many ways that God takes care of those who serve Him.

Discussion Questions:

-Why can it be so difficult to share the Gospel with the people we care about the most?

-How can we maintain an urgency in our Gospel message and yet continue to build bridges with non-believers?

-What experiences have you had sharing the Gospel with your friends and family?

-Which of your friends and family have never heard the Gospel from you?

"Missions are the chief end of the Church . . . . the chief end of the ministry ought to be to equip the Church for this. Each congregation is meant to be a training class."

– Andrew Murray

Give Em' A Survey

"The best thing that we can do for someone is to lead them to heaven."

-Rick Warren

Pastor David Ferrel was very skeptical about the use of surveys for sharing the Gospel.

Doubting their effectiveness, he agreed to give them a try anyway and set off with a partner. And then, his very first survey blew his mind. It was, quite literally, a miracle.

> It was, quite literally, a miracle.

For his first survey, Pastor Dave approached a young man who was sitting on a park bench. As soon as he asked the young man to take the survey, he recognized him. This same young man, a couple of months earlier, had burst into a Bible study that Pastor Dave had been leading and caused a commotion. He had verbally berated the members of the

Bible study for being Christians and had told them how foolish they were for believing in such an outdated and archaic book as the Bible. He had used harsh language in insulting everyone in the room and made it quite clear that he had no respect whatsoever for any Christians. Pastor Dave later admitted that, if he had recognized the young man before he approached him, he never would have asked him to take the survey. However, it was obvious that the young man did not recognize him, and he was willing to answer the questions, so Pastor Dave dove in. If he was skeptical before, now he was certain: That survey was going nowhere. What happened next was beyond what he could ever imagine.

The survey consisted of questions such as these: *Do you believe Jesus is the Son of God? Do you believe in Heaven? Do you believe in Hell?* While asking the questions, Pastor Dave was thinking to himself, *"I can't wait to get away from this guy."* As far as he was concerned, his time would be much better served somewhere else. That's why, when the young man began sobbing and sucking in his breath, Dave wasn't sure what to think. He was quite stunned. The young man, with tears streaming down his face, explained why he was crying. Just ten minutes before Pastor Dave showed up, the young man sat on that park bench and prayed for the first time in a very long time. He had said to God, *"God, if you are there, I need you to show me and show me now."* Pastor Dave had no idea when he approached that he was walking in as God's answer to prayer.

The young man did not hesitate to pray with Pastor Dave to surrender his life to Jesus. In fact, that evening he attended Pastor Dave's church and testified to the congregation about what God had done to reveal

Himself. It was an amazing testimony as to what can happen when a person makes the effort to reach out to others. One might argue that it wasn't necessarily the method of using surveys that made the difference but rather that it was a supernatural move of God, and I would agree. However, I would also argue that people who make a consistent effort to share the Gospel with others will see far more situations in which God moves than people who don't. As with many other methods we have discussed, surveys are one of many very effective ways of putting ourselves in a position to see God's hand move in the lives of other people. As a tool for reaching others, surveys work. I have seen literally hundreds of people pray to receive Jesus as a result of surveys.

> People who make a consistent effort to share the Gospel with others will see far more situations in which God moves.

Surveys or questionnaires are effective for many reasons:

> Doing so with a survey can be considered socially acceptable behavior.

People are used to taking surveys: Between online questionnaires, phone calls, people with clipboards at the mall, and postcards received in the mail, people are used to being asked for their opinions. While it might be considered breaking a social norm to approach strangers cold turkey and ask them about their religious beliefs, doing so with a survey in hand can be considered socially acceptable behavior. Using a survey can tear down walls of discomfort that might be constructed in other approaches.

Surveys encourage active listening: It is easy for Christians to become so focused on the message they want to deliver that they don't take the time to listen to others and find out what they believe. Used properly, surveys focus on listening and responding, which allows us to minister to people in a more personal way.

Surveys teach the art of asking pointed questions: In a previous chapter I covered the necessity of learning to ask good, open-ended questions. Surveys can go a long way in teaching us what questions work well and what questions don't. After doing surveys for many years, if I am ever in a conversation that seems to be faltering, I can just recall questions that I have used in surveys and introduce them into the conversation.

Surveys make a great evangelism training tool: Because people are used to answering survey questions (and some people absolutely love to give their opinions), surveys can be an excellent introductory method of approaching strangers. They give a well-defined format for the conversation to develop, and they can be tailor-made to ask the most important questions. Over time, Christians who often do surveys will have seen many different situations and will be equipped to speak effectively with nearly anyone from any background or point of view. In addition, just asking the questions is a great ministry to make people think about spiritual things. If a Christian gives a survey to someone but then doesn't feel equipped to share the Gospel with that particular person, he or she can always say, *"Thank you for your time"* and walk away. As such, even for Christians who are new to sharing their faith, surveys give the opportunity to engage people in conversation, see if they want to talk further, and decide for themselves to what level they want to go.

So, now that we have established that doing surveys can be an excellent way of sharing the Gospel, where do we go from there? How can we develop them and use them to maximize our efforts?

Come up with a survey: You can develop your own surveys or use someone else's. My personal favorite is one that we have developed for use in our campus ministry. It is available for download on our website at **www.godsgreatestpassion.com**. Regardless of whether you use ours or develop your own, the idea is to come up with questions that will stimulate discussion about spiritual things and segue into direct questions about a person's beliefs and ultimately that person's eternal destination and standing with Jesus Christ.

> Come up with questions that will stimulate discussion about spiritual things.

Come up with a place: Surveys can be done anywhere people gather. As a general rule, public places such as parks, state schools, and street corners can be the best places. In addition, as long as they are done on a more personal level (not a mass of people from the local church) they can also be done in shopping malls, bus stations, and other privately owned places. Just remember, if you are asked not to do surveys in a particular location that is not a public place, be respectful and find somewhere else.

Approach someone: It will be up to you whether you want to approach individuals or groups of people. I have found in years of doing surveys that both can be effective. Often, approaching an individual will encourage free expression, honesty, and intimacy, while approaching a group of people might stifle that a bit but can create other interesting times of ministry. I have seen it many times that a group of friends will take a survey together and play off of one another – *"Don't let him fool you. He ain't a Christian," "What?! I didn't know you believed that,"* or *"Hey, man, hold on a second, let me hear what he has to say."* Different people create different dynamics. I can think of several occasions when I approached a group of people and gave one of them a survey but ended up sharing the Gospel with the rest of the group as several people became interested in what was going on.

Once you have decided whom you want to approach, I have found the easiest way to initiate the conversation is to say, *"Excuse me, have you taken this survey yet?"* If you ask them, *"Do you want to take a survey?"* or *"Do you have time to take a survey?"* many times the answer will be *"no."* *"Have you taken this survey yet?"* seems to generate far more positive responses. Sometimes people will respond with, *"What is it about?"* If they ask this question, I have found it best to say, *"It is asking your opinion on different issues. For example, the first question is . . . ."* I try not to tell them it is a *"religious"* or *"Christian"* survey because many times this will alter their responses.

As a general rule, once someone has agreed to do the survey, it is a good idea to introduce yourself – *"I'm H.L. What's your name?"* Try to use the person's name periodically throughout the survey – *"Joe, how often do you pray – daily, weekly, occasionally, hardly ever, or never?"*

Ask the questions: While asking the questions, do your best not to comment on their answers unless they invite you to do so. (Also, watch your non-verbal communication. If a person says something you disagree with, don't crease your brow, frown, and look at the person with a mean expression. Remain emotionless.) The idea is to go all the way through the survey and then ask for permission to dialogue further. Remember, you invited them to do a survey, not have a discussion. Every survey will be different. Some people will be standoffish, and others will be warm and friendly. Some will be very serious, and some will joke around. When they see that the survey's content is of a spiritual nature, some will become very polite and begin to call you *"sir"* or *"ma'am"*. Others will become aloof and act annoyed. Regardless of their response, the idea is to get through the questions.

Transition: The most fearful part of giving surveys for most people is the end. Many people just don't know what to do. There are several methods, but the one I have found to be most useful is simply to be

> The most fearful part of giving surveys for most people is the end.

honest and straightforward. After asking the questions and completing the survey, I might say to a friendly person, *"As you have probably guessed by now, we are out doing this survey as a way to engage people in conversation about spiritual things. I noticed that you said you grew up in church but haven't been back in a while. Why not?"* To a person who seems more standoffish, I might say,

"I'm sure you have guessed this already, but the reason we are doing this survey is to get out and talk to people about spiritual things. Would you mind if I ask you a couple of questions that aren't on the survey just to clarify a few of the things you mentioned?" (They might nod their head or grunt their approval.) *"I noticed you said that you don't believe Jesus is the Son of God. Who do you believe He was?"* Again, every survey is going to be different, but the transition into further conversation can be the same. Honesty is the best policy.

Talk further: I couldn't tell you how many times I have asked a person to take a survey, and the person agreed but said he or she only had a few minutes to spare or was in a hurry, and then forty-five minutes later that same person was still there actively engaging me in conversation.

Once you have completed the survey, you will have a much better idea where to go from there. If the person is a Christian, encourage him or her in Christian growth and outreach – to read the Bible every day, to attend church regularly, to share his or her faith with others, etc. If the person is a non-Christian who believes Jesus was the Son of God, encourage him or her to surrender to Him by ministering through your testimony or the Word of God. Challenge non-believers with the Law or the ideas of selfishness that we discussed earlier. Challenge them with their need to be born again. If the person is a non-Christian who doesn't believe Jesus is the Son of God, ask his or her opinion on the identity of Jesus. Who was He? Was He a liar? Lunatic? Legend? Or was He Lord? Again, because every survey is different, there is no set way to determine where the conversation should go in each situation. God will touch different people in different ways. However, as we practice and remain faithful, we will learn to hear from God in each particular circumstance, we will learn how to answer the hard questions, and we will learn how to patiently love people and help them in their spiritual journeys.

Pray: At the end of each survey and conversation, when it is feasible, offer to pray. If they have indicated prayer requests, pray for those. If they have never been born again, ask them if they would like to pray to Jesus to come into their lives and make them new. If they indicate they would not, let them know that they can call out to Jesus at any time and encourage them not to delay in doing so.

> Offer to pray with your eyes open.

If the person is uncomfortable praying in public, offer to pray with your eyes open so that those nearby will have no idea what is going on – it will look like you are still continuing to have a conversation. Just remember, prayer works, and prayers where two agree together work even more (Matthew 18:19). If they indicate a desire to receive Jesus, don't hesitate to lead them in a prayer. You can either have them repeat after you or give them some basic instructions and encourage them to create their own prayer. Again, if they do so, try to exchange contact information with them and stay in touch. If they don't have a good local church, encourage them and help them in finding one.

Learn: Take every survey as a learning experience. If you encounter someone of a religion or philosophy that you have never encountered before, don't panic. Share your testimony with the person and then go home and investigate further so that the next time you will be more equipped. If the person is dealing with a particular problem that you are not sure how to respond to, go to the Word of God and also talk with qualified people. The next time you will have Bible verses and advice on hand that can help in that particular situation. If people ask questions that you don't know how to answer, be honest. Tell them you don't know, but offer to find out. Exchange contact info with them, and get back to them after you have researched the answer.

Do some more surveys: The best method of learning how to do surveys effectively is to do them a lot. Do them often. Find a friend who also wants to share his or her faith regularly and set up a weekly time to go out in your community and do surveys. You will be amazed at how many great spiritual conversations you will have and how many contacts you will develop. I am of the opinion that doing surveys is one of the easiest and most effective ways we will see of reaching people with the Gospel in our lifetimes. After more than a decade of doing surveys regularly, I can attest that they are effective. Through regular use, I have learned more about sharing the Gospel with others than any book, seminar, or lecture could ever teach me. My prayer for you is that you will begin doing them and see the same results I have.

You might also consider using a survey to do role-playing with a friend. Whatever survey you choose to use, pretend your friend is a stranger on the street and ask him or her the questions. At first you might designate the kind of person he or she should role-play – *"Okay, this time you are a person who was raised in church but doesn't care about church anymore."* After you have become more comfortable with different types of people, you might give your friend free reign to choose any personality or background they desire. Eventually you might ask your friend to do his or her best to stump you. Practice with your friends at home, and even more regularly in real life, and I guarantee it won't be long before you feel comfortable sharing the Gospel with nearly anyone.

Discussion Questions:

-When was the last time you took a survey of some sort?

-What are some good questions that you might ask on a survey in order to discuss the Gospel message with people?

-Where is a good location in your town where you might do surveys?

-What are some personalities or spiritual backgrounds that it might be useful for your friends to role-play?

(If this book is a part of a Bible study or training course, now would be a good time to do some role-playing.)

"Everybody can be great . . . because anybody can serve. You don't have to have a college degree to serve. You don't have to make your subject and verb agree to serve. You only need a heart full of grace – a soul generated by love."

-Dr. Martin Luther King, Jr.

The Bridge of Service

"If anyone wants to be first, he must be the very last, and the servant of all."

-Jesus Christ

It is Judgment Day.

All the nations of the world stand before the throne of God. Billions of people are on their knees before Jesus, the King of Kings and the Lord of Lords. Some are crying tears of joy as they worship their Savior and view Him for the first time. Others, however, are crying in abject fear. Sweat is pouring from their faces, and they can't seem to catch their breath. They

> Some declare Him Lord out of love; others out of fear.

are nearly in a panic as they realize what is happening to them. Without exception, every individual is declaring the Lordship of Jesus (Philippians 2:10-11). Some declare Him Lord out of love; others do so out of fear, hoping that if they recognize Jesus now it might not be too late.

Suddenly Jesus stands to His feet and begins walking into the crowd. The vast multitude hushes in anticipation. As He walks forward, the crowd stands and begins to part. He looks around into the eyes of those near Him and then turns, nodding toward an angel standing nearby. The angel responds by launching himself high into the air, spinning rapidly as he ascends. On cue, other massive angels, until now unseen, move in from the corners of the crowd and begin to separate people into groups, pressing forward and driving the people before them like shepherds driving sheep. The people are helpless to resist, and it is not long before some begin to wail and scream as they are separated from loved ones. Others are driven ahead by force, scratching and clawing the ground in a useless attempt to prevent the inevitable. Still others walk zombie-like with their heads down and shoulders slumped, their bodies quaking in silent sobs. Jesus oversees the entire process, and slowly but surely the immense crowd is separated (Matthew 13:40-43).

Returning to His throne, Jesus stands and addresses the nations – now in two groups, one on His right and one on His left. His voice is heard with perfect clarity by every soul as He begins addressing those

> On cue, other massive angels, until now unseen, move in from the corners of the crowd.

on His right side. He smiles with unexplainable joy and compassion in His eyes as He speaks: *"My beloved ones. Welcome! You could never know how I have looked forward to this day. I have prepared a place for you, and it is now yours for the taking. It is your reward for following Me. When you saw people hungry, you gave them food. When they were naked, you gave them something to wear. When they were sick or in prison, you visited them and cared for them. Even when they were strangers –*

you didn't even know if you could trust them – you went out of your way to help. In blessing them, you were blessing Me. You have shown your love for Me by loving others. Now, come inside. I have great things in store for you."

Then, turning toward those on His left, Jesus' expression changes. His smile dissolves, and the joy and compassion seen in His eyes vanish. They are replaced by fire as He stares at the crowd. After a silence that seems to last forever He speaks:

"YOU!"

"I showed you nothing but love. I gave everything, even My own life for you, and in your pride you never thought of anyone but yourself. Your punishment is well deserved. Did you not see the hungry people around you? You could have helped, but you were too wrapped up in your own riches, games, and social life to even take notice. Selfish people! All around you people were dying of sickness and rotting in prisons. All they needed was someone to care – someone to reach out in a spirit of love. You couldn't do it because the Spirit of love was nowhere near you. You wanted nothing to do with real love."

> *"All they needed was someone to care."*

At this point, people from all over the crowd begin to yell and scream. Some claim there *"must be some mistake."* Others complain about their circumstances, and still others justify their behavior by claiming ignorance. People begin to push and shove in their attempts to be heard. Some climb on the shoulders and heads of others, screaming out to Jesus. In many places, fights break out as people punch, kick, and shove one another.

"SILENCE!"

The voice of Jesus breaks through with authority, and the crowd is instantly silent. Thousands toward the front are thrown to the ground by the power of His voice. *"I've had enough. I will not hear you any more. Away from Me!"*

At this, the angels begin to prod the crowd on the left toward an unknown destination – *"the eternal fire, prepared for the devil and his angels"* (Matthew 10:41). The crowd on the right is then led to *"eternal life"* (Matthew 10:46).

The above is, of course, a rendition of the parable of the sheep and the goats as told by Jesus in Matthew Chapter 25, which holds particular interest in any discussion about serving others because in this parable Jesus makes it clear that for those who will inherit eternal life, acts

> A person who has been born again through the Spirit of Jesus Christ will be a person who moves from intention to action.

of service are a natural and necessary part of their lives. A person who has been born again through the Spirit of Jesus Christ will be a person who not only desires to serve others but also moves from intention to action. This person's life will show the fruit of service to other people.

In John 13:1-17, Jesus set the example for His followers when it comes to acts of service by washing the feet of His disciples. In verses 14-15, Jesus says, *"Now that I, your Lord and Teacher, have washed your feet, you also should wash one another's feet.* **I have set you an example that you should do as I have done for you.***"*

In the second chapter of Philippians, we are told that our *"attitude should be the same as that of Christ Jesus: Who, being in very nature God, did not consider equality with God something to be grasped, but made himself nothing,* **taking the very nature of a servant.***"* In the first part of this same chapter we are told, *"Consider others better than yourselves. Each of you should look not only to your own interests but also to the interests of others."*

> We must be concerned about the well-being of others in every area.

Jesus desired that His followers be people who take an implicit interest in the wants and needs of other people, not just concerning spiritual things but in every area of life, from emotional to physical and from social to financial. While a life focused on others is primarily concerned with the spiritual well-being of other people, it does not stop there. We must be concerned with the well-being of others in every area of their lives. John said it best in 3 John 1:2 when he said, *"Dear friend, I pray that you may enjoy good health and* **that all may go well with you,** *even as your soul is getting along well."* The truth of the matter is this: As we seek to help others achieve soundness in their spiritual lives, we must also seek soundness for them in every other area. Serving others is the Word of God in action. It is the advancement of God's Kingdom on Earth and a most definite bridge to evangelism. For some people, the best way to reach them is to serve them. With that in mind, here are some practical steps toward incorporating service with evangelism.

Come up with a plan: There are literally thousands of ideas that can be utilized in this area. Servantevangelism.com alone lists hundreds of ideas that can be used to reach people in various settings from sporting events to parks and from high

> Come up with some way, any way, of serving the people in your community.

schools to shopping centers. Their ideas run from giving away free stamps on tax day to dog washing and everything in between. The idea is to come up with some way, any way, of serving the people in your community in a way that is practical and would be appreciated. The following is a small list of ideas designed to stimulate your thinking and help you come up with other ideas.

Service Giveaways: Are you a car mechanic, chiropractor, or accountant? Do you have a set of skills that might be used to bless others? Consider doing so. Contact charitable organizations in your area, let them know that you are available to help people, and see what they might suggest. Consider giving free service to every twentieth or thirtieth customer you serve (or any number of your choosing). Any skill set you have is a skill set that can be used to bless people. Let them know that you are doing so as an example of the love and generosity of Jesus.

Outreach to Internationals: Do you have a college or university nearby? If so, contact the international student department and let them know that you are available to participate in a conversational English class or that your home is available for students studying abroad. Do you speak Spanish and live in an area with a large contingency of Hispanic Americans? Offer to help them learn English, and set up a weekly time to meet with them. Deuteronomy 10:19 says, *"You are to love those who are aliens."* Look for opportunities to serve those around you who come from other nations.

Nursing Home Visitation: James 1:27 tells us, *"Religion that God our Father accepts as pure and faultless is this: to look after orphans and widows in their distress."*

Often in America, because we are so blessed, it is easy to think that there is no one around us who really needs our help. In reality, we need only look to the nearest nursing home to see people who desperately need the touch of someone who will care enough to make a difference in their lives. Many nursing home residents are left completely abandoned and can go months and even years without a loved one stopping by. You can make a difference. Consider scheduling a weekly time to spend your lunch break or some time in the evenings at a nearby nursing home. Ask the nurses which residents rarely see visitors, and make it a point to spend time with them. I guarantee you will be as blessed as the people you visit – probably even more so.

The Service of Prayer: Perhaps you could install a separate phone line somewhere in your home and place a small advertisement in your local paper offering prayer for those who need it. If time is an issue, place the appropriate time in the ad and disconnect the phone during other times, or connect an answering machine with an encouraging note instructing callers to leave a message with the assurance that you will pray for them.

> **People will come to you with their needs.**

The possibility of ministry with this idea is unfathomable. People will come to you with their needs, knowing that they are entering into an area connected to spiritual things.

Not only will you be able to pray with people and serve them through compassion, connection with another person, and even godly advice, but you also will most likely be able to share the Gospel on a regular basis. Liveprayer.com is an excellent example of the service of prayer. It is a website dedicated to helping people by offering personal prayer twenty-four hours a day, seven days a week. At this point, they receive more than 20,000 visitors and 40,000 email prayer requests every day.

Other Ideas: Come up with your own ideas. Next time there is a heavy rain, go to a busy area in town with a huge golf umbrella and offer to walk people to their cars. (Introduce yourself as *"Such-and-such from such-and-such church . . . . We are out here serving people in the community. May I offer to walk you to your car?"* The idea is to minimize their concerns that you are some kind of psychopath.) If you live in an apartment complex or dorm setting, grab a friend, some gloves, and some cleaning materials, and go door to door offering to clean bathrooms. Also try this in public places such as stores and gas stations. You are sure to leave an impression. Consider taking the time to mow not only your own yard but your neighbor's yard as well. Of course, we have not even covered involvement in some of the most important acts of service that take place on a much larger scale, such as medical missions, organizations committed to hunger relief, and disaster recovery services. The idea is to brainstorm and come up with ways to serve others. When in doubt, remember the age-old adage, *"Find a need and fill it."*

Implement your ideas: It is no good to come up with ideas if you are not going to put the ideas into action. It might work best to come together with several believers, brainstorm a list of ideas, and then set a time and date for

> Go door to door offering to clean bathrooms.

your first service project as a team – *"Okay, we'll meet this Friday at 4:30 p.m. for (your activity.)"* Having other people involved can go a long way toward motivating you to get started.

Turn *"Service"* into *"Service Evangelism"*: It is very important that we understand the distinction between acts of service and service evangelism. Just as in relationships, service does not become service evangelism until evangelism is connected with the service. In other words, you can serve people greatly and do very little toward the salvation of their souls. In fact, Christians who serve without any kind of Gospel message may in some ways be sending a message that good deeds are enough and that the Gospel of salvation through Jesus is secondary. We must be careful to always place the message of the

Gospel at the forefront of our efforts. As we have seen time and time again, it is the Word of God planted in people's hearts that helps them spiritually. Every physical, emotional, and financial need of a person can be completely filled, and yet that person can still pass into eternity without Jesus. While service alone is a wonderful advancement of the Kingdom of God on Earth, we must recognize that it is also an excellent way to build opportunities to share the Word of God with others.

When you serve others, do your best to make sure that some kind of opportunity is available for the Word of God to touch their lives. This might be as simple as one or two sentences letting them know why you are serving them, or it might be much more in depth than that. If, after you mow your neighbor's yard, he or she comes to thank you, you might explain that Jesus has blessed you abundantly and you want to share His love with others. Then, engage your neighbor in conversation as we studied in prior chapters: *"Do you have a religious background? Do you have a church you go to around here? What do you think about Jesus? If you died today, what would happen to you?"* As always, if people don't want to hear it, they don't want to hear it, but more often than not, with a good bridge of service to walk across, you will have built some degree of rapport with them that can be used to minister in their lives. If your service involves shortened contact with others (the umbrella idea, for example) you might just tell them, *"Have a blessed day"* and hand them an invitation to your church.

Whatever you do, do it in the love of Jesus Christ with the idea of blessing people, both spiritually and in every other way, and you can't go wrong. In all of your dealings with people, keep in your mind the image of Jesus, the highest authority in the entire universe, on His knees, washing the dirt and grime off His disciples' feet. Mark 10:45 tells us, *"The Son of Man did not come to be served, but to serve, and to give his life as a ransom for many."* If Jesus surrendered His life in service to others, and His Spirit lives in you, then your life is designed not to be served, but to serve. Look for opportunities every day for this to become a reality for you, and use these opportunities to share the Gospel with others.

Discussion Questions:

-Of the ideas presented in this chapter for serving your community, which might be practical for you?

-What are some other needs in your community that might be met by Christians with a desire to serve?

-How are service and evangelism connected? Do you believe service is a bridge to evangelism? Why or why not?

"Never concede to doing something so small that it could be accomplished entirely in your lifetime. Be a part of something that began before you were born, and will continue onward toward the fulfillment of all that God has purposed to accomplish."

-Ralph Winter

New Beginnings

"We have all eternity to tell of the victories won for Christ, but we have only a few hours before sunset to win them."

                 - Amy Carmichael

Chances are, it took you about three seconds to read this sentence.

If you are like me, you may have gone back and read it again, just to see if it really was three seconds. Regardless, you can never have those seconds back. They are gone forever. They have been spent. They have been withdrawn from your account.

> We get one shot at this life.

The point is this: Time is passing us by. We get one shot at this life, and every individual is given an amount of seconds to spend. We don't know how many seconds we have, but for every individual one thing is the same – they are ticking away. They are more valuable than money and more precious than gold or fine jewels. I would imagine there are countless people who, at the moment of death, would trade in all of their material possessions in exchange for more time. In some cases, they would do so for even just a few more precious seconds. There is no getting around it: Our time is our most valuable commodity.

How will you spend your time on Earth?

Will you spend your life in pursuit of personal accomplishments, accolades, and triumphs? How about in pursuit of material things – cars, houses, boats, and other treasures? Maybe you will seek to become famous – to become a household name. Or maybe you will just seek *"security"* – a house, a wife, two kids, a dog, and a picket fence.

Either way, at this point you must ask yourself: Whose kingdom will I build with my life – the Kingdom of God or my own personal kingdom?

> Whose kingdom will I build with my life?

The prologue of this book was titled *"Beginnings"* because it described the beginnings of my life as a soulwinner. It was my story of how God changed my life and challenged me to go out into the world with the message of His Gospel.

This conclusion is titled *"New Beginnings"* because I pray that it will be the beginning of something great in your life. Many times when we come to the last few pages of a book we are thinking, *"Almost done."* We will even flip over a few pages to see how much more we have to read until we are finished. My prayer for you is that the end of this book is not actually the end, but rather a beginning of a lifetime of outreach. Ending this book is not graduation; it can instead be an initiation into an entire lifetime of service in the army of Jesus Christ, advancing His cause and His message.

We have only barely covered the tip of everything there is to know about outreach and evangelism. It is now up to you to find out more. Make it your goal to get your hands on every resource that you can to

> Ending this book is not graduation; it can be instead an initiation.

train you how to share your faith effectively. Don't let this be the last book you read on the topic. Make it one of many. Read this one again in a few months. How much of its content will you have applied to your life in that time?

More important than the need to study and read is the need to practice.

Practice outreach every day of your life. Make it the central theme of your days in one way or another. Come up with new ideas of how to spread the Gospel worldwide and implement those ideas. There are so many methods of reaching people with the Gospel that they never could be included in just one book. We didn't discuss using your talents. (Are you a musician? Go to a park, play guitar, and share the Gospel. Are you a web designer? Design websites that impact the world for Jesus.) We didn't discuss long-term and short-term mission trips, which I believe every Christian should be a part of whenever possible. We didn't discuss opening your home up for the Kingdom by hosting neighborhood Bible studies or sheltering those in need. There are thousands of ways to spread God's love and message to the world. It is your job to find out what God would have you do, and then do it.

You have been called as an ambassador for Christ, spreading His love, power, and grace into the world around us. You are His agent and designed to be on His mission. You can make a difference in the world. Don't let anything get in the way of God's ultimate mission for your life – *"to seek and save what was lost."* God has given you a certain amount of time to spend on planet Earth, and it is ticking away. I challenge you in the name of Jesus Christ to spend it wisely, in complete surrender to His greatest passion - reconciling man to God.

Speaking Engagements:

Do you want to encourage and equip your congregation, youth group, or conference attendees to actively share their faith on a regular basis?

H.L. Hussmann is available for speaking engagements throughout the U.S. And internationally.

Conferences, services, and seminars can include the following:

-Powerful motivation toward living an outreach-centered life

-Dozens of practical ideas for reaching people with the Gospel

-Tangible tools that can be used for opening conversations and sharing Jesus with others

-A course in basic or advanced apologetics (defending the faith)

-Hands-on outreach opportunities in the local community

-Information about sharing the Gospel with various people groups (Muslims, Mormons, Atheists, etc.)

-Dealing with objections to evangelism

-Opportunities for questions and answers

We are committed to reaching people with the Gospel of Jesus Christ and to helping pastors by training congregations in personal evangelism.

For references and more information, please see our website:

http://www.godsgreatestpassion.com

God's Greatest Passion

H.L. Hussmann

BULK COPIES:

Are you interested in using *God's Greatest Passion* for a weekly Bible study, small group, workshop, or other situations with several in attendance?

Bulk copies of *God's Greatest Passion* are available at a discount for pastors, Sunday school teachers, youth leaders, and anyone wanting copies to give away as gifts. See our website for bulk ordering.

3-10 copies	25% Off	$14.99 each
11-25 copies	35% Off	$12.99 each
26-50 copies	40% Off	$11.99 each
50+ copies	50% Off	$9.99 each

http://www.godsgreatestpassion.com